What Is an Environment?
A Study in the New
Comparative Interpretation

Clayton Shoppa

William Zanardi

Published in the USA in 2015 by Forty Acres Press
2246 Guadalupe Street
Austin, TX 78705
www.fortyacrespress.com
ISBN-978-1-61043-027-2

Cover and Layout: Leigh Kosloski

Table of Contents

INTRODUCTION

This is the third in a series of books experimenting with the new comparative interpretation. The two previous efforts applied the new practice to traditional puzzles in philosophy and theology.[1] This volume contains applications to fields beyond those two. Our primary aim is to test the usefulness of this form of comparative interpretation against a wide range of intellectual puzzles. In doing so, we hope to attract the attention of scholars as yet unfamiliar with this new practice.

In keeping with its title, this work both explores the meaning of "environment" and envisions a new environment for doing scholarly work. Fantasizing about future practices needs some grounding in actual performance; hence, this book series has been an attempt to surpass conventional scholarly practices by demonstrating a more promising alternative. We are under no illusions that those unhappy with current comparative practices are numerous or that more than a few are eager to depart from them. Still, we offer an alternative for the discontented few. For example, the meaning of "environment" is not summarily stated anywhere near the beginning of this work. As opposed to a conceptualist tradition dominant in much of the philosophical literature, we believe that a serious concept is reached only after a difficult climb through raising and answering questions, slowly amassing a nest of related insights and categories and thus only gradually approximating a comprehensive understanding of the object under study. Instead of beginning with an easily repeatable word definition, we review the multiple uses of the term across the histories of several disciplines and only in the final chapter work out a complex meaning arising from that historical survey and the developments we have detected within it.[2]

---

1   *The New Comparative Interpretation: A Primer* (Second, revised edition, 2014) and *Cracking the Case: Exercises in the New Comparative Interpretation* (2014). Both are published by Forty Acres Press (Austin, TX).
2   "People who ask for definitions are usually crazy. It is a waste of time, because definitions haven't got a precise meaning unless you have a fundamental set of terms and relations, with the terms fixing the relations and the relations fixing terms, and the whole lot verified." Ber-

We invite readers to track these developments in meaning along with us and so to undergo a similar development both in their understanding of the meaning of environment and in their understanding of how they go about understanding. This two-part invitation may seem strange to those unfamiliar with the first two books in this series. Its novelty lies in asking readers to keep track of how they are operating in relation to the ink marks on these pages. As we will see in subsequent chapters, a common-sense usage of environment is that of an imaginable totality (think of earth as photographed from space). That is, an environment is what bounds or contains whatever appears. What happens, however, when we come across claims that an environment is neither an entity nor an aggregation of entities? What then might it be? Does an environment even exist if it is not something perceptible? Might it be similar to words like "society" and "institution" that, some say, are not realities but simply convenient ways, or nominal terms, for referring to aggregates of peoples and customs?

Answering these questions involves moving beyond a common-sense horizon and making at least a slight entry into the horizon of theoretical understanding. Then the focus of inquiry becomes not imaginable objects but intelligible patterns of relations within and among things. Self-consciously making this transition and controlling how one is relating to ink marks and the meanings one makes of them require some understanding of how it is possible to intend the same objects in two different ways. Thus, entry into a third horizon of intentional operations becomes part of the process of tracking the shifting meanings of environment. Is it too much to ask of readers that they pay attention to their own performance in moving among all three horizons? Admittedly there are few precedents for such a request. However, we believe this book series points ahead to what one day will be conventional practice in scholarly reading and writing.

That day is not here, so we need to acknowledge obstacles to gaining a hearing for the new comparative interpretation. To begin with, the meaning of "comparison" in this new practice departs from ordinary usage. We envision comparative interpreters of the future relying upon a developmentally ordered sequence of the best interpretations of some issue and so comparing any new viewpoints or previously neglected ones to that sequence. Gone will be the days of comparing two or more authors' views to one another or of debating obsolete views appearing early on

nard Lonergan, *Caring about Meaning: Patterns in the Life of Bernard Lonergan.* Pierrot Lambert et al. (eds.) (Montreal: Thomas More Institute, 1982), 24.

in such sequences. Instead, interpreters will be alert for whatever seems a promising addition to that developmental sequence and thus worthy of attention. Chapters in this book sketch such sequences of views before comparing and criticizing recent interpretations. But our borrowing and even "invention" of such sequences is scarcely the stuff of a future, mature practice. In our defense, few disciplines in the Humanities even attempt such developmental orderings. Common-sense eclecticism and randomly related views are characteristic features of journal articles and collected essays in the Humanities. To use an analogy Philip McShane is fond of, the sequentially ordered views of how puppies develop into healthy dogs and the sequentially ordered views of how veterinarians should treat them when ill have no parallels in most scholarly fields. More directly, the latter lack anything similar to the Standard Model in contemporary physics.

But how many of us in scholarly disciplines even have a sense of what is lacking? As the previous books announced, one feature in the new comparative interpretation is pushing beyond "rich description" into the explanatory categories of the horizon of theory. How many scholars are familiar with the difference between the two? How many think theory in a strict sense is the province of the natural sciences and irrelevant, or even harmful, to the "art" of interpretation? Does talk of a science of interpretation set off alarms in some scholarly circles? If it does, then these experimental works, for all their immaturity, might be worth reading, if only to point out any mistaken aims and flawed means and so save a new generation from attempting such follies.

There is a sense of fantasy and folly in composing these pages. For example, what Chapter One sketches as the five "elements" of the new practice include a universal viewpoint (UV) as an affirmation of basic meanings of the terms "reality," "knowing" and "objectivity." The earlier books offered more details, but even then a critic might wonder how a viewpoint could be universal when so few shared it. Then there is the element of the new practice referred to as Generalized Empirical Method (GEM) which few have heard of and even fewer practice. Our response is a challenge to the reader: just as questions precede answers so performance precedes commentary on it. Get to know your performance, your questioning and the proper objects intended by it, and you may find that talk of UV and GEM is not all that remote from what you have been doing, no matter what you may have been saying about your performance.

Directly addressing the reader with this challenge reveals another departure from convention. The earlier *Primer* repeatedly invited readers to pause and reflectively work through various puzzles, e.g. Hegel's first three stages in his dialectic of consciousness. Such pauses are part of the pedagogy in learning GEM.[3] In contrast, a doctrinal mode of presentation is far more pervasive in and expected of scholarly works. But that conventional mode easily leaves readers comfortably at home in whatever common-sense horizon they happen to occupy. It also tends to disguise the limited effectiveness of arguments in displacing readers from faulty stances on basic issues. Nonetheless, because these books are transitional works, they rely heavily on doctrinal discourse and only occasionally exhibit direct address. So making the transition to a new practice involves compromises; it also entails risks. Moving toward a science of interpretation is like climbing a mountain aware that surprises are likely, especially if there are few well-trodden paths to follow. But our efforts are not solitary. A small but growing number of scholars are writing about what Bernard Lonergan called "functional specialization." The previous books have located the new comparative interpretation within that larger methodological framework as the fourth specialty or what Lonergan called "dialectic." Chapter One will reprise some of those earlier comments.

Part of the fantasy of functional specialization is that institutional practices in academia and at research centers will become increasingly communal, collaborative enterprises as opposed to remaining individual fiefdoms or "Lone Ranger" research projects. Imagine a group of specialists understanding their distinct aims, committed to explanatory understanding in their own fields, convinced that functional collaboration is the best use of their diverse talents and believing that such collaborative efforts are a way of making history better, if only for anonymous future generations. The fantasy, then, is that the collaborative efforts now quite common in the natural sciences will one day be common in the human sciences. A future science of interpretation will require as much. Is such a science worth pursuing? Again, there are risks, but actually taking them becomes more probable as dissatisfaction grows with the enduring intellectual impasses and fragmentation current practices promote.

If fantasy is ever to turn into reality, the first steps lie in doing something new, in attempting to depart from current routines, in daring to strike out in new directions. An Introduction is appropriate for informing

---

3   To repeat the description of that pedagogy found in the previous books: one begins to understand what it means to understand by reflecting on the act of understanding, i.e. *intelligere*. But *intelligere* has a history; so re-enacting the journey from common-sense understanding through theory to the self-knowledge of intentional operators is part of knowing *intelligere*-in-act.

readers what departures and novelties to expect in the coming chapters.

The first chapter condenses the descriptions of the new comparative interpretation found in the two previous books. Even in abbreviated form, the challenge of the new practice appears a steep climb. Its five elements are like a series of camps marking stages in the ascent. To raise the level of one's performance by internalizing methodical controls over that performance is usually a climb occurring during years of graduate studies. Present-day graduate programs in the Humanities rarely include the first element in its technical sense, namely, entry into the horizon of theory. This book series, therefore, may be an invitation to return for missed training or even to remedy mis-education. In writing these books we have found ourselves making such a return and occasionally wondering how much further along we might be if our earlier graduate studies had been different. Again, we expect only a few at first to be willing to accept the invitation. Most will be far too busy on the academic treadmill of scholarly productivity. Others will not see the need to depart from settled routines; for commonly, "what is lacking is knowledge of all that is lacking, and only gradually is that knowledge acquired."[4] Still, we can point out some of what is lacking and at least make it a topic of wider conversations. Our hope is that eventually the few may become a wider audience.

Chapter Two attempts a widening of the audience by reviewing a recent work on art history and environmental movements during two decades of the last century. That work and another survey of different meanings of "ecosystem" trace how artists and ecologists have understood their own fields and practices. Analysis of those different meanings yields a pair of different developmental orderings of the meanings of ecosystem and environment. That is, we find two competing claims about which views are more advanced than others. These orderings or sequences become materials for applying comparative interpretation to a basic puzzle in the field of ecology. In the future such sequences of views will be part of the standard models of disciplines, but for now we have to cobble together orderings from works not indebted to functional specialization. All the same, the second chapter does identify a variety of basic issues relevant to understanding what an environment is. It serves, then, as a way of framing the order of subsequent chapters.

The third chapter focuses on questions in political science and sociology or, if you like, questions about social environments. For example, in what sense does a society or an institution exist? If one holds

---

4   Bernard Lonergan, *Insight, CW* 3 (Toronto: University of Toronto Press, 1992), 559.

that persons are perceptible but institutions are not, is it plausible to withhold the category of "real" from the latter? A similar puzzle recurs in later chapters in talking about organisms and ecosystems. One never sees an ecosystem just as one never sees an institution. What then is the ontological status of an institution or of an ecosystem? In response to this question, Chapter Three identifies three different views of institutions and then excavates their underlying assumptions about reality, knowing and objectivity. It, thus, becomes an exercise in applying UV to a basic intellectual puzzle within two distinct disciplines. This application is part of the climb toward a serious concept of environment.

Chapter Four at first seems a digression from the title question of this book. The focus is on issues in psychology (e.g. the origins and limits of the language of self-interest in describing human behavior) and in economic theory (e.g. the methodological purposes the language of self-interest and rational agency play in supposedly making economics a predictive science). Exploring these issues will prove useful in criticizing some views of an economic environment and in detecting how economic realism consistently overlooks conditions for the emergence and survival of economies. Among those conditions are persons-at-liberty who are capable of radical displacements from conventional beliefs and practices. The fourth chapter's sketch of what these authors call the "Education of Liberty" is a hope-filled fantasy that large numbers of persons will one day understand how a market economy functions and will act intelligently and responsibly in adapting to its rhythms. An enlarged perspective on history as "environment" is part of this fantasy. In rejecting talk of market mechanisms and impersonal laws of the economy, this chapter rejects a deterministic and non-historical understanding of markets. In doing so, it provides a transition to the next chapter's focus on developments in environmental history and its recognition of the need for a better language in talking about environments.

Chapter Five investigates what environmental historians have thought about their field over the past forty years. What has been going forward in these decades of environmental studies? Have there been advances both in the practices of historians and in their understanding of what an environment is? Two major figures in the field composed surveys of the literature and offered answers to these questions. In doing so they supplied materials anticipating what we have been calling developmental sequences of views. Worth special attention is one conclusion; namely, some of the categories commonly in use are "undertheorized." Exposure to the natural sciences has led historians to recognize that, as commonly used, the terms "environment," "nature" and "agency" are far too undifferentiated to serve as basic categories. The authors of both surveys, as well as these present writers, take this turn to questions about language as a sign of maturation in the field. Entry into the second horizon usually requires such a move away from ordinary language and toward talk of intelligible patterns of relations among variables. The fifth chapter considers a further step already under discussion by some historians, namely, adoption of a "relational ontology" in thinking and talking about organisms, ecosystems and the environment.

The sixth chapter advances the inquiry into the meaning of environment by taking up two puzzles in contemporary neuroscience. Reductionist analyses tend to conflate psychological states and intentional acts with neurobiological processes; so the first puzzle is whether common-sense views of human control are illusory. Whatever relations of dependency may exist between psychological and neurobiological processes, the current terminologies in the field are a muddle of mechanistic metaphors, remnants from faculty psychology and borrowings from computer-based information theory. The two puzzles are translatable into questions about an environment: Is an environment reducible to its components? Can we find a better language for talking about relations among organisms, ecosystems and an environment? Thus, answers to the puzzles in neuroscience may be relevant to these further questions about an environment.

The seventh chapter is finally able to give a direct response to this book's title question. After reviewing the previous, partial responses to the question and earlier developmental orderings of them, the chapter concludes by presenting a much expanded understanding of the meaning of environment. What results is a new theoretical meaning, one surpassing various common-sense usages and even departing from technical usages in some fields.

An Epilogue restates some of our reasons for being disenchanted with current practices and then estimates the prospects for what we believe is a way forward. Those prospects require an expanded view of human history and a belief that it is more than "a tale told by an idiot, full of sound and fury, signifying nothing." Why else would we or anyone else continue to ask questions and seek ways to improve scholarly performance? The following chapters represent our trust that the efforts are worth making.

CHAPTER ONE:
OVERVIEW OF COMPARATIVE INTERPRETATION

The two previous books in this series presented introductions to and case studies in the new comparative interpretation. This first chapter cannot summarize all that those works contained; however, new readers unfamiliar with them may benefit from a review of the five elements of this new practice and what it hopes to achieve. Subsequent chapters will introduce further refinements to the procedure and new case studies testing its worth.

I. A Framework for Comparing Interpretations

What are the "elements" of this new practice? For new readers the following list will seem vague; however, sections dedicated to expanding on these initial descriptions follow below. The five elements are: explanatory understanding pursued within the horizon of theory (H2);[5] generalized empirical method (GEM); a universal viewpoint (UV) composed of basic positions on the meanings of reality, knowing and objectivity; a developmental ordering or genetic systematics (GS) of interpretations and lastly functional specialization (FS), with comparative interpretation as the fourth of eight related specialties. Together they form a critical procedure for comparing different interpretations: (1) by tracing some of their differences to disagreements over what their authors meant by reality, knowing and objectivity and then comparing them to UV and so diagnosing and evaluating sources of those differences; and (2) by comparing those different interpretations to what eventually will emerge as developmental sequences of views (GS) on some issue ranging from less developed views to more developed ones.

---

5   The first horizon (H1) pertains to common-sense forms of understanding and descriptive formulations.

The two parts to the preceding description of the procedure reflect two different temporal frames of reference. At present this new practice is experimental and proceeds without the collaborative results from numerous functional specialists that will someday be available. Consequently, contemporaries doing comparative interpretation (FS4) cannot readily draw upon the refined sequences of interpretations that historians doing FS3 will someday produce. We anticipate that eventually such sequences will undergo "recycling" through all eight functional specialties and that all specialists working on a common issue will be familiar with the sequences relevant to that issue. Clearly the second frame of reference is a distant time and a remote practice. As anticipated but not yet achieved, that envisioned practice serves as a guide to our present efforts, even if they fall far short of the ideal. Still, experiments can go forward, and, as in any process of inquiry, new insights can refine initial and even clumsy efforts.

Case studies in the previous books and new ones in the following chapters are experiments in applying this procedure and thereby assessing its merits. The earlier tests of its usefulness gradually refined the meaning of this way of doing comparative interpretation. Five steps outline how doing FS4 initially proceeds: (1) it begins by summarizing different orderings of interpretations handed on from historians doing FS3; (2) it identifies similarities and differences in those materials; (3) by raising further why-questions, it seeks to explain those similarities and differences; (4) it does so by reducing some similarities and differences to their origins, e.g. by relating some differences among the sequences of interpretations to variable background stances, some of which are at odds with basic positions the practitioner of FS4 explicitly adopts regarding questions about reality, knowing and objectivity (UV); (5) after identifying which similarities and differences are compatible or incompatible with these basic positions, the specialist in FS4 proceeds to evaluate them as reflecting more developed or less developed viewpoints.[6]

Here the fantasy is that future specialists will not repeatedly go over the same old debates; instead, they will operate with developmentally ranked interpretations of some issues and will likely accept that some previously debated questions have been settled. That is, they will

---

6   These initial ways of proceeding will eventually produce cumulative and progressive results. For example, after future specialists in FS4 have recycled their re-orderings of views from FS3 and have received criticism and made revisions, future practitioners of FS3 will have these improved results available to them. One improvement over current practice is that they will not squander attention on views left behind by such evaluative rankings. Instead, their focus will be on what views promise to add something positive to the best understanding to date of some issue.

rely on an acquis, i.e. an acquired normative viewpoint, and presuppose that some issues are no longer worth debating. One consequence will be that future specialists in FS4 will compare authors not by directly relating them to one another but by situating them in relation to what those specialists accept as a normatively ordered sequence of interpretations of a particular topic. Is this pure fantasy? An analogy to developmental psychology may be helpful. Theorists in that field operate routinely with "stage theories" employing genetic frameworks. For example, they situate instances of moral decision-making and the rationales for them along gradients from least to most developed. When those frameworks are relatively comprehensive accounts of the forms moral decisions and their rationales can take and when those applying the frameworks correctly diagnose specific instances, they have significant control over the "readings" of multiple cases. A similar "control over meaning" is envisioned for the future practice of comparative interpretation.[7]

Why should control over meaning be important? First, major thinkers have thought it so. As Socrates sought to expose the limits of common-sense speech, as Aristotle formulated logical steps to order otherwise undisciplined inferences, as the medievals used questions and answers to organize their inquiries, so contemporary methods are ways of controlling the making and evaluating of meanings.[8] What begins as the random questioning and guessing of children can and has historically become the intelligently designed and more efficient procedures disciplines adopt in raising and answering questions. Absent such procedures, fields of inquiry resolve few questions and, instead, continually revisit the same old issues. External critics and a few bright undergraduates wonder if any advances in understanding ever occur in those fields. They may even dismiss entire fields as unproductive in contributing to human progress in understanding.

Whatever one's view of human progress, the desire to know and to know more than we currently understand seems fairly widespread. If this desire for more comprehensive understanding is a datum to be integrated into whatever our stories are about our times, our tribes and our shared

---

7   As noted in the Introduction, Philip McShane draws an analogy between control over meaning and practices in veterinary science. The healthy dog is an ideal type, and veterinarians operate with the best views to date on both what patterns of development dogs undergo and what therapies to employ when they are sick. Treatment of a sick puppy is, thus, not a comparison of it to some other puppy but to standardized "lore" in the profession. More importantly, careful attention to new specimens may lead to new insights that develop or correct the prior understanding of dogs, their development and treatment. If we generalize beyond providing better days for animals, we can imagine how a mature practice of FS might provide better days for the human species. *Futurology Express* (Vancouver: Axial Press, 2013), 14-18.

8   In the previous books this was the meaning of "normative objectivity."

futures, then there is a second reason for seeking further control over meaning. This reason is part of a broader historical viewpoint that is worth making explicit. "The challenge of history is...progressively to restrict the realm of chance or fate or destiny and progressively to enlarge the realm of conscious grasp and deliberate choice."[9] In other words, the challenge is to replace haphazard coincidence with meaningful cooperation, to help ourselves and subsequently others understand, reflect and choose to do what was previously only a remote hope for intelligent collaboration. Inquirers operating without any methodical controls can scarcely hope to meet this challenge.

II. Implementing the Fantasy

A. The First Two Elements: H2 and GEM

Supposedly it took Augustine of Hippo decades to realize that what was real was not identical with imaginable bodies. The same shift from common-sense "picture thinking" to a world of contemporary physics took much longer.[10] Such personal and historical developments are relevant to understanding how a radical change in one's thinking, e.g. a departure from common-sense estimates of what is real, is possible. How does the possible become probable?

What occurred very slowly in Augustine is not achieved exclusively by logical arguments. Lonergan noted the difficulties on the side of the one arguing and on the side of the audience.

> The problem is not having people repeat with Augustine that "The real is not a body, it is what you know when you know something true." The problem is to get people to mean as much as Augustine meant when Augustine spoke about truth. And that's a transformation of the subject. It is bringing a subject up to the level of

---

9   *Insight*, 253.
10   "St. Augustine of Hippo narrates that it took him years to make the discovery that the name 'real' might have a different connotation from the name 'body.' Or, to bring the point nearer home, one might say that it has taken modern science four centuries to make the discovery that the objects of its inquiry need not be imaginable entities moving through imaginable processes in an imaginable space-time." Ibid. 15.

thought of a Plato and an Aristotle and an Augustine and an Aquinas, and that's a terrific development in the subject. And there is no automatic, no surefire means of bringing that about. You push people along the way as far as you can. It is just as in teaching any particular point, putting any particular point across: the teacher can utter the sounds and make the gestures and draw the diagrams[,] but he cannot guarantee that people are going to understand. He can repeat himself over and over again, but their understanding of it is an immanent activity of their own....[11]

The main insight here is that something external to an argument, i.e. a development in the audience, is a precondition to the de facto persuasiveness of an argument. The persuader can "utter the sounds and make the gestures," but there is still the question of whether an audience is going to grasp the intended meaning. To grasp meaning is an act immanent in hearers or readers. The arguments, whether written or oral, may be necessary but not sufficient conditions for the assent of the audience. What arguments do is limited: they set up some conditions favorable to assent, but the act of assent requires fulfillment of still further conditions external to the content of an argument and immanent in the audience.[12]

Formulated arguments employ words, but the same words may mean different things to different audiences. In the extreme, words that represent insights from a context remote from that of an audience will seem puzzling and even at odds with that audience's "facts." Arguments representing remote contexts will not be compelling because they will be largely incomprehensible to the audience. The fundamental issue will not be one of logical validity or resistant bias; instead, the issue will be one of developmental differences between the one arguing and the audience.

---

11   Bernard Lonergan. *Phenomenology and Logic. CW* 18 (Toronto: University of Toronto Press, 2001), 132.

12   Why are there further conditions? Oral argumentation in part is the emitting of sound waves by speakers. Likewise, written argument is the production of ink marks on pages. The intelligent hearing or reading of either is dependent on immanent acts by listeners and readers. The medievals made the same observation with their maxim *quidquid recipitur ad modum recipientis recipitur*. They recognized that the capacity of an audience for "receiving" a text affected what sense they could make of the text. The implications are significant (1) for understanding the limits of arguments in evoking assent and (2) for recognizing that developments and even radical displacements in audiences can be preconditions to understanding and assent. This talk of further conditions to assent anticipates insights leading to the meaning of "environment" worked out in Chapter Seven.

How plausible does all this seem? With the passing of nine-teenth-century positivism, it no longer is controversial to assert that there is an existential dimension to all theorizing and that there are limits to argumentation such that no amount of evidence and no argument by itself will "compel" assent to some fact or course of action. Put simply, facts do not speak for themselves, and arguments per se do not always persuade.[13] So the more developed the listeners and the more expansive their horizons of understanding, the more capable they will be to recognize sound arguments and to judge between competing claims. Of course, some will worry that this conclusion makes "subjectivity" the measure of truth and moral rightness. But the issue is not whether decisions and commitments are decisive for judging but whether they are arbitrary.[14] Put another way, the issue is whether the decisions and commitments reflect sufficiently developed subjects. Reasoned discourse, then, becomes not a matter of moving from premises to conclusions but of carefully pursuing further insights, especially ones that expand initial horizons and so leave behind less developed viewpoints. Any shifting of viewpoints presupposes judgments: negative ones about positions left behind and positive ones about replacements. An example of such judgments occurs in the first element of comparative interpretation, namely, the shift from descriptive to explanatory understanding, from an initial horizon of common sense to the horizon of theory.

One author provided a broad historical account of this expansion beyond an initial horizon. Bernard Lonergan wrote of the two times of the human subject.[15] The first category in his historical sketch refers to the spontaneous wondering of practical living. Here persons ask how they are to meet the challenges of surviving, whether they are hunter-gatherers or suburban parents juggling family dinners, the kids' soccer schedules and piles of laundry. This is the horizon of common-sense living and practical problem solving. The second category refers to the slow emergence of sustained reflection on how we operate in understanding. In brief, the two times correspond to (1) a common-sense horizon of practical concerns and (2) a reflective horizon of wondering about wonder, of attending to what we are doing in understanding, and so of focusing on

---

13   Deciding to assent is distinct from understanding the arguments, just as knowing what can and should be done is distinct from consenting to do it. *"What Are Judgments of Value?"* in *Bernard Lonergan. Philosophical and Theological Papers: 1965-1980. CW* 17 (Toronto: University of Toronto Press, 2004), 149-150.

14   "Is It Real?" in ibid. 127.

15   *The Triune God: Systematics. CW* 12 (Toronto: University of Toronto Press, 2007), 399-413. He subsequently wrote of three "stages of meaning" in *Method in Theology* (New York: Herder and Herder, 1972), 81-99.

intentional acts.

Why did a shift from one time or horizon to the other occur? Between the two times is an intermediate stage of theoretical inquiry, i.e. the horizon of theory (H2). In this long intermediate period occurs the production (with ever increasing acceleration since the sixteenth century) of multiple hypotheses, interpretations and scientific theories. A much earlier diversity of viewpoints and a babble of voices gave rise to the question of how to control any flood of meanings. The Greek philosophers' puzzling about the status of myth was an early sign of tension between commonsensical and theoretical meanings, a tension giving rise to formal logic as a means of controlling whatever one asserted. Galileo's demotion of secondary qualities from the status of what was "objectively real" was a further sign of tension between common-sense understanding and theoretical claims. Eddington's puzzle about his desk reflected a twentieth-century version of the same tension.

Such puzzles can shift an inquirer's focus to questions about knowing, objectivity and reality: Just what am I doing when I am trying to understand? How is my common-sense knowing related to my theoretical knowing? Is one way of making meaning alone reliable? Are the sciences the road to knowledge while common sense settles for something less? Or are the sciences "abstract" while common sense comes to grips with what is concretely real? And just what do I mean by "concrete" and by "real"? The realism of common sense affirms that what is real must be observable or at least imaginable, but the generalizations of the scientists seem to affirm a different measure of what is real.

Such questions and the different viewpoints concerning what is real and objectively knowable can prompt a new shift to reflexive operations, to self-attention on the part of inquirers. Suppose this new focus of concern is called the "horizon of interiority."[16] The puzzles about different types of knowing and different types of realism can lead confused inquirers to shift their attention from any original object of attention to how they are operating on the object. Entry into a horizon of interiority need not occur, but the alternative is to experience on different occasions something akin to Eddington's bafflement over how to understand his own writing desk.

To this point, we have a preliminary framework for comparing interpretations: the two times of the human subject and the three stages or historically sequential appearances of horizons of common sense, theo-

---

16   The terminology is borrowed from Lonergan's *Method in Theology* and later essays. Entry into this third horizon is not a matter of "peering inside" but of reflecting on personal and historical developments in human inquiry. (Cf. *Insight*, 441.)

ry and interiority. They provide a first approximation to "framing" the methodological question of how to order and to evaluate philosophical differences. For example, one can ask in what horizon authors were operating when they composed their works.[17]

Three further claims begin building a more detailed framework. First, while philosophical questions may emerge spontaneously as a symptom of human curiosity responsive to any number of different concerns (practical or otherwise), they historically undergo a radical shift when the demand for understanding becomes a demand for explanatory understanding, i.e. when the horizon of theory, with its goal of answering further why-questions, emerges.[18] Second, the demand for explanatory understanding will initially be at odds with the demand of practical living for tangible benefits and answers within the reach of common-sense understanding.[19] The tension between the two demands will generate any number of puzzles and intellectual impasses; however, given sufficient time and ingenuity within the human species, questions pertaining to the horizon of interiority are bound to receive increasing attention. So, thirdly, one can anticipate a time when common practice will more often exhibit something similar to the methodological injunction phrased as generalized empirical method (GEM), a practice requiring familiarity with this third horizon. Lonergan formulated such an injunction.

> Generalized empirical method operates on a combination of both the data of sense and the data of consciousness; it does not treat of objects without taking into account the corresponding operations of the subject; it does not treat of the subject's operations without taking into account the corresponding objects.[20]

---

17 As a result, one might discover and provocatively assert that, even though J.S. Mill is said to formulate a theory of liberty and John Rawls a theory of justice, both wrote within the first horizon.

18 Aristotle was aware of how we begin by inquiring about objects in relation to us, but he also observed how we later consider them as related among themselves. The medievals wrote of the same two orientations toward objects: *priora quoad nos* and *priora quoad se*. All the same, many thinkers over the centuries have neglected the distinction and its implications.

19 In the earlier texts, these demands for understanding appeared as distinct imperatives: Be Practical! Be comprehensive! Aristotle's reach for systematic knowledge of the cosmos was his response to the second imperative. Plato before him knew that mathematics and geometry pushed beyond both the limits of practical living and what was available to the senses. A tension between two types of reality and two types of understanding, present earlier in Parmenides' work, was historically becoming more explicit.

20 Lonergan. "Second Lecture: Religious Knowledge" in *A Third Collection* (New York: Paulist Press, 1985), 141.

What difference can entry into the third horizon make in doing comparative interpretation? Operating in the horizon of theory is part of the intermediate period, and, as already noted, it produces an ever increasing flood of hypotheses and competing theories. One control over theoretical meanings is to link explanatory or theoretical terms to the categories of intentionality theory. Doing so can ground the former terms in what all common-sense thinking and theory construction presuppose, namely, the structured performance occurring in raising and answering questions. This effort at linkage permits some criticism and control over formulations at odds with the performance that produced them. How well such control will work in a variety of disciplines remains to be seen. Experiments in the following chapters will suggest some applications, but future practices may provide far more reasons for adopting this part of the procedure. For now we can offer only a glimpse of the possibilities if scholars operated with an awareness of all three horizons, tracked their performance in relation to them and recognized their slow emergence as instances of historical development.

Perhaps the description of the sequential emergence of the three horizons is not controversial. Might it offer clues as to how to construct a genetic sequencing of philosophical differences? What might it be like if new generations were at home in all three horizons when they began to compare and to evaluate different interpretations? Fantasize, if you will, how some future generation of inquirers might employ an interpretive framework to control their questioning, their expectations about what would count as adequate answers and how they distinguished between less advanced and more advanced interpretations. The first two elements would be parts of a model, a normative reference point, for comparing both questions and answers and for judging their adequacy in terms of what "has been settled."

This fantasy presupposes that the first two elements will someday become part of conventional practice. That is, GEM and operating in the second horizon will become common measures of scholarly competence. Then, something similar to Lonergan's canon of explanation might become one of the accepted standards for scholarly practice.

> The interpreter's differentiation of the protean notion
> of being must be not descriptive but explanatory. It will
> aim at relating, not to us, but to one another, the con-
> tents and contexts of the totality of documents and in-
> terpretations. As long as interpretation remains on the

descriptive level, it may happen to be correct[,] but it cannot escape the relativity of a manifold of interpretations to a manifold of audiences; in turn, this relativity excludes the possibility of scientific collaboration, scientific control, and scientific advance towards commonly accepted results.[21]

But this standard is not yet in place, and most contemporary interpreters probably have no expectation that such a standard should be part of their scholarly practice. However, expectations change, and slowly more interpreters may notice that descriptive interpretations fall short of explaining anything, i.e. they fall short of answering further why-questions. Some may then begin to wonder about future possibilities and a time when mixing theoretical and common-sense orientations will be less commonplace.

Perhaps it is easier to identify what future interpreters will not be doing in their works. No longer will scholarly studies reflecting a confused mixing of theoretical and common-sense horizons be so commonplace and so commonly accepted as competent work. When Plato depicted some rare individual leaving the cave, he was anticipating what the sciences are doing in reaching for explanatory correlations and statistical frequencies. If comparative interpretations are to proceed at the level of the best science of the day, can they continue to be descriptive studies? If they do, will they be taken seriously? If alchemists were to address a conference of chemists, would they be taken seriously?

To take a methodological stance, competent interpretive work should at least: (1) be responsive to the further questions that belong to an explanatory or theoretical horizon and (2) should take seriously the claim that the complete data of any inquiry include the data of the inquirer and, thus, should employ GEM. What follows from these two elementary stances? Since any answers presuppose questions about puzzling "objects," interpreting someone's text requires attention to and retrieval of the questions leading to the answers. Furthermore, since the formulations of questions and answers vary with authors and audiences, a partial evasion of such relativity may be available by operating in the horizon of theory and attempting to recast questions and answers in explanatory terms.[22] However, these as well can vary, so employing GEM and linking

---

21   *Insight*, 609.
22   It would be a significant improvement in practice, for example, if interpreters routinely asked in what horizon an author of a text was operating. To ask this question presupposes that the questioners have already asked it of themselves.

explanatory categories to intentional acts and the functional relations among them, either directly or by way of analogy, is a way of constructing a useful interpretive framework for exploring both original questions and answers. The results of case studies are the tests of its usefulness, but, even in advance of those outcomes, the first two elements of the framework provide some control over the making of meaning.

B. A Universal Viewpoint

The pedagogy of the two previous books invited readers to re-enact the cultural journey from the first to the second time of the subject and thereby to experience their own developing subjectivity.[23] More specifically, the invitation was to pay attention both to selected cases and puzzles and to the readers' own performance in making sense of them. Again, GEM is the practice of doing both. One attends both to how one is operating, i.e. one's intentional acts, and to the objects on which one is operating. This dual attention is especially important in meeting the challenge of erecting a critical interpretive framework. Why is this so important?

Descartes opened the modern period of philosophy with his search for a method revealing a bedrock truth. Contemporary interest in a "metamethod" continues this search for a critical framework that would stand to procedures in inquiry as biology stands to organisms. As an element of the critical framework being sketched here, GEM asks readers of these texts to be attentive to themselves as specimens of what they are reading about. Three reasons for imposing this burden on readers appeared in the earlier works.

First, just as questions precede answers and concepts, so intentional acts precede theories. This includes theories about intentional acts. If readers are to evaluate different theoretical views about those acts, it helps if they have some understanding of their own performance in making sense of such theories.

---

23   Lonergan wrote: "one knows intellect by reflecting on its act, *intelligere*." [*Verbum: Word and Idea in Aquinas,* CW 2 (Toronto: University of Toronto Press, 1997), 238.] Since *intelligere* has a history, re-enacting the journey from common-sense understanding through theory to the self-knowledge of intentional operators is part of knowing "*intelligere*-in-act." In making the journey, one becomes an instance of development in what one is studying, i.e. *intelligere*. This was the primary pedagogical aim of the preceding case studies and of those that follow. They are invitations to personal development. To draw a parallel: just as intellectual history records some advances, so re-enacting some portion of that dynamic process can move one from less developed to more developed performance in inquiry.

19

Second, understanding their own intentional operations is a step toward eventually answering questions about the intended objects of those operations and, more generally, about what they mean by reality, knowing and objectivity. Presumably they will already have implicit views about all three. Readers of the earlier case studies and puzzles have perhaps found their views becoming more explicit and even more problematical. At least, they may no longer be complete hostages to the muddles of un-examined polymorphic consciousness.[24] Still, the views they do have may be a mixture of their own self-discoveries and what they have borrowed from other writers on epistemological and metaphysical issues. Since theories are multiple, readers can ask why they should choose theory x instead of theory y. Having some self-understanding of the operations that generate such theories is one step toward a non-arbitrary defense of whatever choice a reader makes.

Third, the various meanings persons attribute to reality, knowing and objectivity affect how they answer further questions about ethics, politics, theology and the sciences.[25] If they operate with unexamined and faulty notions of the former, they will likely arrive at unnecessary impasses in regard to the latter. At least this is one plausible diagnosis of why debates in some fields are interminable.

Critics will quickly point out that there is little agreement on the meanings of reality, knowing and objectivity. Why are thinkers so often at odds with one another on these topics? The general response here is that development in inquirers, as historical "contexts" for questioning, varies, and so their answers vary. This general claim is consistent with Hegel's dialectic of consciousness, assuming it is read as a genetic sequence of ever more comprehensive viewpoints on the relation of consciousness to its objects.[26] As a caveat, talk of such a genetic sequence need not assume that one can map developing viewpoints along an unbroken timeline.[27]

A further reason for the disagreements among philosophers is that accepting the invitation to re-enact the cultural journey between the two

---

24   The different ways people have understood and talked about the sun supply a simple exam-ple of polymorphic consciousness. Besides relating to objects in commonsensical and theoretical ways, we can also relate to them in psychological, moral, aesthetic and religious ways. If speakers are not tracking their diverse ways of relating to objects, confused discussions and confusing opinions are likely to follow.

25   *Insight*, 412.

26   This view of Hegel's dialectic was part of Chapter Two in the *Primer*.

27   One implication of noting how each new generation relives its predecessors' confusion of meanings about reality, knowing and objectivity is that there is no such chronological pattern of historical development. In the history of philosophy the intentional breakthroughs to the second and third horizons by "three weird Greeks" were forgotten or misunderstood by later generations of thinkers. So much, then, for any chronological model of intellectual development.

times of the subject or even attempting the climb through Hegel's early stages of the dialectic is rare. The simple reasons for either's rarity are that (1) both are daunting and (2) no one can re-enact or climb for another. The labor of self-attention and self-discovery is difficult and a private task. Someone can invite readers to reflect on their own intentional operations and on the history of attempts to do so, but no one else can do the work for them.[28]

The absence of that labor is part of an answer to questions about why each new generation seems to relive the confusions of the past and why the common performance of inquiring subjects is not commonly known. What is commonly known is what has repeatedly been attended to and queried. If most persons never reflect on their own mental acts (due perhaps to their prior education being largely a repetition of the results of others' mental acts), their own performance will likely remain *terra incognita*. Then, each new generation, even if not totally unfamiliar with the theoretical pattern of experience, will be strangers to the horizon of interiority and so strangers to that which is closest to them, their own mental acts. GEM may be not an alternative tried and found wanting but one found difficult and so not tried. The result is that polymorphic consciousness remains both in charge and unexamined. The different demands and tensions within it continuously generate differences in viewpoints and expressions.[29]

Still, the earlier books invited readers to undergo the climb toward a more comprehensive and even universal viewpoint regarding the meanings of reality, knowing and objectivity. To undergo the ascent is to become a "moving viewpoint." What might this mean? The earlier analogy to theories of developmental psychology suggested an empirical basis for ranking diverse views. That is, just as those theories identify earlier and later stages of intellectual and moral understanding and so presuppose judgments about less developed and more developed views, so the flood of philosophical opinions may be subject to similar judgments. Personal experiences in detecting developmental differences among viewpoints about reality, knowing and objectivity can ideally

---

28   As a corollary, moving to more comprehensive viewpoints does not occur deductively or automatically but is a matter of raising and answering questions, and some of the questions may be threatening, may intimate displacement from familiar ways of thinking and so portend a type of homelessness.

29   "Just as the earth, left to itself, can put forth creepers and shrubs, bushes and trees with such excessive abundance that there results an impenetrable jungle, so too the human mind, led by imagination and affect and uncontrolled by any reflexive technique, luxuriates in a world of myth with its glories to be achieved and its evils to be banished by the charms of magic." Bernard Lonergan, "Dimensions of Meaning" in *Collection* (New York: Herder and Herder, 1967), 258.

become empirical and personal reference points for beginning to depart from a flat landscape where multiple opinions are equally plausible. Together those experiences can become the material for understanding the meaning of a developing or moving viewpoint.

Three basic positions identified with UV presupposed such movement and became the third part of the framework for doing comparative interpretation. Without this experiential "measure" many intellectual impasses remain so-called "incommensurable differences." With this measure divergences from any of the positions identified in UV are evidence of a less adequate viewpoint. A further step (GS) will be to relate competing interpretations originating in such divergences to one another and to order them as reflecting varying degrees of development.[30]

Before turning to that fourth element (GS), we can review the various formulations of UV that appeared in the earlier books. Lonergan offered the first formulation of the three basic positions.

> It will be a basic position (1) if the real is the concrete universe of being and not a subdivision of the 'already out there now'; (2) if the subject becomes known when it affirms itself intelligently and reasonably and so is not known yet in any prior 'existential' state; and (3) if objectivity is conceived as a consequence of intelligent inquiry and critical reflection, and not as a property of vital anticipation, extroversion, and satisfaction.[31]

The contrasts in this formulation distinguish less and more developed positions. The first realism identifies the real with what is immediately present or can be imagined as presentable to extroverted consciousness. In contrast, the position of UV identifies the real with whatever is intelligible and affirmable in true judgments. The model of reality for extroverted consciousness favors a view of knowing as some immediate grasp of whatever is real. In contrast, the position of the second type of realism affirms the mediation of whatever is given in sensation by further intentional acts. Knowing, then, is not a single type of intentional act but a series of distinct but related acts. To know is to reasonably affirm one's understanding of some experience. The first realism, again, assumes the immediate presence to consciousness of the real object. Objectivity,

---

30   At present such ordering is a function of historians doing FS3, but, in the mature practice of FS, the recycling of such developmental sequences through all the specialties will make them a common possession for all of those engaged in any of the eight functional specialties.
31   *Insight*, 413.

then, must be a property of a sensible object "out there" or of a feeling "in here." In contrast, the third position in UV is that objectivity is a consequent of distinct types of intentional acts meeting the demands of their various operators. To say that objectivity is a "consequent" is to assume the preceding meaning of knowing; namely, objectivity is a product of multiple intentional acts that together constitute knowing.

This synopsis of UV may unintentionally mislead readers into settling for a nominal understanding of the three positions instead of personally acquiring the insights they formulate. However, one way of determining whether one has won through to a more developed viewpoint, as opposed to being able to quote someone else's position, is to compose a personal narrative about what experiences and insights sparked doubts about one's first estimates of reality, knowing and objectivity. How did one respond to any doubts? Was there a "startling strangeness" in departing toward a more developed viewpoint?[32] If the answers are "yes," then the following claims may be close to what readers have already discovered for and about themselves and so can affirm in direct address.

> 1. By "real" we mean whatever is affirmable in correct judgments, and by the "known" we mean whatever meaning is correctly affirmed regarding intended and understood objects or events of experience.

> 2. Our knowing is not a single type of intentional act; instead, it is an order or pattern among distinct but related types of such acts. In abbreviated form, by "knowing" we mean the process of intelligently grasping and reasonably affirming our understanding of some content of experience.

> 3. What do we mean by the third term, "objectivity"? In keeping with the preceding meanings of "real" and "knowing," we understand it to be a consequent of intelligent inquiry and reasonable judgments. Put another way, objectivity is not a property of an "object

---

32   Ibid. 22. For one of these writers, a first experience of strangeness was walking through a nature preserve with some limited understanding of the nitrogen cycle and wondering what the plants he saw actually were. Later experiences in clinical psychology and the neuroscience of attention provided more complex puzzles that helped stabilize his own developing understanding of the three basic positions.

out there" but a characteristic of how our distinct but related types of intentional operations are related to the objects we intend.[33]

Why is this third element (UV) a basic requirement for doing comparative interpretation in a new way? The answer has four parts. First, given multiple differences among horizons, varying degrees of development among audiences and variations in modes of expression, we need an interpretive framework broad enough to include such diversity. Second, if applying such a framework to incompatible differences is to yield defensible results, it must contain "common grounds" that precede all of these differences. Third, if there is an invariant pattern to the intentional operations that precede explicit conclusions and are constitutive of knowing, then basic positions formulating an understanding of such functionally related operations and their implications for the meanings of reality and objectivity can provide the needed common grounds. Fourth, from that viewpoint, one can go on to trace some of the differences among interpretations to stances consistent with or at odds with the formulated basic positions.[34]

The earlier texts offered far more details in support of these four claims. Here we simply assume that implicit notions of reality, knowing and objectivity often make a difference in explicit positions regarding questions in ethics, politics, theology and the sciences. Such differences appear in the cases studied in this series. However, in contrast to the usual state-of-affairs where these three notions remain hidden assumptions, the case studies make them explicit. Thus, a critical interpretive framework should be able both to acknowledge diversity of views and to trace the origins of some differences to tacit notions about the three basic issues. Failure to locate these fundamental sources of disagreement leaves them in the background, unarticulated and unexamined; but to do so is to proceed uncritically in doing philosophy.

Why is there the further expectation that practitioners of FS4 will explicitly state their own positions on these three questions? To evade

---

33   For a review of distinctions among four types of objectivity, see *Cracking the Case*, 26-27.

34   Are formulations of the three basic positions to function as transcultural categories in a science of interpretation? Someone may quickly object that any formulated position will be but one of any number of possible formulations. After all, an indefinite number of descriptions can be generated about any object of experience. A first response is to note how operating in an explanatory mode, and so defining terms in relation to one another, can partially escape the variable meanings of common-sense language. A further response points out that persons attempting to argue that the basic positions of the universal viewpoint are unjustified will proceed to operate with the very structured operations they are denying.

this challenge is to hide from the spontaneous questions for judgment that press for more than simply cataloguing the diversity of historically available interpretations. They are different, but why and can they be evaluated? While research specialists may assemble divergent views on any topic, eventually other specialists raise questions about the plausibility of those views. Then questions about signs of development in those views are inevitable, and judgments about advances and retreats in understanding will become the focus of inquiries. Thus, at least some interpreters should attempt critical judgments within comparative interpretation and communicate their results to specialists in other areas.

An added reason for being explicit about one's own positions is that leaving them unexamined may entangle one in seemingly endless debates that invite ridicule. Of course, to accept the challenge of direct speech on these three questions is to invite criticism of whatever positions one does take. Such self-disclosure is atypical amid current scholarly conventions. However, if such personal positions are never to be topics for discussion because of possible embarrassment, what hope is there for moving past conflicts originating there? Again, at least some interpreters should make comparative interpretation their specialty. To identify and to evaluate diverse interpretations on any number of topics, including one's own positions on the three basic issues, and to circulate one's conclusions for peer review offer some hope of resolving puzzles and avoiding impasses.

Still, no one should underestimate the reluctance of scholars to expose their potential lack of development by taking public stands on basic questions.[35] Admittedly, doing comparative interpretation requires some degree of direct discourse, of self-disclosure. Conventional academic practices provide all sorts of "defense mechanisms" for the reluctant. Still, the common ground that allows for comparison of differing views will be, for instance, what one means by "real." To paraphrase Lonergan's comments from a slightly different setting, practitioners of the fourth specialty must not conceal their assumptions but lay their cards on the table.[36] So it is not enough to possess mastery of the primary and secondary literature on authors and selected topics. It is not even enough to have a grasp of the spectrum of variant opinions on the three basic questions. What will be crucial are: (1) locating oneself within that spec-

---

35   Added to this reluctance may be the presence of some forms of bias. Despite the cliché about all persons being biased, the basic question to ask is whether interpreters are "on the move" in raising new questions. As long as this is the case, there is the possibility of developing beyond any initial limitations in present understanding, even if some types of bias are among those limitations.

36   *Method in Theology*, 193.

trum of less and more developed stances, (2) objectifying that self-understanding in how one explicitly evaluates competing views and (3) being open to further development as one's work is recycled by and among other specialists.

C. Genetic Systematics

Comments on FS3 and FS4, especially in regard to developmentally ordered sequences of views, have already introduced GS but not as a distinct fourth element of the new practice. Those comments were further specifications of what Lonergan listed as preconditions to doing dialectic or comparative interpretation.

> First, there is the genetic sequence in which insights gradually are accumulated.... Secondly, there are the dialectical alternatives in which accumulated insights are formulated, with positions inviting further development and counterpositions shifting their ground to avoid the reversal they demand. Thirdly, with the advance of culture and of effective education, there arises the possibility of the differentiation and specialization of modes of expression....[37]

To distinguish these tasks even further, suppose practitioners of FS3 have a broad enough historical perspective on some issue so that they can organize diverse interpretations into a genetic sequence of viewpoints leading, according to their best judgments, from the least developed to the currently most developed. Again, the temporal frame of reference matters here. At present functional specialists must first invent such sequences of views. In the future such orderings will be common possessions or models imparted in graduate studies and routinely employed in assessing new or previously neglected views. But for now we assume experiments in constructing such sequences are worth trying. This general supposition could cite as a precedent Hegel's dialectic, assuming it is read as a genetic sequence of ever more comprehensive viewpoints on the relation of consciousness to its objects. Again, talk of such a genetic sequence need not assume that one can map developing viewpoints along an unbroken timeline.

---

37   *Insight*, 609-610.

Since the basic positions (UV) identified in Section B represent performatively based meanings of reality, knowing and objectivity, they can serve as measures of what otherwise would remain incommensurable stances on those three issues. The implication is that divergence from any of these positions is evidence of a less developed viewpoint. A further step will be to relate the multiple viewpoints among themselves as reflecting varying degrees of development. In effect, this frame of reference for comparing views includes not only the positions one has affirmed but also an acquired understanding of the range of alternatives to those positions.

The practice of GS is a remote goal and clearly beyond the competence of one person, so the teamwork of functional specialization is a precondition to its attainment. In pursuit of this remote goal, specialists in FS3 will situate new contributions within a genetic sequence. Determining whether a new interpretation was properly situated in the sequence would be one more task for comparative interpreters in FS4. But, as with their other tasks, recycling of their works will be routine. And here is the further implication of doing so: recycling will gradually produce increasingly detailed genetic orderings of explanatory interpretations of various topics. As those accumulate and undergo recycling and refinement, future specialists in comparative interpretation will have them as a further basis for evaluating new interpretations.

D. Functional Specialization

The previous books offered little more than a sketch of the first four of eight functional specialties and omitted any descriptions of the last four. This review chapter goes no further. What follows is an effort to link comparative interpretation (FS4) to the three preceding specialties. As a further limitation, what follows describes FS in relation to the first temporal frame of reference. In the absence of a more mature practice, it describes what is presently possible to achieve. Someday practitioners will rely on the cumulative and progressive results of numerous collaborators, but those results and those numbers belong to the future. So what is possible today?

Research (FS1) identifies and assembles the various texts and loci pertinent to a common topic. Especially if the topic is as broad as the history of hermeneutical practices, researchers would have to rely on a team effort. When the literature on the topic is ever expanding because of new contributions, research will be ongoing and intergenerational. Consider how assembling a variorum edition for a literary classic may be an ongoing enterprise as new materials surface that were unknown to previous researchers. Biblical studies provide numerous cases of archaeological and textual discoveries adding new materials for inclusion in the resources scholars have been consulting. Experiments in particle physics sometimes produce anomalous data that generate excitement among those whose task is to make sense of, to give an integrated account of, all the available data. That is not the task of someone engaged in pure research, and so one can begin to imagine how the findings of the first specialty become the materials passed on to the next specialty.

The tasks of specialists in interpretation (FS2) include taking the researchers' assembled materials and "lifting" them into the horizon of theory (H2). Doing so calls ideally for transposing the pre-theoretical modes of discourse that will be prevalent in the assembled materials. Experimenting with various explanatory categories to discover their usefulness in "framing" or relating all the diverse materials will likely follow. As noted before, basing these category schemes on an understanding of intentional operations is one way of evading some of the problems of relativity to audiences and to varying modes of expression.

Still, different categories are likely to be in use, and interpreters, manifesting different degrees of development, will produce different viewpoints on a number of issues. Thus, multiple interpretations, ranging from the marginally different to those that are incompatible with one another, will result. Specialists in interpretation do their work by making the best sense they can out of the materials researchers pass on to them. Whatever diverse results they produce, they, in turn, pass on to the third functional specialty.

The primary task of historians (FS3) is to take the currently available works of interpreters and "order" them into plausible sequences of increasingly more adequate interpretations. Assuming historians are also operating in the second horizon, their judgments about which explanatory interpretations are more and which are less developed will indirectly reveal something about their own development within the second and third horizons. Again, differences in development will yield different orderings, so what one historian judges to be the most advanced interpretation to date may to others seem less so. At least there will be some explicit reasons for multiple rankings, and appeals to matter-of-fact differences may not get the final word.

When historians doing FS3 produce different orderings of explanatory interpretations, these become materials for the fourth functional specialty. Lonergan labeled it "dialectic." Because of the diverse uses this term has had in the history of philosophy, these authors have preferred the label "comparative interpretation." Whatever the label, how is dialectic or comparative interpretation distinct from other specialties?

First, what are the tasks for comparative interpreters? Suppose they are comparing the views of historian A and historian B (both specialists in FS3) on developments in the historical interpretations of some common topic. They want to know something about what each author understood about the history of those readings. They proceed to notice similarities and differences in the two historians' ordered sequences of interpretations. However, suppose the comparative interpreters have some familiarity with GEM and so recognize that they are actually comparing and contrasting their own different acts of understanding. They know, in other words, something about how they are operating in relation to texts. Their integrations of ink marks are relatively self-luminous operations; they recognize their constructive operations in making sense of whatever materials they have "to hand." Furthermore, they appreciate the difference between interpretive acts of synthesizing and reflective acts of judging. As a result, they bypass clichés about it all being a "matter of interpretation" or "cultural perspective." They go on to ask whether their understanding of the two historians' meanings was the latters' intended meaning (or a plausible implication of what the two authors intended). They are attempting to know what was on the mind of each author (or what further insights eluded but were implicit in what either author did affirm).[38]

How are comparative interpreters able to know what the historians were thinking? Suppose that at first they cite their years of scholarly research in primary and secondary sources regarding both the writers and their common topic. They may even marshal specific texts as proximate criteria supporting their judgments about the authors' meanings. In both activities, they will be demonstrating scholarly expertise. However, assuming the canon of explanation is conventionally accepted and so is part of their standard practice, they will go on to ask further questions. For example: "Within which horizons did the two historians write?" "What were their positions on basic questions about the meanings of reality, knowing and objectivity?" "What are our own horizons of operations and basic positions on the three questions?" By asking such

---

38   The comments in parentheses reflect the adage that sometimes interpreters know authors better than they knew themselves.

questions future scholars will be acknowledging the "existential dimension" of comparative interpretation. They will be asking about degrees of development, and so of competence, both in themselves and in authors they study. By explicitly taking a stand on the three basic questions, they will be revealing something about their own development.

This descriptive account of some steps in the fourth functional specialty points beyond current practices.[39] Perhaps the key innovations are (1) the shift to operating in the second horizon and (2) the effort to trace some differences among historical explanations back to variable stances on the questions of reality, knowing and objectivity. Note that "comparison" now has a new meaning; namely, reducing differences among explanations to underlying stances on the three questions is actually comparing them to one's explicit answers to the three questions.

How does one justify this new way of comparing interpretations? One response is to repeat the claim that, just as questions precede answers, so operations precede outcomes. To work out the pattern of operations presupposed by all forms of knowing and to recognize its implications will be to find the *tertium quid*, the common ground, to which one can relate opposing answers. In addition, this framework for comparing views includes not only the positions one has affirmed but also an understanding of the range of alternatives to those positions. So part of a second response is to raise and answer a question about how universal or comprehensive one's viewpoint is. Does it leave out or fail to consider any of the less developed stances on the three questions?

Publicly answering this question opens one up to criticism and potential embarrassment; however, this may be the price of making progress in one's field. Why might this be the case? To engage in the new type of comparison, specialists in FS4 disclose what explanatory orderings of stances they think are consistent with or at odds with what they themselves affirm as basic positions. Since there will be disagreements in many cases (ranging from slight differences to incompatible views), the practitioners of comparative interpretation will be supplying new materials for further rounds of assembling, interpreting, ordering and comparing. In other words, by recycling different views through the first four specialties and inviting criticism and correction, the participating specialists may be developing, making more comprehensive, their own viewpoints.

---

39   This account is an abbreviated version of steps that Lonergan laid out in *Method in Theology*, 249-250.

Why should anyone believe such recycling will go anywhere, will achieve any "cumulative and progressive results"[40] and so justify this new way of doing comparative interpretation? The ethos of peer review in the natural sciences provides grounds for hope. For example, at a conference a research team may report some recently acquired data that seem at odds with prevailing views in the field. Everyone in the field expects peers will quickly attempt to replicate the anomalous data. If they succeed in producing the unexpected data, whatever hypotheses they advance to account for the data will provoke a new round of efforts to test them. Common practice, then, already includes recycling and is a precondition to the ongoing development of various fields of inquiry.

III. Summary of Comparative Interpretation

The pedagogy of the *Primer* dictated a slow approach to the meaning of comparative interpretation. An author operating within a conceptualist tradition might have begun with a definition of the phrase and then proceeded to specify what the definition implied. Missing in that case would be any record of the slow climb through multiple insights into the meaning of the definition or concept (assuming it was more than a descriptive formulation). In contrast, the *Primer* invited readers to work toward a serious concept of comparative interpretation by gradually accumulating a series of insights into its five elements.

This review chapter has necessarily abandoned that slower pace and instead has used the doctrinal mode of discourse to summarize much of the two previous texts. All the same, the abbreviated results provide a basis for moving on to the case studies in the following chapters. Earlier case studies and the new ones to follow are experiments in applying this framework. From the earlier tests of its usefulness emerged a third approximation to the meaning of comparative interpretation. Five steps outlined how doing FS4 will proceed: (1) it begins by summarizing different orderings of interpretations handed on from FS3; (2) it identifies similarities and differences in those materials; (3) by raising further why-questions, it seeks to explain those similarities and differences; (4) it does so by reducing some similarities and differences to their origins, e.g. by relating some differences among the historians' sequencings

---

40   Ibid. 4.

of interpretations to variable background stances, some of which are at odds with basic positions the specialist has explicitly affirmed regarding questions about reality, knowing and objectivity; (5) after identifying which similarities and differences are compatible or incompatible with these positions, the specialist in FS4 proceeds to evaluate them as reflecting more developed or less developed viewpoints; (6) even if an ordering of interpretations is less developed than another, the specialist may find some part of it is worth retaining and developing.

To understand comparative analysis in this way promises to solve a number of problems. Descriptive comparisons tend to vary relative to modes of expressions, the capacities of anticipated audiences, the horizons of the interpreters and the presence or absence of bias in them. These multiple sources of variability are obstacles to comparative interpretation ever becoming a science of interpretation.[41]

To take up the first two obstacles, how might comparative interpretation avoid relativity to mode of expression and audience? The third element (UV) is responsive to this question. If all common-sense meanings, all theories and all implicit viewpoints presuppose intentional acts, and if there is an invariant pattern in the relations among those acts, then there is something in all inquirers that is invariant. However, to formulate this invariant pattern is to put into one set of words what others may express differently. What then is invariant? The second element (GEM) is responsive to this problem, and its solution is to distinguish between variable expressions and a single insight, or between different sentences and a single proposition. While formulations can be recast in any number of ways, the pattern of operations that generate meanings is not open to radical variation. The performative argument for this claim is straightforward. Any attempt to disprove the claim would make use of the very patterned operations being denied. In addition, while insights into the process of making meaning may be expressed in various ways, the appeal to audiences to reflect on their own performance is one check on the adequacy of the various formulations.

These, then, are partial responses to the question about the possibility of a science of interpretation. While no more than basic elements of such a science, the five components of the new comparative interpretation, including the affirmation of an invariant pattern among intentional operations, provide some "control" over modes of expression in doing this new science.

---

41   *Insight*, 587.

An earlier claim was that a type of developing human inquirer was a criterion for evaluating some philosophical differences. The third approximation now allows for greater specificity. The criterion is the self-reflective subject: (1) "at home" in the three horizons, (2) operating from the universal viewpoint, thereby (3) able to anticipate the range of often hidden assumptions at the origins of many explicit philosophical differences and so able to correct those at odds with UV. Of course, we foresee further developments in both subjects and their practices. Again, the temporal frame of reference for this volume is predominantly what is presently within our reach. We can anticipate more refined and standardized procedures that later practitioners of FS4 will exhibit, but the following chapters reflect experiments in what for now is an innovation still finding its way in the world.

CHAPTER TWO: ART AND ECOLOGY

This chapter experiments with applying the new practice of comparative interpretation to art history, the history of ecology and the varied meanings of "environment" in both. Section I draws upon a recent work surveying competing understandings of ecology that affected how artists understood their own works and practices during two decades of the last century. In section II those competing views of ecology and a second historical survey of competing meanings of "ecosystem" supply the materials for composing different genetic sequences of less and more developed views and, thus, for doing FS3. In section III those different sequences become the materials for applying FS4 to different views in the history of art and in the history of ecology.

I. Nisbet's Work

A recently published work by the art historian James Nisbet provides the background for identifying both diverse views of ecology and different ways artists conceived of their works in relation to environments.[42] The author's purpose is to understand how different views of ecology affected the understanding and practice of artists in the 1960s and 1970s. He finds four "clusters" of views and practices[43] and, without judging the correctness of any of them, surveys how artists participated in or resisted different ways of thinking about ecology.[44]

---

42   *Ecologies, Environments, and Energy Systems in Art of the 1960s and 1970s* (Cambridge: MIT Press, 2014).

43   With some modification of the original author's categories, the four clusters are: environmental art, land art, ecological art, process art.

44   Nisbet, 11. At the same place the author states what he means by "ecology." It refers "not only to concerns about pollution, resource management, and earthcare in general, but also to how information travels and coheres into historical explanation. If the fundamental insight of ecology is that all forms of matter upon our planet are connected to one another, the unfolding of ecology as an intellectual field over the past century and a half has sought explanatory models to account for this sweeping interconnection." One implication here is that ecology is a

He notes one source of diversity and resistance in a basic puzzle concerning how to understand environments and ecological systems. On the one hand, there is plenty of evidence of temporal changes and flexibility in ecosystems; but, on the other hand, the tendency is to talk of them in mechanistic terms, i.e. as constituting "closed, entirely self-serving cycles."[45] Early on in the book the author notes a similar problem in acquiring an understanding of time and finding a language appropriate for talking about art history. If that history is thought of as reflecting regular patterns of development, then the metaphors drawn from botanical cycles of emergence, growth and decay will seem appropriate. Thus, the history of art may be analogous to the relative order of an ecology. However, if art history is thought of as far more diverse, even chaotic, then physics may supply more appropriate metaphors, e.g. energy impulses, resistance, increments and losses.[46]

In fact artists employed metaphors from both fields during the 60s and 70s. The results were both vagueness in the categories in use and competing ways of talking about ecosystems, e.g. ones that emphasized their stability and continuity versus ones that favored their openness and flexibility.[47] As a further instance of what previous books in this series have termed "multiplicity," early discussions of environments and ecological systems lacked both a critical language and agreed upon meanings for whatever terms were commonly in use. It is no surprise, then, that, when artists in the 60s and 70s inquired into how their practices were related to broader material conditions, they employed multiple terms such as "whole earth," "environment" and "ecosystem" and often did so without close attention to the meanings of those terms.

All the same, Nisbet does suggest a pattern of increasing complexity in how artists understood the material conditions for their works.[48] The

term relevant to understanding not only biological systems but also the social development of intellectual fields. How the latter manifest ecological patterns of relations will be exemplified in section III and its remarks on FS.

45   Ibid. 209.

46   The author cites George Kubler as a defender of this second way of speaking about art history (ibid. 2). Cf. the latter's *The Shape of Time: Remarks on the History of Things* (New Haven: Yale University Press, 1962).

47   As examples of these contrasts between "closed" and "open" systems, Nisbet cites Norbert Wiener's works on cybernetics and Ludwig von Bertalanffy's general systems theory. Ibid. 6-7. Section III will offer a third option termed "emergent probability."

48   "By following the rise of systems thinking and its interaction with emerging communications technology, this book will trace a turn from art that addresses artificially confined environments and simplified allegories of the planet to art that increasingly attends to the more 'unruly complexities' that bind global ecologies of information and power." Ibid. 12. As will appear in Section II, the implicit criterion of comprehensiveness is at work in constructing this pattern, and, while Nisbet is reluctant to pass judgment on which trains of thought were superior to others, his language does reveal an implicit normative ordering of views of art and ecology, an

simplest expression of the pattern begins with artists expanding their understanding of "environment" beyond the much older view of the earth as landscape or backdrop for paintings. To anticipate later developments: the changes were from that ancient view to understanding environment, first, as bounded space and then as self-enclosed whole.[49] Next was the view of ecological systems as open and interrelated and finally as ecologies of energy and information exchanges.

A traditional view of nature as supplying a panoramic setting or wide-angle landscape for artistic expression precedes these more recent views. While landscape painting has a very old history, the vistas of nature portrayed by Western artists were often not "pure" landscapes but backdrops for subjects and events, real or imagined. The earth, then, was understood as a stage upon which actors performed. The earth provided the stage props, but the drama, historical or mythical, was the focus of attention. While admittedly a too simple view of the broad range of landscape paintings, this traditional view of the earth as at the service of the artist antedates a series of contrasting views that gradually emerged in art history.[50]

Nisbet uses the category of <u>environmental art</u> to denote the first cluster of new views of the earth affecting artistic practices. The term "cluster" alerts the reader to expect divergent views and practices even within the same category. The legitimacy of the category depends upon some commonality despite the divergences. The unifying feature of the environmental cluster is the ideal of total art (*Gesamtkunstwerk*). That is, the art work is not something simply looked at (think of a conventional picture gallery in a museum) but something that one enters into, participates in, interacts with. Allan Kaprow's *Yard* provides one example. The artist filled the courtyard of a gallery with debris, primarily used tires, and invited visitors to walk over and among them, and even to rearrange the tires at their discretion. The environment he created was a space to be entered much as one moves through a neighborhood or one's home. In some environmental works artists added sound and lighting effects to complete or round off a total sensory experience.[51] Creating a total environment became the elusive ideal.

---

ordering that makes his study an approximation to FS3.

49   Once photographs from space became available, the earth could be conceived quite literally as an imagined sphere, a unified whole, containing discrete objects, both natural and artificial.

50   The Judeo-Christian understanding of a divinely bestowed human sovereignty over creation probably reinforced in the West this view of how the artist was related to materiality.

51   Nisbet, 12-22.

What do such works reveal about an understanding of earth as environment? Presumably the ordinary features of daily experience, e.g. the sights and sounds of street life and the tools and tasks of practical living, are features of environments we experience. Environmental art, then, aims at mimicking the objects and activities that constitute ordinary living, that surround us within the "bounded space" of that living. Suppose the guiding question asks: How do we interact with our bounded environments? To focus simply on visual experience will fall short of an adequate answer. Judging the conventional gallery experience to be too incomplete, Kaprow and others pursued an immersion experience of art, one appealing to all the senses.

However, gallery installations such as *Yard* evoke further questions. Is it possible to create an environment?[52] An artificial installation can provide a bounded space containing multiple types of sensory experience; however, is that focus on human sensory responses adequate in understanding what makes an environment what it is?[53] Nisbet cites Rachel Carson's *Silent Spring* (1962) as influential in expanding the view of environment beyond that of bounded space. She portrayed the environment as a unified, living whole such that major changes to even one part might "alter its larger relationships permanently."[54] Clearly modern technologies have generated new artificial environments (think of the chemically accelerated productivity of agriculture), but humanity's effects on natural environments were what alarmed Carson.

Given the limited purposes of this chapter, contemporary debates about environmental degradation and sustainability are not immediately relevant. Our first purpose is to trace changes in the understanding of the environment, and what Carson's work signals is the grasp of a natural environment as a systematic unity in which interconnected parts are mutually dependent. Questions of human mastery and exploitation of the environment, for good or ill, are secondary to recognizing the broadening perspective on the earth.[55] That perspective leaves behind the notion

---

52   Nisbet remarks that the answer to this question tended to be affirmative in the 60s but negative by the early 80s. (Ibid. 22.)

53   Asking what makes something what it is should bring to mind what the two previous books presented as basic distinctions between the orientation of common sense and the orientation of theory and between the subsequent differentiations of descriptive and explanatory modes of understanding.

54   Nisbet, 24.

55   Rachel Carson's words explicitly capture the sense of danger while also revealing the implicit theme of interdependence. "We still talk in terms of conquest. We still haven't become mature enough to think of ourselves as only a very tiny part of a vast and incredible universe. Man's attitude toward nature is today critically important, simply because we have now acquired a fateful power to alter and to destroy nature. But man is part of nature, and his

of a bounded space, whether artificial or natural, and represents a broader ecological reading of the whole. In place of discrete environments and autonomous objects within them, the expanded view is of a whole earth comprised of interacting systems, chemical, biological and technological.

What difference did this enlarged perspective make for the practices of artists? The change in practice was not immediate. The sculptures of David Smith represented something of a transition between a modernist claim for the autonomy of the artwork from its surroundings and the use of landscape for displaying those works. Beginning in 1954, he installed many of his sculptures in fields near his studio exposing them, as a result, to the vagaries of light, weather and changing seasons. Nisbet notes that Smith's arrangement of works outdoors anticipated "the importance of environmental sites in the installation of minimalist sculpture and then land art in the 1960s." However, the works were not "site specific" in that they could be and were moved without ceasing to be the same artworks.[56] Still, this was step toward understanding the mutual conditioning of works and settings. Visitors to those fields with their sited sculptures could not avoid experiencing the works with all the attendant changes in light, weather and seasonal colors. The effect was to join the visual experience of the sculptures with the varying conditions of an outdoor environment. Such variable conditions erode a sense of the artwork as a static object, the meaning of which is solely under the control of the artist.

The relativity of the art work to so many variables seems a barrier to any search for its meaning in the intentions of the artist. At a minimum, the localizing of the work entails that speaking about it will include an understanding of the empirical features of a particular site. Furthermore, the dynamic or fluctuating relation of the work to the changing conditions of its outdoor environment implies that, whatever part of the whole experience is dependent on artistic creation, it is not separable from the environment in which it is embedded. But then the environment altered by the work's placement is also inseparable from whatever has been created. Put simply, environments are understood as both found and made, discovered and invented.[57]

A further insight marked an even clearer shift from the initial understanding of environment as spatial container or boundary. Nisbet

---

war against nature is inevitably a war against himself." Concluding remarks from *CBS Reports*, "The Silent Spring of Rachel Carson." (1963). Quoted in ibid. 30.
56   Ibid. 34.
57   In Section III these insights into functional relations between works and settings will play a role in estimating the degree of development differing views of environment exhibit.

cites Marshall McLuhan's quip that "environments as such are imperceptible."[58] What might this mean? The old contrast between Being and beings offers a clue.[59] To manipulate an environment, for example by digging an irrigation canal, is to change what is perceptible, is to alter the visual environment. The field of perceptible objects is no longer the same. So it is that placing a piece of art in situ introduces something new into an audience's visual field. However, the environment itself is not an object for perception just as Being is not a determinate "what" or specific being. The implications are that an environment is not an entity alongside other objects for perception, and to site new objects in an environment both changes what is and leaves the environment something still unperceived.[60] This way of thinking about environments implies that earlier efforts to create a total environment or total art by manipulating sensory experiences were bound to fail.

The meaning of environment is shifting again. What began as environmental works such as Kaprow's *Yard*, sited within enclosed gallery spaces, gave way to placements outdoors reflecting how artists began to understand the interdependence of works and their sites. The most general change was from thinking of the works as discrete, autonomous art objects to grasping how they continually interacted with their sites. Furthermore, their environments were not fixed spatial boundaries but material conditions altered by and altering those works. If there was no "immaculate perception" of the work without its local material conditions, perhaps the next insights would challenge the notion of the earth as a materially "given" whole containing the works of the artist.[61]

The gradual emergence of these insights occurs in Nisbet's second cluster, land art, as artists deliberately "began to incorporate the existing environmental conditions of outdoor locales into their work."[62] It was not enough to place works "out in nature." Instead, the material conditions of their settings were to be part of the works.[63] Far from being an effort

58   Ibid. 63.
59   Chapter Six of the second book of this series, *Cracking the Case*, argued for this distinction and worked out some of its implications.
60   Niklas Luhmann's distinction between an ecosystem and its environment (Nisbet, 110) may derive from a similar insight. To differentiate objects or ecosystems would seem to require relations to some shared reality that itself is not another object or ecosystem.
61   To anticipate comments in Section III, the challenge is to move beyond the model of the world of immediacy such that one understands earth and environment not as imaginable givens but as data to be understood.
62   Nisbet, 42.
63   One land artist describes his own work in a way that illustrates Nisbet's point. He writes: "My sculpture [...] joins the kind of land art characterized by temporality and emphasis on the local. The landscape sustains art and becomes art. Human control relaxes. Environmental forces share in the creation of the work and its evolution." John Huddleston, *Healing Ground:*

to control the environment, the practice and product of the artist were dictated by the specific conditions of a locale. This meant the work was dependent on external conditions and so mutable in its form and hardly a finished product indebted solely to its creator's intentions.[64]

This recognition of mutability and dependence met resistance. Nisbet locates one source of resistance in disagreements among advocates and practitioners of minimalist sculpture. As part of "object aesthetics," the pure minimalist stance declared the artwork to be autonomous. For example, the critic, Robert Smithson, argued for the otherness of minimalist sculptures insofar as sufficiently astute viewers could perceive them without attending to historical or environmental settings. Presumably this argument was easier to make when the sculpted figures were cubes or other geometrical shapes exhibited in a gallery. "[Such] sculptured objects are internally devoid of all drama: they are mute, inert, and plain."[65] Peter Hutchinson initially held a similar view of minimalist sculpture: "The works reject emotion and display none. There is nothing obviously human about them or the abstract geometry, topology, algebra and crystal symmetry on which they are constructed."[66]

This stance was under siege in the 1960s because of the increasingly vocal environmentalist movement and because of the fascination with space travel.[67] Some minimalists were not immune to the effects of both. Photos from space suggested that the earth was a physical whole, a single object. But how were artists to relate their works to such an immense mass? For some minimalists this question initiated a departure from their focus on the discrete work independent of its surroundings. Placing minimalist sculptures in situ was one way of incorporating works and environments, hence the experiments with land art and earthworks. The transition to thinking of art as dynamically related to ecological conditions was underway.

What positive understanding of environment emerges for practitioners of land art? Just as the "unruly complexity" of biological diversity pushed biologists toward new ways of thinking and talking about eco-

Walking the Farms of Vermont (Chicago: Center for American Places, 2012), xiv.

64   This relation of artistic intention and local conditions is explicit in Michael Elmgreen and Ingar Dragset's 2005 "Prada Marfa," an installation sculpture that appears to be a luxury retail store set in the unlikely habitat of west Texas. Its desert setting reveals an intention to criticize consumer behavior in the marketplace. The fact that in time the desert will decompose the sculpture signals the work's dependency on local conditions and the limits of human control.

65   Nisbet is commenting on Smithson's views at ibid. 92.

66   Quoted in ibid. 98.

67   Nisbet comments at length on the "planetary visions" popularized by Stanley Kubrick's *2001: A Space Odyssey* and by Stewart Brand's famous cover for *Whole Earth Catalog*. Cf. ibid. 71-86.

systems, ones emphasizing their openness and flexibility, so art history exhibited its own unruly complexity and demanded new practices. For example, Nisbet investigates the appearance of postminimalism with its move away from the rigid forms of minimalism and asks what new insights were at work in this movement. A too simple answer would be the generality about what artists do; namely, they eventually "break the crust of convention" by transcending established techniques and forms. The author's more detailed diagnosis cites criticisms of the rational design of the Aspen Project[68] as misreading how ecologies function. The tendency of industrial engineering to assert control over materials and to impose order on them was the target of the critics.[69] Counter to the "top-down ideals of design," critics emphasized artists' dependence on raw materials and on unconscious processes within the artists (their psychic depths) and beyond the artists (their Zeitgeist and access to technological innovations). The general insight was that no one was in control of the whole process.[70]

The ideal of designing and controlling environments proved elusive. However, Nisbet cautions against assuming this repudiation of engineering or controlling environments was linear or without resistance. He cites experiments with psychedelic art and hallucinogens in the 60s as efforts to design and to control artificial environments that, by altering neuromolecules and behavior, would expand the meaning of reality beyond the mind. Altering "the boundaries of subjective identity and relationship to place" was one goal of manipulating sound and light, images and body chemistry. Nisbet's judgment, however, is that these artificial environments failed inasmuch as they eliminated the diversity of both subjects and environments.[71] Additionally, they marked a retreat from the earlier insights that environments (1) are more than

68   The reference is to the collaborative efforts of designers and industry to create ideal and total environments, "to control ecology by shaping the form of the earth's physical environment." The design of the campus for the Aspen Institute was to fulfill this ambition. Ibid. 136.
69   Ibid. 137.
70   Talk of "process" discounts talk both of the artist's intentions and of any conception of the artwork as a static object. Examples of land art that were subject to erosion and eventual disappearance undermined the latter view while interactive works inviting audiences to move through the works and even rearrange them undercut claims to the primacy of the artists' intentions. Cf. ibid. 137-139.
71   Cf. ibid. 42-52. Nisbet's judgment of their failure is important for what it reveals about his assumed position regarding the meaning of reality. He cites as a "false analogy" the belief "that to feel vibration was to feel the being of the world itself, as if life was merely a pulse and the earth a unified subject–a Mother Earth, a Father Nature–that could take in all other subjective multiplicities." (62) Some readers of Chapter Two of the *Primer* may recall how the immediacy of feeling belongs to the first stage of Hegel's dialectic of consciousness and to the first type of realism.

spatial boundaries, (2) are not entirely subject to human control and, yet, (3) are not separable from the human works placed "in" them.

Nisbet's third cluster, <u>ecological</u> <u>art</u>, represents a loose class of artists and works exploring a more complex understanding of relationships among variables, one in which the focus shifts from singular objects to patterns of relations.[72] Dennis Oppenheim's *Oakland Wedge* is perhaps one work signaling the transition. The work, "a wedge-shaped space cut away from the upward slope of a hill," challenged the autonomy of the art object, as independent of its environment. The triangular hole or "purely negative space" turned the contiguous environment into a periphery and exposed both the wedge and its surroundings to ongoing change.[73] What is clearly a minimalist work was at the same time part of a changing ecological setting and so no longer the autonomous object envisioned by Smithson and Hutchinson.

What some critics cite as a transitional piece between land art and ecological art, Helen and Newton Harrison's *Shrimp Farm: Survival Piece #2*, arguably represents a clear instance of the latter. It consisted of "four ten-foot-by-twenty-foot containers…each filled to the depth of eight inches with water that increased in salinity from one pond to the next. Given these '[simple] discrete ecosystems,' of brine shrimp, algae, and salt water, each pond achieved step degrees of redness, modulated by the amount of stress placed upon its population of algae by its salinity level."[74] In effect, the artists constructed an ecosystem as a work of art.

But the Harrisons and others soon recognized the limits of such artificial, closed ecosystems. Much like the enclosed, miniaturized biosphere of a terrarium, their ecosystem was too simple a simulation of the more flexible and dynamic ecosystems in nature. But to abandon artificial ecosystems and to embed art works in the more fluid ecosystems of nature raises a new question. How does the artwork retain its identity once integrated with a natural ecosystem? Niklas Luhmann proposed an answer in terms of types of systems. Ecological systems and artworks are two distinct kinds of systems capable of interacting while not being reducible to one another.[75] This proposal raises even further questions. How is one to conceive of an artwork as a system? If so conceived, all the while being distinct from ecological systems, what do both types of

---

72   Nisbet's astute diagnosis of the limitations of this second cluster is succinct: "Land art … was handcuffed by the constraints of a world constituted by singular objects and contained by a similarly solid sphere." Ibid. 127.

73   Ibid. 105.

74   Ibid. 99.

75   Ibid. 109. This claim about the irreducibility of distinct types of beings will reappear in Section III.

systems have in common? What similarities do they share such that any analogy is defensible?

Answers to these questions emerged as part of Nisbet's fourth cluster, <u>process art</u>. He cites Robert Morris as a peripatetic figure whose works and writings at various times reflected the different views associated with several of the clusters.[76] His association with process art lies in identifying material systems and artistic production as mutual exchanges of energy.[77] As flows of energy they have both similarities and differences. Regarding commonalities, both are mutable, dynamic, fluid.[78]

Nisbet describes an example of what Morris meant by a non-fixed, fluid artwork. One design of that artist's multiple versions of *Steam* is "a square bed of stones through which a plume of steam continuously rises." Breezes, fog and changes in pressure within heated water tubes alter the plume of steam, thus embedding the artwork in and having it mutate with conditions in the local environment.[79] This work is compatible with an understanding of ecosystems as fluid, dependent on variable conditions and enjoying only a relative stability. In turn, *Steam* represents artistic production as a process not of top-down control by the artist-producer but as one of collaboration among producers, available materials, current technologies and the history of art. Just as an ecological system endures through adapting to mutable environmental conditions, so the artwork as embedded in complex processes emerges from and remains dependent on mutable conditions.[80]

Nisbet notes that this understanding of a work's entanglement with so many variables contributes to the difficulties in identifying the boundaries of this fourth cluster; indeed, "its elusiveness and constant change are characteristic features."[81] What in nature's ecological systems

---

76   Ibid. 129.
77   Ibid. 131.
78   Robert Morris was emphatic about the mutability of the artwork and hostile toward any view of it as some fixed work "out there" the meaning of which was somehow permanent. He wrote: "Under attack is the rationalistic notion that art is a form of work that results in a finished product.... What art now has in its hands is mutable stuff which need not arrive at the point of being finalized with respect to either time or space. The notion that work is an irreversible process ending in a static icon-object no longer has much relevance." (Quoted in ibid. 145.)
79   Ibid. 146.
80   Ibid. 176-77. Hans Haacke captures this sense of interconnectedness between the artwork and its environment. A "sculpture" that physically reacts to its environment and/or affects its surroundings is no longer to be regarded as an object. The range of outside factors influencing it, as well as it own radius of action, reach beyond the space it materially occupies. It thus merges with the environment in a relationship that is better understood as a "system" of interdependent processes. "Untitled Statement" in *Theories and Documents of Contemporary Art: A Sourcebook of Artists' Writings*. Kristine Stiles and Peter Howard Selz (eds.) (Berkeley: University of California Press, 1996). Quoted in ibid. 202-03.
81   Ibid. 131-132. Elsewhere, Nisbet comments that the variety of practices within process

are material exchanges of energy are in cultural systems the control of energy and the processing of information. Yet this distinction between nature and culture is under attack among some advocates of process art.[82] Composing an artwork is not mastery of materiality. Morris, instead, understands it "as a kind of ecological composition; of work taking shape through the interaction of decisions made on the part of the artist, the inherent biogeochemical properties of the materials involved, and the conditions of the work's environmental situation over time."[83] This complex series of relations sheds light on the notions of energy exchanges among systems and of "ecological composition." Rather than top-down control, the artist's intended production is dependent on more complex processes involving materials in use, variable conditions in a specific locale, available technologies, sources of financing and past achievements of artists.

But if we talk of inorganic, organic, technological, economic and historical ecologies, has the term "ecology" grown so expansive as to be meaningless? Analogies are definitely in use, and the relevant similarity in play seems to be energy exchanges. Nisbet refers to Robert Barry as one who recognized that energy is a type of information such that cultural and institutional processes could be understood as similar to biochemical processes.[84] Barry experimented with this notion of energy as information in an exhibition that at first must have seemed quite strange. Visitors to his show perceived empty rooms; placed out of sight in closets were machines emitting carrier and ultrasonic waves. While inaudible to visitors the waves were forms of energy existing in the rooms along with the visitors and whatever sights and sounds they could perceive.[85] The experiment, then, was an instance of conceptual art. That is, the appeal was not to the senses of visitors but to their understanding. Could they conceive of how both the emitted electromagnetic waves and they themselves were bundles of energy moving about in continuous flows that only sometimes were sensible? While the limits of human sensibility can be supplemented by sophisticated detection and measuring devices, the generalized insight was that, whether in visible or invisible form, currents of energy were the foundation of whatever we perceive, think, make

---

art resist easy classification. Given the "unruly complexity" of biosystems, art historians perhaps should not expect to find less in their field. Cf. ibid. 176-177.
82   Chapter Five will comment on how environmental historians during this period were also criticizing this conventional distinction and replacing it with talk of "hybrid environments."
83   Nisbet, 139.
84   Ibid. 153.
85   Ibid. 156.

or become.[86] With Gregory Bateson we might conclude that "mental and material operations [are] interrelated events of transferring energy...."[87]

But this emphasis on energy transfers as well as Barry's experiment will evoke new questions. If energy transmission per se is invisible, has the sensory experience of process art been lost? Has conceptual art, pushed to an extreme, lost touch with any experienced environment?[88] Has art dematerialized? The questions became more pointed after Barry went on to photograph his rooms and their invisible electromagnetic waves. Why take photos of what ordinary cameras and the unassisted human eye cannot detect? Was it to underscore the dematerialization of art? Was it to record the setting for the electronic emissions rather than to depict an experience any viewer might have?[89]

Nisbet's responses to both questions are quite original and helpful in revealing the understanding of ecology at work in process art. Both questions presuppose that Barry's photos were "documents" meant to convey information about events. However, Nisbet suggests an alternate purpose, namely, to exhibit how "photographic processes are continuous with the actual energy events that they mediate via printed images."[90] Rather than documenting what dematerialization means or the setting for invisible transmissions,

> [the photos] model an alternate form of electromagnetic movement within the same space. Whereas photography is typically employed to capture static objects, Barry's photographs create a literal *medium* for empirically registering energetic change within an environment. Light does not reveal a subject in these works, but is itself the evidence of one electromagnetic presence that exists among others.[91]

---

86   Admittedly this is an expansion of Nisbet's reading of Barry's experiment at ibid. 156-157. However, it anticipates some of the evaluative remarks in Section III.
87   This is Nisbet's reading of Bateson. Cf. ibid. 157.
88   Nisbet reviews the interest in mental energy and health at the Esalen Institute (163-167) and experiments in body art that joined internal and external forms of energy (167-173). Both can be understood as attempts to link the invisible (energy) and the visible (health and body) such that persons are both subjects and environmental objects, producers and products, i.e. minds and bodies—to use the older terms.
89   These questions represent the two readings of Barry's photos that were commonly given but which Nisbet rejects. Cf. ibid. 195-196.
90   Ibid. 196.
91   Ibid. 197.

The thesis is clear: forms of energy, whether light or ultrasonic waves, are the ground of all environmental processes, whether visible or invisible. More specifically and in regard to similar photographic projects by John Hilliard and Jan Dibbets, "photographic prints are the result of chemical transformations intimately connected to the fluctuating photoenergetic conditions of the ecological world."[92] Clearly the understanding of artworks in relation to environments has shifted from pictorial or sculptural objects placed in gallery spaces or outdoors. They are no longer autonomous but continuous with environments understood as systems of energy exchanges.[93] At a deep level, the unity of art and world appears complete. Or does it?

At the start of his study Nisbet observed that reflection on art and ecology during the 60s and 70s exhibited the instability and unexpected mutations akin "to the life of an ecosystem itself." He later cautions against privileging talk of ecosystems and their energy exchanges to the neglect of categories appropriate to the different contexts – "political, geological, vegetable, atmospheric" – in which exchanges occur.[94] This cautionary note is renewed when he ends his study with remarks on unresolved tensions in process art.

A first tension is between generalities and the specific cases they are supposed to explain. To advance energy exchanges as fundamental to understanding ecosystems risks losing touch with the diversity of both human subjects and systems interacting in environments. What the category of "energy" gains in extension comes at a price, namely, the loss of details about the "unruly complexity" among so many distinct classes of particular objects and processes.[95] Nisbet discerns that energy exchanges are "animated" by specifics, whether they are technologies, organisms or persons.[96] The worry that conceptual art lost contact with the sensual experience of specific works and environments reflected this concern that concrete experiences that are "situated, perceptual, durational" can

---

92   Ibid. 203.
93   Nisbet identifies shifts in Eugene Odum's influential writings on ecology. He notes two major developments compatible with process art: "first, he incorporates social activity within the scope of ecology; and second, he alters the fundamental basis of ecosystems from cycles that synthesize biological, geological, and chemical components to a system that distributes energy." Ibid. 205.
94   Ibid. 177. Section III will put forward a theory of emergent probability as a way of respecting the diversity of contexts and their mutability while also being a way of talking about ecosystems from within the second horizon.
95   A similar criticism will appear in Chapter Five, Section II, in relation to the categories of "nature," "environment" and "agency."
96   To anticipate the language appearing in the next section, specific things exist in and through ongoing exchanges, but the latter are not things but schemes of recurrence that do not exist independently of specific things.

vanish amid generalities.

A second but related tension was mentioned at the beginning of the chapter. The question of whether systems are open or closed is not resolved by saying energy exchanges are at the root of all ecological events. The category "energy" cannot do the work needed to understand "how ecosystems are subject to temporal change" if at the same time one holds that energy exchanges occur "in closed, entirely self-serving cycles."[97] Further categories must be in use if we are to have an adequate understanding of how ecosystems develop.

A third tension remained largely out of view until the final paragraphs of Nisbet's study where he cites several environmental disasters occurring in the late 70s and mid 80s.[98] Questions of how artists' practices changed in step with their changing views of environment seem less significant in the face of mounting threats of environmental catastrophe. The practical concern becomes how to acquire an ecological knowledge adequate to meeting such threats. However, there is the further question of how to make any such knowledge effective in moving persons to take action. As Plato well knew, arguments are of limited use with most audiences; instead, affect-laden images are the key to moving persons out of their caves. To that end an aesthetics of environments can make a contribution. At least that is the hopeful note on which Nisbet ends his study.

II. Two Genetic Sequences

A. Nisbet's Sequence

Recall a central problem in this chapter: granted the meanings of earth, environment and ecology have changed over time, are we limited to recording matter-of-fact differences in meaning or can we detect any pattern of development in those meanings, i.e. a sequence of views approaching more comprehensive understanding? An earlier claim was that, though Nisbet professed not to judge the correctness of any of the different views of ecology he surveyed, he implicitly operated with a principle of comprehensiveness and so left clues to an ordering of those views from least developed to more developed. Indirectly he performed

---

97   Nisbet, 209.
98   As will appear in Chapter Five, environmental history arose in the 60s and 70s as a specialty largely in response to perceived environmental degradation.

one of the tasks associated with FS3.

This section reviews the meanings of environment found in his four clusters and identifies the genetic sequence implicit in his survey of a brief period in art history. It then outlines a recent history of changes in the meaning of "ecosystem," notes differences among them and proposes a sequential ordering of those usages. Having these two developmental readings out in the open allows for the practice of FS4, e.g. tracing some differences in the two orderings back to their origins in competing views about reality, knowing and objectivity.

The understanding of environment found in Nisbet's first cluster, environmental art, is that of encompassing or bounded space within which objects appear. Persons moving through and interacting with their familiar surroundings provide experiences of such an encompassing space.[99] Environment in this sense is a setting or background, e.g. a panoramic landscape, in which objects are situated. Visual experience tends to dominate in presenting examples of such settings and their "contents." Talk of a panorama containing diverse objects and events relies on this initial understanding of environment as boundary.

Land art was, according to Nisbet, indebted to the writings of Rachel Carson and the newly available photos of the earth taken from outer space. The latter provided an image of the earth that many read as depicting a single sphere, a material unity encompassing many diverse objects and processes. As diverse as the parts might be, they still belonged to a unified, living whole. This broadened perspective lent itself to talk of the environment as a single living ecology wherein all parts were connected. Hence, Rachel Carson's concern that changing a part could change the whole made sense because one assumed the earth as a unified environment formed a single system. Visual experience (the imagined whole) was here supplemented by a common-sense notion of causal relations, e.g. discrete human actions were those imaginable efficient causes that, for good or ill, changed the earth.

The understanding of environment found in the third cluster, ecological art, departed from talk of an imagined unity and, instead, favored talk of interactions among diverse systems. Physical, chemical, biological, technological and industrial systems form a series of interdependent

---

99   One could use the term "horizon" in a literal sense (i.e. "as far as one can see") to refer to this understanding of an environment. These authors have avoided this usage because of the differentiated meanings of "horizon" they repeatedly use in this book, namely, one's orientation toward an object of inquiry. Is one considering the object in relation to oneself (H1)? Is one considering objects in relation to each other (H2)? Is one considering how one is operating intentionally in relation to an object (H3)?

and <u>mutable</u> <u>ecosystems</u> that were far from being a complete unity. The emphasis within ecological art on mutability and incompleteness seems to be an acknowledgement of randomness as a genuine feature of inter-actions among systems. The same recognition of "surprises" occurring within dynamic environments helped undermine the ideal of humanly designed and controlled "total" environments.[100] Here visual experience and description give way to explanatory understanding. Causal relations need not be imagined as physical motions that either by design or by accident change an imagined whole; instead, they can be understood as intelligible relations of dependency among variables.

Process art operated with the most generalized and hence abstract understanding of environment. The focus was on what is common to all ecological systems, namely, <u>energy</u> <u>exchanges</u>. The study of ecology becomes the study of how diverse systems distribute energy, e.g. how stars consume fuel, plants absorb and release nutrients, industries con-sume one form of energy and produce another. Much like "force" in the third stage of Hegel's dialectic of consciousness, the constitutive element of every ecological process is energy. Here the explanatory category has broken with imaginable events in picturable settings, and the symbolisms of physics and biochemistry become more appropriate ways of conveying an understanding of what makes an environment what it is.

What developmental ordering of these four views of environment is implicit in Nisbet's study? One clue lies in his reading of art history as mimicking the "unruly complexity" of ecological processes. What is "unruly" would seemingly resist any ordering; however, science without any regularities at all would be impossible. As well, the history of science has presumably been less chaotic than the history of art. Even if one dis-putes the latter surmise, to speak of the history of something presupposes some continuity among instantiations of that something. The question, then, is whether different understandings of environment have shown any historical development. The differences among views are easy to cite, whether in the arts or in the sciences. But have any of those different views marked advances or developments in understanding?

What marks an advance? Suppose the expectation is that an increase in comprehension, in the intelligent integration of more of the available data, is one measure of a discipline's progress. The earlier claim was that Nisbet operated in his study with a criterion of comprehensiveness. His presentation of the four clusters occurred roughly along a time line

---

100   Nisbet's description of Kaprow's *Echo-logy* is suggestive of how an indefinite number of variables conditioning ecological outcomes will make human prediction and control of them problematical. Cf. Nisbet, 64-66.

extending over two decades. However, the linear model was secondary to what did take time to emerge, i.e. an increasingly more complex understanding of an environment and its conditioning of artworks. Robert Morris was a curious figure "on the move," not confined to just one of the clusters but experimenting in several of them. He was an instance of developing understanding. Additionally, the linear model breaks down when Nisbet notes how practitioners associated with an earlier cluster resisted a later one well past its initial appearance.

These authors conclude that, for Nisbet, process art and its understanding of environment represent the most advanced views of art and ecology during the two decades under study. Since he does not explicitly say as much, readers may wonder why we conclude this. We offer three reasons.

First, just as land art moved beyond the static perspective of its predecessor, environmental art, so an understanding of environment as interconnected systems forming an imaginable unity is an advance over a conception of environment as encompassing or bounded space. More diversity is recognized in the later view than in the earlier. Still, while the second cluster represents environments as more dynamic settings for objects, its holistic view is still indebted to an imagined unity or totality of objects and events.[101] An ecological view of environment as comprised of a series of diverse, interdependent systems, flexible in their interactions and open to novel changes, is more compatible with the "unruly complexity" of biochemical mutations, global extinctions and artistic experiments departing from prior conventions. However, talk of ecological systems ranging from biological cycles to cultural institutions rests upon analogical thinking. The further question is what similarity allows for such analogical comparisons? To this question the fourth cluster provided an answer in terms of what all biochemical and cultural systems had in common, namely, the absorption and distribution of energy.

What goes forward in these historically emergent estimates of environment is an expanding, increasingly more comprehensive viewpoint. In its generalization about a common ground for all environmental processes, the fourth viewpoint seems the most comprehensive one in the series. Still, Nisbet voiced some reservations about the fourth viewpoint. First, talk of energy flows among systems omits too many specific differences among types of systems and things. He cautioned against neglecting the categories appropriate to talking about geological, botanical, atmospheric and political systems, categories not reducible to talk of energy

---

101   This reliance on the part-whole metaphor will be left behind in Chapter Seven.

transmissions.[102] Second, the single category of "energy" is inadequate by itself to resolve the puzzle about open and closed systems. While some botanical cycles are relatively closed, few would say the same about agricultural and political ecosystems. Finally, insofar as energy crises and environmental disasters in the 70s and mid 80s helped recruit new members for vocal political movements focused on environmental issues, the what-to-do-question became paramount, and talk of energy exchanges as matter-of-fact processes did not supply the answers alarmed persons were seeking.

For these reasons the fourth view of the environment seems more comprehensive than the other three but is far from complete. To detect even further limits, we next survey a second reading of the history of ecological thought to extract a sequence of views on ecosystems, again looking for evidence of greater comprehension.

B. A Second Sequence

In *A History of the Ecosystem Concept in Ecology*, Frank Benjamin Golley traces developments in the understanding of ecosystems during a time frame roughly equivalent to that covered in Nisbet's study.[103] He warns that his readers should expect neither a single history of ecology studies nor a linear pattern of development in how ecologists have understood ecosystems. All the same, he does operate with two criteria in selecting materials for his story. The first criterion is of interest in our search for signs of sequential development in understanding ecosystems. In Golley's words, this criterion is one of generality: "Does the study open the window to larger vistas? Does it provide links to other events occurring at the same time"[104] Using the wording of this chapter, the criterion is one of comprehensiveness.

This criterion is the basis for his sketch of three stages in the development of the concept of ecosystem: a formative period, an initial growth stage and a time of rapid growth.[105] The formative period precedes the

---

102   Consider how different categories are in play in talking about plate tectonics and the formation of mountain chains, the nitrogen cycle and plant growth, depletion of energy resources and economic crises, weather patterns and demographic pressures, environmental disasters and detectable shifts in political opinions, including the rise of new political movements. While one may talk of all these processes as "energy exchanges," the differences among them are lost in such talk.
103   (New Haven: Yale University Press, 1993).
104   Ibid. xii.
105   Ibid. 185.

Second World War. While historians debate who the precursors to ecological studies have been, Golley begins with late nineteenth-century figures. The assembling of studies and their results for later organization under the heading of ecological studies was going forward, but the discipline, its objectives, terminology and methods were in formation and not yet a distinct field of inquiry. The minimal meaning of ecosystem was an understanding of how organisms were embedded in and dependent on environments.

The initial growth stage was marked by efforts to integrate various forms of inquiry and their objects, and the term "ecosystem" lent itself to this unifying function. In particular, it was broad enough to include findings from physics, chemistry and physiology, and by its inclusivity it evaded some of the dichotomies of previous debates, e.g. the divisions between "terrestrial and aquatic habitats, vertebrates and invertebrates, field natural history and physiology."[106] But this generality came at a price. Golley notes the frequent use of loose analogies (e.g. the world as a heat engine) while advocates claimed the new discipline was relevant to more problems than it could solve.[107]

The "time of rapid growth" saw the maturation of ecosystem studies. Analogies were still in use but under more control, and the understanding of ecosystems as "flows of energy and cycles of materials in well-defined systems" was, with some dissenting voices, widely shared.[108]

Again, the sketch does not present an unbroken line of increasingly more comprehensive viewpoints. For example, cybernetics for a time provided an analogy for how ecosystems functioned. However, the mathematical model of computers and their information flows proved unable to capture all the details of complex ecosystems and to generate testable predictions. One response to this difficulty, already noted in Nisbet's study, was to create artificial, controlled ecosystems, but the price in doing so was to close off such experimental settings from the interference of other systems and variables found in nature that introduced random variations and the probabilistic outcomes found in natural ecosystems. In short, the lab settings did not produce the knowledge of natural eco-

---

106   Ibid. 188.
107   Golley writes: "The condition of ecosystem studies at this time might be characterized by Claude Lévi-Strauss's term *bricolage*, which refers to the construction of an object or a theory from a variety of unrelated, found materials. The *bricoleur* arranges these and creates something new and unexpected from the disparate materials. Ecosystem theory was constructed from thermodynamics, from physical equilibrium theory, from information theory, from evolutionary history, from field natural history, and so on. In 1965 it did not yet form a coherent, organized body of knowledge." Ibid. 109.
108   Ibid. 204.

systems ecologists were seeking.[109]

Golley remarks that this disappointment led many to adopt reductionistic methods in ecological studies. An as yet unresolved conflict, already present in early ecological studies, is the dichotomy between research focusing on ecosystems as complex unities and studies attempting to explain macro-phenomena in terms of constitutive components. This ongoing tension Golley labels a conflict between holistic and reductionist approaches to ecology.[110] Despite this unresolved issue, his main observation is that the "mature" phase of ecological studies (at least as of the early 90s) witnessed the appearance of many types of ecologies. He attributes this multiplicity to an understanding of nature as complex and ever changing. We quote his remarks in more detail since they are relevant to the next section of this chapter.

> In the Heraclitian interpretation, the real world "out there" actually consists of fields of energy, matter, and information, which we stop in thought and language as if we were taking a snapshot of reality. The methods we use tend to enhance our capacity to see these "objects," whether we use a microscope that lets us see into a cell or a telescope that enables us to see into the universe. But we do not have equally powerful methods to see flux. What would our worldview be if we could do so? Intuitively, the field ecologist senses flux in nature and sometimes uses the ecosystem concept to express this sense of dynamism.[111]

The preceding sketch of Golley's history of ecological studies cited three stages but did not isolate the distinct meanings of ecosystem in use during them. What usages were in play and how were they distinct? Arthur Tansley coined the word "ecosystem" in 1935, partly to move beyond internal disputes that were negatively affecting the reputation of

109   "Of course, a system's behavior can never be fully determined, because it entails many interactions, and there are always stochastic elements to be considered. The only way to improve the predictability of a system's behavior was to take the system out of nature and confine it in a controlled environment, where it could be manipulated experimentally. [...] The isolation and closure of the ecosystem ignores the role of systems that control system behavior and introduce stochasticity. Ecosystems are open systems. Thus, neither the laboratory nor the modeling analogies led to the anticipated advances in knowledge of the ecosystems." Ibid. 189.
110   Robert P. McIntosh reviews some of the figures in this ongoing debate. Cf. *The Background of Ecology: Concept and Theory* (Cambridge: Cambridge University Press, 1985), 200-201 and 224-225.
111   Golley, 204-205.

ecology as a serious discipline.[112] The new term in this formative period referred to an understanding of how living organisms were integral parts of their habitats or physical environments, together forming hierarchical systems that were "the basic units of nature on the face of the earth." Of many sizes and kinds, ecosystems were one among many kinds of systems in the universe.[113] In the formative period, then, the meaning of ecosystem stressed the interdependence of organisms and habitats, with lower-order systems supporting more complex ones and making patterns of relations within and among such systems the "objects" of ecological studies.

Eugene P. Odum's work after the war increased the popular usage of what initially was a technical term. Golley suggests the meaning of ecosystem gradually underwent more theoretical development and became an accepted paradigm for ecological studies.[114] Notoriously "paradigm" suffers from overuse and vagueness; however, two necessary conditions for achieving that status in a field of inquiry are institutional acceptance of (1) common parameters and (2) shared theoretical and practical objectives. Ecologists met the first condition by agreeing that genuinely scientific ecology required detailed investigation of mutually conditioning exchanges between biological and non-biological components of bounded environments, e.g. ponds or watersheds; hence, the terms "ecosystem" and "ecosystem ecology" became common parlance. Evidence that many believed ecologists were meeting the second condition appeared with the post-war funding of ecological research by the Atomic Energy Commission, the International Biological Program (1968-1974) and the U.S. National Science Foundation. Practical objectives attracted the funding and permitted better organized and longer-term studies that, in turn, became models for future research projects.

---

112   Ibid. 27 and 34-35. By "ecosystem" Tansley meant "the whole *system* (in the sense of physics) including not only the organism-complex, but also the whole complex of physical factors forming what we call the environment of the biome – the habitat factors in the widest sense." Quoted in McIntosh, 193.

113   Golley, 8.

114   "During this period of about fifteen years [1950-1965], the ecosystem concept became established as a scientific paradigm in ecology. This paradigm described an ecosystem as an ecological machine constructed of trophic levels that were coupled through flows of energy. Ecosystems were in a steady state when the input and output of energy [were] balanced and no accumulation of biomass through productivity was observed. If there was an accumulation of energy and materials, as in successional ecosystems, the system would expand in biomass and species diversity until a steady state was reestablished." Ibid. 104-105.

[Especially in America,] the ecosystem concept appeared to be modern and up to date. It concerned systems, involved information theory, and used computers and modeling. In short, it was a machine theory applied to nature. The concept promised an understanding of complex systems and explicitly promised to show how Americans could manage their environment through an understanding of the structure and function of ecological systems and by predicting their responses to disturbances.[115]

The practical ambition to control and even design environments was already part of the American mindset, from city planners to agricultural agencies. In the background was an understanding of nature as an object to be understood and then manipulated for human benefit. As noted in Nisbet's study, a holistic view of the earth as a unified network of systems was part of this implicit worldview. Ecologists were to play a role both in understanding this complex web of relations and in preserving the equilibrium of the whole. With the rise of the environmental movement in response to Rachel Carson's work, the idea of ecosystems as self-regulating systems liable to disruption became even more popular. Threats to them were to be detected and reversed; practical benefits to be extracted from them were likewise worth funding, as in cases of managing water systems, forests and fisheries.

The common understanding of ecosystem in the second period reflected two perspectives on ecological research. Theoretical developments allowed for sustained inquiries into (1) how ecosystems functioned, (2) what disturbances occurred in them and (3) what responses the latter provoked, responses usually effecting a return to a relative equilibrium. Ecosystems, thus, were dynamic patterns of relations among organisms and environments, flexible enough to survive most disturbances but occasionally succumbing to catastrophic breakdowns due to natural or human interventions. The second perspective reflected practical ambitions to do more than learn how ecosystems functioned: the further purpose was to learn how to preserve and exploit them for human benefit. The machine analogy lent itself to both perspectives since breakdowns were conditions to be avoided while understanding regular functioning could lead to greater productivity.

Difficulties arose for both approaches to ecological studies. Golley notes two of them: (1) the abstractness, i.e. the simplicity, of the models

---

115   Ibid. 2.

ecologists employed for understanding ecosystems and (2) the reliance of many of them on a deterministic understanding of the relations among environmental and organic variables.

> The complex systems, sometimes consisting of thousands of species, were simplified by the theoreticians to sometimes as few as three or four components. The myriad environmental interactions between ecosystem components were reduced to a few flows of energy. The dynamic response of natural systems was made deterministic, being consistent with physical theory. The ecosystem was conceived as a machine, represented as a computer model.[116]

Dissatisfaction with both limitations inaugurated Golley's third period in modern ecological studies and with it a changed view of ecosystems. The introduction of evolutionary thought into mainstream ecology reflected a recognition both that simplified models missed too many of the real processes occurring in nature and that reliance on deterministic models from physics missed the temporal features of ecosystems, e.g. their evolutionary history.

The understanding of ecosystem during the intermediate period (approximately 1950-1965) had focused on how organisms and environmental conditions exchanged energy (e.g. nutrient exchanges), much like the moving parts of a machine.[117] As well, it had emphasized the departure from and return to equilibrium.[118] In contrast, the view of ecosystems in the third period focused on variations and developments within ecosystems, with equilibrium or steady states often being relatively short-lived phenomena. Resistance to this new view could cite the difficulties

---

116   Ibid. 4.
117   Eugene Odum's definition of ecosystem as the basic unit for research broadly defined the latter as "'any unit that includes all of the organisms (i.e., the 'community') in a given area interacting with the physical environment so that a flow of energy leads to clearly defined trophic structure, biotic diversity, and material cycles (i.e., exchange of materials between living and nonliving parts) within the system.'" Quoted in Donald Worster. *Nature's Economy: A History of Ecological Ideas*, second edition (Cambridge: Cambridge University Press, 1994), 364-365.
118   Golley raises difficult questions implicitly critical of this earlier emphasis on equilibrium. "What do we mean by equilibrium? First, what is the subject of our attention? Is it the genuine properties of the ecosystem? the secondary properties derived from the sum of the parts? or the property of a component such as a species population? Second, recognizing that the environment is continually variable and that biological organisms continually are born, die, adapt, and evolve, what limits in variance in space, time, and response do we accept with the concept of equilibrium?" (195.)

in detecting major changes in ecosystems.[119] An additional difficulty was the necessity for a division of labor in doing evolutionary ecology. Understanding complex and dynamic systems and their histories was beyond the competence of any single researcher and any one discipline. Physical, genetic, chemical, biological, atmospheric and human variables might all be relevant to understanding how an ecosystem functioned and underwent changes.

Golley identifies "relativity" as one characteristic of the third understanding of ecosystem. For him the term appears to have at least two meanings. First, given the diversity of disciplines contributing to an understanding of ecosystems, one should expect that different fields will produce accounts relative to their specialized perspectives.[120] Here relativity seems to mean "partiality" in the sense of incompleteness, i.e. each field's contribution will be a partial step toward a more comprehensive understanding of complex systems. Second, in contrast to deterministic views of relations in ecosystems, the new view endorses relativity as a common feature of evolutionary processes involving random variations. Here the term appears to be a synonym for probability. Golley goes on to survey a number of studies and arguments for rejecting a deterministic stance in regard to ecosystems and for preferring a probabilistic one.[121]

What stance does Golley take respecting these different ways of understanding an ecosystem? He first observes that "ecosystem" has served various purposes in ecological studies. "As a philosophical idea, it animates research and application in environmental studies and management. As a concept that identifies a physical object (in Tansley's sense), it is the subject of much scientific study. As a scientific paradigm, it structures scientific organization and research."[122] Our primary concern has been with the second purpose, i.e. treating an ecosystem as the basic intelligible object of ecological research. Golley gives a qualified endorsement of the holistic view of this object.[123] Citing the famous Hubbard

---

119   Golley notes the length of time it would take to determine something like a relatively steady state or equilibrium: "If it requires ten to fifty years of monitoring an ecosystem's properties to determine the equilibrium conditions of the ecosystem, we could consider equilibrium to be the history of the system. It is a statement about its past performance, not a prediction about its future state. Can we predict the future state? No, but we can describe broad limits of probability." Ibid. 196. Worster describes the decline of the equilibrium model at 391-394 in his *Nature's Economy*.
120   Golley, 189-90.
121   Ibid. 202-203.
122   Ibid. 200.
123   "The holistic view is not the 'right' view, it is merely another way of looking at the world. If we can agree that there are whole systems, with genuine properties, then we can investigate them with the reductionist scientific method and, within the limits of this method, discover useful things about them." (Ibid. 195.) Presumably the reductionist stance is also not the "right"

Brook study, he distances himself from the earlier focus on equilibrium models and thinks it better to talk of "response" systems that at any period are conditioned by their histories and habitats. In his words: "Ecosystems are loose systems, we could call them weak wholes, as compared to a strong whole such as an individual or a city. The changing environment in which the ecosystem is placed (that is, its landscape or biome) creates a dynamic response of the system as a whole."[124] Despite this acceptance of conditionality and variation, Golley decries the application of "evolution" to ecosystem in the 1970s, and, instead of "evolutionary ecology," prefers to speak of "ecosystem development."[125] Strangely, after offering these positive characterizations of his view of ecosystems, he writes at the end of his book: "the ecosystem concept is merely one more device for thinking about the world and ourselves."[126] We will return to this closing remark in the next section for what it reveals about Golley's implicit realism. First, however, there is the question of sequencing the three understandings of ecosystem identified by Golley.

What are those three views? The first conceived of ecosystems as objects embedded in landscapes[127] and contributing to the functioning of higher order systems. The second reflected the joining of physics, information theory and mathematical modeling and represented ecosystems as closed, self-regulating systems tending toward equilibrium. The analogy of the "ecological machine" with energy exchanges occurring among its parts, i.e. species types, was commonly used. The third view Golley identifies is somewhat continuous with the second since both views focus on energy flows (e.g. exchanges of nutrients) and cycles of materials (e.g. water flows and dispersal of nutrients) within systems. However, a new emphasis on ecosystem development and history and a de-emphasis of equilibrium reflect a non-deterministic understanding of ecosystems as dynamic and conditioned wholes with emergent properties.[128]

---

view. Still, at 191-195, Golley defends the holistic view.

124   Ibid. 196.

125   "Evolution has a distinct scientific meaning relating to genetic variation, natural selection, and the formation of new genotypes and phenotypes. Since ecosystems have no genetic structure or even an analogous genetic structure, there can be no ecosystem evolution in the same way that there is evolution of a biological species. Still, ecosystems do change over time, and we can speak of ecosystem development." Ibid. 197.

126   Ibid. 204.

127   Golley points out the absence of a common terminology for talking about the larger context within which an ecosystem functions. "Biosphere" and "landscape" were but two of the terms in use in the time frame he surveys. "Environment" remained an alternative but was probably no more precise in its meaning. Ibid. 199.

128   Ibid.191-192. Talk of emergent properties signals part of the debate between holism and reductionism in ecological studies. To affirm the reality of emergent properties is to side with the former.

What sequencing of these views does Golley endorse? Answering would be easier were it not for his remark that "the ecosystem concept is merely one more device for thinking about the world and ourselves." Nevertheless, without comparing this "device" to any alternatives, we can surmise that his comments critical of the equilibrium model and his positive remarks about holism and ecosystem development are evidence that he thinks the third understanding of ecosystem is more advanced than the two views that antedated it. As suggested at the start of this review of his history, Golley, along with Nisbet, operates with a criterion of comprehensiveness. Measured against that standard, the third view is more developed than its predecessors. It evades the deterministic commitments of the machine analogy found in the second use of the term and, instead, incorporates historical variations and developments in its understanding of the relations between biological and non-biological components of an environment.

III. Doing FS4

This section applies the critical apparatus of UV to the two sequences the preceding section identified. Differences in those orderings record variations both in understandings of environment (or ecosystem) and in judgments about how comprehensive those understandings have been. Prior to those varying judgments were various questions. To begin with Nisbet's implicit sequence, his general question was what debts to the material world did artists recognize they had in creating and later sustaining their works. Let this be the question of the conditionality of the artwork.[129] A more specific question he asked was how artists integrated art, biology and social dynamics.[130] Let this be the question of integration; namely, how is any work or thing a unity or whole when it has so many antecedent conditions and ongoing dependencies? His answers to both questions formed four clusters distinguished by different views of the connections among art, biology and social processes.

The first cluster of environmental art reflected pre-ecological thinking inasmuch as it presupposed the first type of realism. That is, both the

---

129   This question of conditionality will return later in this section. The issue will be whether any views of classes or kinds of things as stable unities or of ecosystems as closed systems are defensible if their antecedent conditions are subject to random variations.
130   Ibid. 2-3.

work as a discrete object and the environment as a picturable setting for the former belong to a world of immediacy. The works with their surroundings or boundaries were assumed to comprise a field of objects "out there" to be sensed. Since vision is but one mode of experience, the ideal of the total artwork, one providing a more complete sensory experience of the object and its settings, proceeded from the same realism. Sound and light shows followed in efforts to reach this ideal of immersion in multi-sensory experiences of art.

A problem implicit in this first cluster begins to appear when the question arises about the possibility of creating a total environment. To ask the question is to ask implicitly whether there can be mediation of immediacy. With this question one moves away from Hegel's stage of Sense-certainty and begins to recognize intentional acts as constitutive of whatever meanings works and worlds have for us. As noted above, there is no "immaculate perception" of the artwork, no immediacy in recognizing, i.e. understanding, what is sensibly present; but this is one step toward a broader generalization about environments, both natural and artificial; namely, as understood they too are mediated by intentional acts. Quite literally, an environment is not a sensible object.[131]

The second cluster, land art, mimics the shift to Hegel's second stage, Perception. No matter what material conditions and works the artist perceives, they have meaning only because of acts of sensing and acts of understanding. To recall the sketches of UV in the two previous texts of this series, any environment as recognized is part of the central nervous system of the one recognizing it. Succinctly put: what is apparently outside is inside. It is this second type of realism that is compatible with talk of a web of intelligible dependencies, of conditionality, entangling and sustaining works, artists, material conditions, art history and future developments. Any extensive range of linked variables eludes immediate sensible presentation; one has never literally seen a relation or pattern of relationships. Insofar as the conditionality of works includes such variables, it makes good sense to deny that those works are ever fixed or final.[132] Practitioners of land art explored such dependencies and explicitly

---

131   Nisbet, 64. Raymond Williams' thesis that there is nothing natural about nature (ibid. 4) reflects historical insight into the varying meanings of "nature" while also being compatible with an understanding of reality as mediated by intentional acts. It also points to this chapter's previously identified central problem: granted the meanings of earth, environment and ecosystem have changed over time, are we limited to recording matter-of-fact differences in meaning or can we detect any pattern of development in those meanings, i.e. a sequence of views gradually approaching more comprehensive understanding?

132   This theme of the conditionality of artworks anticipates the general meaning of environment that Chapter Seven isolates.

denied the notion of the self-enclosed artwork. Still, they continued to be tied to what Nisbet calls the "imaginary" of the earth as a solid sphere, a unified whole containing singular objects. All the same, they were slowly pushing beyond sensory experiences and environments as "containers" toward an understanding of dynamic relations among variables.

The third cluster, with its incomplete and mutable series of interdependent ecological systems, represents a breakthrough to thinking about art and environment in terms of constitutive relationships. For example, the question about what makes an artwork what it is now anticipates an answer in terms of ecological relations among significant variables. The advance over the imaginary of the previous cluster lies in a more refined focus on identifying the environmental conditions that constitute, sustain and modify artists, works and their settings. Talk of physical, chemical, biological, political and technological ecosystems, for all its reliance on analogies, is a more comprehensive way of accounting for things. Their conditionality comes more into focus as complex patterns of relations extending beyond the range of what is imaginable.

The fourth cluster with its talk of energy flows approximates Hegel's third stage, Understanding and Force. Biological organisms supposedly emerge and subsist through energy flows without themselves being the self-generating sources of such flows. Here we detect an increasing distance from the first realism of picture thinking. Just as Hegel's contemporaries thought of "force" as the invisible sustainer of objects and events, so talk of energy flows assumes that phenomenal organisms and artworks exist in and through what eludes sensory detection.

To the three reservations voiced by Nisbet, these authors want to add another. Does the focus on energy as the basic category for explaining ecosystems mark a retreat to the Pre-Socratic search for the "common matter" that made all things what they were? Or is energy to be a contemporary version of Aristotle's prime matter, i.e. the Scholastics' pure potency? Why might these questions be relevant to understanding an environment?

Aristotle held that "being" was said in many different ways, e.g. there are many kinds of beings. He held that what distinguished one individual instance from another in the same class was matter, i.e. what located it "here and now" versus "there and then." However, what made each individual what it was as a member of a class or kind was not matter but form, or better, a combination of forms. Form, not matter, grounded the differences between kinds.

Presumably contemporary audiences will balk at using the binaries form and matter, form and pure potency. Still, the insights formulated in these distinctions are worth preserving.[133] What-questions ask, first, for descriptive answers, ones that identify something by its observable properties. But persons asking these questions may not settle for the conventional labels achieved by sensitive apprehension and formulated in everyday terms. Their questioning may pursue explanatory understanding; then the anticipated answers, as noted in the third cluster, will form patterns of relations among relevant variables.

Now, as already claimed, energy is not sufficient as a category to explain the diverse forms of ecosystems. Why not? Recall how explanatory understanding presupposes further why-questions and that they anticipate the form of any answer will be a correlation or pattern of relations among basic or derived variables. Someone may suggest that forms of energy will be such derived variables. Consider how Barry's photographed experiments made use of invisible carrier waves, ultrasonic waves and photoelectric energy. One concern was that his experiment amounted to the "dematerialization" of art. However, one could come to Barry's defense: (1) all matter is energy; (2) we are historically accustomed to artworks being materially sensible; (3) but, if we are sufficiently astute observers, we will grasp the first fact and discount the pre-scientific habit of the second; and (4) we will thereby recognize that conceptual art, much like contemporary physics, is more mature than its historical predecessors. Still, one might ask whether this defense is repeating Galileo's mistake in dismissing secondary qualities as ultimately "real." Is there no limited but legitimate role for common-sense understanding in comprehending what is real? Returning to earlier comments about UV, the meaning of real is whatever can be intelligently conceived and reasonably affirmed, and not simply what can be understood in explanatory terms. More simply, Eddington had not two but one desk that was knowable, reasonably affirmable, as real in either of two ways.

If we accept the "duality" implied by the meaning of real, we can fault some practitioners of the fourth cluster for discounting the legitimacy of common-sense knowing in favor of talk of energy flows as the right way of understanding artworks and their environments. One implication of this criticism is that ecological art, the third cluster, may offer answers to the question of conditionality superior to those of process art. Among the relevant conditions for making sense of artworks are the describable materials available to audiences. Without access to those

---

133   The problem of finding a new vocabulary to convey such insights is not limited to philosophy. Michael S. Gazzaniga ended his 2009 Gifford Lectures by saying a related problem in the neurosciences was "the scientific problem of this century." *Who's in Charge? Free Will and the Science of the Brain* (New York: HarperCollins, 2011), 220.

materials audiences will have nothing to puzzle over, nothing to make sense of, but then also nothing to return to in checking any guesses they may make. Thus, we suggest a modification in the first sequence, one that demotes the fourth cluster from its status as more developed than the third.

In returning to Golley's sequence, we begin with a short review of its three ways of understanding ecosystems. The view he associates with the formative period was the simplest of the three. The term "ecosystem" referred to an understanding of how organisms were dependent on biotic and abiotic components of their environments and how there were hierarchies of systems within an ecosystem, with simpler ones supporting more complex ones.

The view Golley detects in the initial growth stage reflects a cross-disciplinary object of inquiry. Multiple specialists were needed to investigate the relations among elements of complex systems. The inquiries were guided by machine analogies derived from physics and information theory and by the assumption that systems were closed or deterministic and tended toward equilibrium.

The period of rapid growth operated with a fairly uniform view of ecosystems as energy flows and cycles of materials. As well, though there were dissenting voices, most ecologists came to accept: (1) a holistic versus a reductionist viewpoint, (2) an understanding of systems as open versus closed and (3) multiple types of ecologies, including evolutionary or developmental ecology. These differences Golley loosely labels as "relativity." As noted above, one of his uses of the term may be as a synonym for probabilistic relations among the constituents of an ecosystem. In any case, he appears to endorse this third view as the most comprehensive of the three he identifies.

The review of Golley's history cited two passages from his work that we promised to revisit in this final section.[134] He talks of a real world "out there" which we "stop in thought and language as if we were taking a snapshot of reality." He adds elsewhere: the concept of ecosystem is "merely one more device" we use to impose order on reality. What are the implicit meanings of "real" and "knowing" at work in these passages?

---

134   The first passage was: "In the Heraclitian interpretation, the real world 'out there' actually consists of fields of energy, matter, and information, which we stop in thought and language as if we were taking a snapshot of reality. The methods we use tend to enhance our capacity to see these 'objects,' whether we use a microscope that lets us see into a cell or a telescope that enables us to see into the universe. But we do not have equally powerful methods to see flux. What would our worldview be if we could do so? Intuitively, the field ecologist senses flux in nature and sometimes uses the ecosystem concept to express this sense of dynamism." (204-205)

Talk of "taking a snapshot of reality" is a clue to both meanings. At first one might suspect the metaphor reveals Hegel's stage of Sense-certainty and the belief that knowing is simply sensing what is immediately given to consciousness. However, Golley's reference to concepts as devices complicates the diagnosis. As a first step, recall earlier objections to the assumption within land art that the earth was a "given whole," a visible sphere that photographs from space made present to audiences for the first time. Those objections faulted this view as belonging to the world of immediacy, but they went on to claim that an environment was also not something given. In support of this claim we could have referred to performative differences between seeing and understanding, but our shortcut was a reference to psychology of perception. Where is the environment as recognized? Where is the earth as a recognized sphere? The outside-inside puzzle followed.

Golley makes no references to the puzzle, but his talk of concepts as "devices" is a clue that he recognizes the constructive or synthetic role of acts of understanding. Thus, the second step in our diagnosis suggests an implicit debt to Kant. Golley holds that concepts order experience, but, since they are constructs of minds, he probably thinks that, in adding something to experience, they are not contributing to a correct understanding of things themselves. Perhaps a twentieth-century constructivist version of Kant is at work behind the scenes. That is, just as it is possible to give any number of descriptions of the same things, so it is possible to apply any number of concepts to the same things. The term "ecosystem" is useful in emphasizing "a sense of dynamism;" however, it is merely a device and not a partial grasp of what makes something what it is. But implicit may be unquestioned expectations that real things are out there that ideally we should be able to apprehend directly by some kind of "super look." Since we cannot, we infer what we do understand must be different from the real things; they must be our own "constructs."

Might both these expectations about knowing and reality and this inference be the source of Golley's remarks? In the two previous books in this series, the authors affirmed old distinctions as part of UV. Two types of apprehension (sensitive and intellectual) paralleled the distinction between descriptive formulations and explanatory formulations. A further distinction between acts of understanding and acts of judging allowed for the earlier claim that environments are both made and found, both invented and discovered. These distinctions are relevant in understanding ordinary language uses of the term "concept." Descriptive terms are highly variable, and few would claim any one description of a sensitively apprehended object is privileged. What of formulations based on intellectual apprehension? Again, terms may vary with the theories they belong to; however, linking such terms, directly or indirectly, to categories derived from intentionality theory is one way of controlling meanings. For example, Golley argues in defense of holism by defending the notion of emergent properties. One way of strengthening his argument would be to ground talk of emergent properties and wholes "greater than the sum of their parts" in the distinction between images and insights. While dependent on the former, the latter are not reducible to the puzzling sights and sounds that give rise to questions.[135] Insights are integrations emerging from inquiry into puzzling images but are not themselves more images.

To return to the two passages, our question was what views of reality and knowing were implicit in them. If our surmise is correct, Golley assumes part of the infantile model of reality, i.e. what is real is what is out there to be confronted by inquirers, but he rejects the other part that identifies knowing with looking. Thus, he concludes that, since knowing is not a grasp of what is immediately given, what we talk about (our concepts?) are not to be identified with what is real. Concepts that in some cases are the results of intellectual apprehensions of what makes something what it is are instead mere devices for expressing meanings we have imposed upon the flux of experience.

Now these alleged deficits in his view of ecosystems and what ecologists are achieving in studying them are not fatal to the claim that his third view of ecosystems is more developed than its two predecessors. His brief excursion into generalities about concepts and knowing are at odds with his own performance. All the same, the third view of ecosystems he endorses is arguably superior to the alternatives known at the time he ended his survey. Presumably further developments in the understanding of ecosystems have occurred since the early 1990s. What they may have been is beyond the ambitions of this chapter.[136] However, there was an earlier promise to include in this final section an alternative to the dichotomies between thinking of ecosystems as open or closed systems, as probabilistic or deterministic in their relations, as better suited to

---

135   The same maneuver could be tried regarding talk of energy exchanges. Recall Nisbet's reservation that such talk tended to ignore the diversity of kinds of things. Might a defense of the irreducibility of distinct types of being also begin with an appeal to the irreducibility of insights to images? If whatever meaning "energy exchanges" has depends upon insights, might the study of how we reach insights provide a methodological guide to what meanings we defend?

136   In reviewing forty years of environmental history, Chapter Five will identify some developments occurring after the 1990s.

holistic or reductionist analyses.

Keeping this promise returns us to our earlier text, *Cracking the Case*. Chapter Two of that text surveyed Michael Gazzaniga's view of human consciousness, and his comments provided clues to thinking our way past dichotomies and any purported impasses. For him consciousness is emergent and modular, i.e. a large number of distinct systems at various brain locales in both hemispheres interact and give rise to new "levels" of organization that are not reducible to the properties of the originating subsystems. How does this happen? Presumably the subsystems are "far from equilibrium" and allow "the amplification of random events."[137] That is, as yet unorganized materials in such subsystems are available for new patternings or forms of organization that can emerge as a matter of probability.

This perspective offers clues to a third way of thinking about developing organisms and ecosystems, as both internally and externally functioning in relation to one another. Without mentioning natural selection and the question of survival, we can surmise that random variations within organisms and within the abiotic components of ecosystems sometimes significantly alter the original conditions that made those organisms and ecosystems what they had become. New conditions may evoke new responses from organisms that in turn alter other components of a wider environment. This surmise is not arbitrary. It is not much of a stretch to recognize that chemical resources in soil, air and water are capable of supporting a range of possible forms of plant and animal life. Which forms of integration have been realized to date was a matter of probability; given that those resources or prior conditions are subject to change, what future integrations will appear will also be a matter of probability. Deterministic "laws" only apply once specific conditions have been met, but meeting those conditions occurs not of necessity but as a matter of probability.[138] In contrast to talk of closed, deterministic systems subject to mechanistic laws, we can talk of a number of possible ways of ordering available materials; some are more probable than others; in time some become actual orderings, i.e. distinct types of organisms

---

137   *Who's in Charge?* 124.
138   Gazzaniga cites two cases of how one outcome may be reachable in an indefinite number of ways (i.e. "multiple realizability"). The hypothesis is that a more elementary system sets a range of possible combinations that may occur as a more complex system; however, which ones actually occur is not predictable from the laws applicable to the first system. He cites in support the work of Eve Marder on the nervous system of the spiny lobster and John Doyle's example of how, from nine letters in English, 362,880 sequences of just those nine letters are possible. Which of those many possibilities become actual words in the language cannot be predicted by simply knowing all those possible combinations. Ibid. 130-132.

and distinct types of ecosystems.

This perspective breaks with any research project trying to reduce organisms and ecosystems to ever smaller parts, e.g. to ever simpler forms of energy. Instead, the question becomes how do we understand the appearance of new integrations in nature? Still, to affirm emergence from underlying conditions "far from equilibrium" is not to explain the detailed genesis of any type of natural phenomenon. In addition, finding a language alternative to the mechanistic metaphors of an older physics and of contemporary information theory is an unmet challenge.

Talk of emergence and of probability will reappear in coming chapters. Both terms will acquire more technical meanings. This chapter has avoided the element of the second horizon (H2) in talking about art and ecosystems, but later ones will not. For now, we can end by returning to our beginning: the relation of art to ecology. As there are multiple unrealized possibilities in any environment and existing conditions subject to random variations, so among artists there are unrealized possibilities and existing conditions open to new experiments.

CHAPTER THREE:
THE ONTOLOGICAL STATUS OF INSTITUTIONS

This chapter builds upon the meanings of ecosystem and environment identified in the preceding chapter by focusing on a related question in political theory: What is the ontological status of institutions? Three competing answers representing a longstanding intellectual debate follow and so provide a further opportunity to test comparative interpretation as a promising way of evading or resolving such disputes. Section I offers a brief introduction to the debate. Section II presents details about and arguments for the three competing answers to the focus question. As well, it connects that question to the preceding chapter's developments in understanding organisms and their environments. Lonergan's notions of schemes of recurrence and emergent probability provide a "bridge" between discussions in biology and political theory. Section III formulates the controversy over institutions as two different sequences of views about persons and institutional relationships. Finally, Section IV applies FS4 to both sequences and evaluates their underlying assumptions about RKO.

I. Overview of the Controversy

The question of the ontological status of institutions is broader than asking whether one type of institution, namely a political one, exists. Still, the latter type is part of a broader class, and what is said about the class may apply to its members. If this possibility is granted, and, while admitting we have not yet said what we mean by "institution," we can proceed to sketch contrasting views of institutions.[139]

---

139   Delaying any definition of institution is part of the pedagogy of this book series and its rejection of the conceptualist tradition in mainstream philosophical work.

Classical Liberalism and contemporary libertarianism have been fairly consistent in understanding modern liberal political institutions as humanly designed instruments. They are not "organic" wholes the parts of which are citizens; rather, they are tools to serve the desired ends of citizens. Their legitimacy derives from the "consent of the governed," either through actual historical compacts or through implicit ratification. Tacit ratification supposedly occurs because post-contractual generations accept benefits from the established political order and so owe a "fair return" as a matter of reciprocal justice.[140] The consent of contracting parties, whether explicit or implicit, proceeds from an expectation of benefits flowing to them via the institutional set-up. Repeated failures to provide the expected benefits erode the legitimacy of and loyalty to the institutions designed to meet those expectations.

The descriptive narratives of Hobbes and Locke take for granted that individuals (or perhaps small groups) come first and political institutions appear as later inventions. Subsequent criticisms of these narratives or "contract theories" often were part of a debate between atomistic and organic views of the state. Twentieth-century forms of fascism and Marxism routinely defended an organic view. For them the state is a unity greater than its parts, much as a body as a living whole is more than its members. Cut off from the whole the severed part or individual member is useless and soon dies. Thus, it made no sense to claim individuals had rights against the state. With the demise of its political champions, the organic model of the state fell from favor; today the atomistic view seems triumphant. Individuals with natural rights come first; states function primarily to protect those pre-legal rights and any subsequent legal rights. "Rights against the state," enshrined in legal restrictions on state intrusions, are evidence of belief in the priority, both temporally and morally, of individuals over political institutions. While individuals may voluntarily sacrifice their private goods to protect the latter, doing so further demonstrates that a legitimate political order *ceteris paribus* owes its existence and continuance to the free consent of individuals.

While admittedly but a synopsis of one enduring view of political institutions, the preceding description probably grounds statements about society and individuals that allot the term "existence" to the latter but deny it applies to the former. Margaret Thatcher supposedly held that "there is no such thing as society, only the individuals who

---

140   This view of implicit consent because of received benefits has its critics within modern libertarianism. Robert Nozick quipped: "tacit consent isn't worth the paper it's not written on." *Anarchy, State, and Utopia* (New York: Basic Books, 1974), 287.

constitute it."[141] Robert Nozick and Milton Friedman endorsed similar distributions of "existence." The former asserted, "But there is no social entity with a good that undergoes some sacrifice for its own good. There are only individual people, different individual people, with their own individual lives."[142] As well, he identifies the state as a tool or instrument with "side constraints," i.e. the rights of individuals.[143]

Milton Friedman was similarly insistent that society is an instrument of its members and no more than an aggregate of its "ingredients."

> To the free man, the country is the collection of individuals who compose it, not something over and above them. He is proud of a common heritage and loyal to common traditions. But he regards government as a means, an instrumentality, neither a grantor of favors and gifts, nor a master or god to be blindly worshipped and served.[144]

Friedman's references to both "country" and "government" suggest that he is not limiting his view of institutions as aggregations of individuals to political orders. The implication of treating all institutions as aggregations is that they are not distinct realities. A pile of rocks is hardly a new entity if a rock is added or subtracted.

To identify a second, dialectical view of institutions, we begin with a primitive form of the question about how individuals are related to institutions: Which come first – individuals or institutions? Advocates of a contract theory of the state assign priority to individuals since persons precede contracts. Someone may object that, except for feral children, the institution of the family precedes individuals. One response to this objection is that the question of priority will receive different answers depending on the type of institution one is considering. While in ecology it makes no sense to think an organism is intelligible apart from its niche in an ecosystem, and in sociology or social psychology it would be strange to study individuals apart from an institution such as the family, still in political philosophy Nozick and others[145] have insisted that one

---

141   Attributed in Paul Ormerod. *The Death of Economics* (London: Faber and Faber, 1994), 34.
142   Nozick, 32-33.
143   Ibid. 31.
144   *Capitalism and Freedom* (Chicago: University of Chicago Press, 1962), 1-2.
145   Some Christian traditions hold that political institutions are post-lapsarian necessities. Had humans not fallen from grace, there would be no need for the executive functions of political orders, i.e. for asserting and exercising a monopoly over the power to coerce recalcitrant beings into behaving.

type of institution, namely the political kind, is a secondary phenomenon dependent on founding actions or agreements among antecedent individuals.

Here we apparently have another intellectual impasse. Which has priority-individuals or institutions? An earlier book, *A Theory of Ordered Liberty*,[146] evaded this impasse by shifting to a dialectical analysis of the issue. To quote Berger and Luckmann's formulation:

> *Society is a human product. Society is an objective reality. Man is a social product.* It may also...be evident [that] an analysis of the social world that leaves out any one of these three [dialectical] moments will be distortive.[147]

The language of dialectic is apt for talking about the relations between individuals and political institutions. It offers a way past an avoidable conundrum in political theory. If we start with the question of priority, we might be reminded of the old chicken and egg puzzle. How do we get beyond it? If we think of individuals as saying and believing different things, where did they acquire their languages and beliefs-from family upbringing, schools, the popular media? But, if we think of institutions as established, understood and agreed upon ways of doing things, who first does the establishing, understanding and agreeing? Dialectic offers an alternative to an either-or phrasing of the question in the sense that priority need not be assigned to either term. Individuals are not the sole "primordial facts" nor are the institutions to which they belong.

Besides the question of priority, there is the question of the ontological status of institutions. On this question sociologists are justifiably silent leaving it to some other field's line of inquiry. Social phenomena produced by human beings are legitimate objects of sociological inquiry. Still, it is one thing to say societies and their practices are human products; it is another to explain how they emerge and act back on their producers. Can what is non-existent "cause" changes in what does exist?

---

146   William Zanardi, second, revised edition (Austin: Forty Acres Press, 2011).
147   Peter Berger and Thomas Luckmann. *The Social Construction of Reality* (Garden City, N.Y.: Doubleday, 1967), 61. They add the following critical remarks in an endnote. "Contemporary American sociology tends toward leaving out the first moment. Its perspective on society thus tends to be what Marx called reification (*Verdinglichung*), that is, an undialectical distortion of social reality that obscures the latter's character as an ongoing human production, viewing it instead in thing-like categories appropriate only to the world of nature." (Endnote 29, 197-198) In contrast, Nozick and others tend to ignore the second and third moments, at least in regard to political institutions. Is it possible that competing viewpoints may be correct in what they include but defective in what they exclude?

Writers such as Jerome Bruner and Bernard Lonergan respond to such further questions and so present a third view of institutions. Bruner employed Karl Popper's "world three" to distinguish cultural institutions from both natural phenomena and interior mental states. In contrast to world one (nature's display) and world two (the interior life of the psyche), institutions were objectively real sets of relations constituted and sustained by human decisions and actions.[148] Bernard Lonergan agreed in talking of three worlds, though his typology differed somewhat from Bruner's. The former wrote of a world of immediacy (e.g. the infant's prelinguistic world), a world mediated by meanings (e.g. both commonsensical and theoretical inquiries into natural phenomena) and a world mediated and constituted by meaning (i.e. human acts of meaning and their cultural products, including the institutional set-ups constituted by such acts).[149]

According to Lonergan, adults only intermittently live in the first world; dreamless sleep, a coma and "zoning out" at the beach under a baking sun are examples. Primarily adults live in the two worlds of meaning because they ask questions, express ideas, share common beliefs and agree to cooperate in creating and maintaining social enterprises. Evidence of such shared realities abounds in the care-filled efforts of activists and civic leaders to maintain what they consider more important than their private lives. Still, the infant's first experiences in the world of immediacy and subsequent estimates of what is real live on into adulthood. Then many continue to assume that anything that is real must be at least a sensible object "already out there." Visual experiences tend to predominate, so the real objects are those that are visible or at least imaginable. A naïve empiricism seems plausible, i.e. we can assess the reliability of truth-claims by tracing them back to the sensate experiences they supposedly refer to.[150] A problem, thus, lies just beneath the surface. Strictly speaking, no one has ever seen a meaning, a relationship, a ratio or a correlation. More to the point of this chapter, no one has ever seen an institution. Once past the brick-and-mortar image of a bank, a school, a church or a library, the puzzle may become explicit: What are institutions if they are not visible? Common sense may assume that persons are observable, but what about a political party, a labor union or even a marriage?[151]

---

148   "Possible Castles" in *Actual Minds, Possible Worlds* (Cambridge: Harvard University Press, 1986), 44-45.
149   "Dimensions of Meaning,", 252-255.
150   Chapter Two of the *Primer* identified this model of reality as a characteristic of Hegel's first stage in the dialectic of consciousness.
151   The preceding chapter raised a similar question regarding the imperceptibility of an

With such puzzles we enter into the focus question of this chapter: What is the ontological status of institutions? There are secondary questions: Individuals exist, but do institutions exist in the same sense? How are individuals related to institutions? Are the latter adequately understood as instruments much like hammers and cars that persons create and control?

The questions are plentiful. Whether answers are as abundant will be one of the challenges facing this chapter. Its goals are to test the capacity of comparative interpretation to evade impasses in how these questions are answered, to shift reflection on some of the questions into the horizon of theory (H2), to present various answers as sequences of views that specialists doing FS3 will someday produce and to apply FS4 to those sequences.

II. Three Competing Views of Institutions

Already noted was the view attributed to Margaret Thatcher that society is not a reality; only the individuals who constitute it are. Nozick similarly asserted there is no society over and above "individual people, different individual people, with their own individual lives." Why entertain this view?

Perhaps Nozick's view is dictated by his purpose, namely, explaining "how a state would arise from a state of nature without anyone's rights being violated."[152] While he affirms that one type of institution, namely a state, is a "bit of the real world,"[153] the question of its ontological status is not something he explicitly explores, and it is not clear what he means by "real world." What is clear is that he begins his inquiry into the legitimacy of the political state by assuming individuals already have rights in something akin to Locke's state of nature. Additionally, he criticizes Rawls for populating his "original position" with groups rather than with individuals.[154] In accounting for the emergence of a state, he employs an "invisible hand explanation." That is,

> [W]ithout anyone having this in mind, the self-interest-
> ed and rational actions of persons in a Lockean state of

environment.
152   Nozick, 114.
153   Ibid. 9.
154   Ibid. 190.

nature will lead [first] to single protective agencies dominant over geographical territories [and eventually to the
appearance of the state as an] institution (1) that has the
right to enforce rights, prohibit dangerous private en-
forcement of justice, pass upon such private procedures,
and so forth, and (2) that effectively is the sole wielder
within a geographical territory of the right in (1)....[155]

Presumably individuals, consulting their own perceived self-interest, find institutional set-ups (having such a monopoly "with side constraints") an
acceptable solution to living in proximity to one another.[156]

This first view of institutions focuses on their "ingredients," i.e.,
if they exist, they are equal to their component elements. Thus, a state
or a society exists only as an aggregation of its members. This view is
attractive since it seems quite concrete.[157] Individuals, or perhaps small
groups, are the basic imaginable units of a society or state. Since they are
distinct entities in their own right, to talk of them as some type of unity is
but a shorthand way of saying that they are in proximity to one another
and have, by design or by accident, become related to one another. To
make the subsequent relations or any unity among them objective realities is to mistake "ideas" for reality. No one perceives ideas. When asked
to say exactly what one perceives in talking about societies or states, a
clear-headed response would produce descriptions of particular individuals, their behaviors and locales. Lists of such descriptions may lead
to talk of communities, nations and institutions, but these will be abstract
terms. Their empirical base will remain their ingredients.[158] The latter

---

155   Ibid. 119. As a necessary condition for being a state, Nozick specifies that it must have a
monopoly as "the sole effective judge over the permissibility of violence." (118)
156   Here critics often object to an ahistorical analysis that begins with the Lockean story. The
history of any society contains skeletons in the closet. Not only individuals but entire groups have
preceded the formation of a particular political order. For many their experience was of oppres-
sion and dispossession. This question of the historical legacy of past injustices is a puzzle that
Nozick took more seriously in later works, but in *Anarchy, State, and Utopia* it was not his central
focus. For example, he casually writes: "In the state of nature, property is acquired initially, let us
suppose, in accordance with the principle of justice in acquisition, and thereafter in accordance
with the principle of justice in transfer, by exchanged property for owned property or for services
or commitments, or by means of gifts." Ibid. 280.
157   Near the beginning of a section on civil society, Hegel notes the difficulties in holding
to this first view: "Individuals, as citizens of this state, are *private persons* who have their own
interest as their end. Since this end is mediated through the universal, which thus *appears* to the
individuals as *means*, they can attain their end only in so far as they themselves determine their
knowledge, volition, and action in a universal way and make themselves *links* in the chain of this
continuum [*Zusammenhang*]." *Elements of the Philosophy of Right*. Allen W. Wood (ed.) H.B. Nisbet
(trans.) (New York: Cambridge University Press, 1991), §187, 224.
158   The second text in this series contains a lengthier discussion of this view. Cf.

exist as concrete particulars, but an idea is an abstraction. To hold otherwise is to lapse into some form of idealism or, perhaps, to use ordinary language carelessly.

Many analyses of the debates between the preceding view and its opponents have used the distinction between atomistic and organic models of society. It is possible and important to avoid this way of framing the debate. First, we need additional views that are less tied to picture thinking and the first type of realism. To begin with a story about imaginable individuals meeting to discuss ways of organizing themselves for mutual protection is part of the history of Classical Liberalism. Whether treated as a methodological tool for answering questions of legitimacy[159] or assumed to be historical fact, the narrative already presupposes answers to questions raised in this chapter. For instance, the narrative portrays individuals with rights as being prior to at least political arrangements. As well, the narrative describes political institutions as instruments for the benefits of their makers and their successors. How could either of these stances be controversial?

A dialectical view of institutions provides challenges to both. Each new generation finds institutions already in place and experiences them as "objectivated realities" that demand their cooperation in sustaining a "given" social order. Their elders expect them to internalize, i.e. to understand and agree to, the various intelligible relations among assigned roles and to play their parts in maintaining these social patterns of interaction. Repeated "testing" of how well they have internalized the "rules" or conventions of society will be ways of assuring the continuance of the institutional orders that ensure a society's survival.[160]

Talk of "objectivated realities" returns us to the earlier question of the relation of individuals to institutions. In the dialectical understanding of institutions, individuals are not the sole "primordial facts" but neither are institutions. The "we" is *temporally* first in the sense that

---

Cracking the Case, Chapter Six, Part III, section C, 254-262.

159   Questions about the legitimacy of a particular form of political organization and it enactments are beyond the scope of this chapter. Thus, there is no attempt to discuss and evaluate Nozick's or anyone else's views of what kinds of political set-ups might be legitimate.

160   In theoretical fields the means to this end will include "patterned resources" transmitted to a new generation through graduate programs, specialized journals, professional associations and their annual conferences. Graduate schools and research institutes represent institutional means for "inducting" trainees into the procedures, terminologies and accumulated understanding (the acquis) of various specialties. Where a clan inducts its new members by repeating its oral history, teaching hunting skills and conducting painful rites of passage, specialized fields employ classroom hours, collaborative research projects and the strenuous "exit tests" of dissertations. In both types of cases, the capacities of a new generation receive training and then testing to see if candidates have successfully internalized the patterned resources of a community.

parents beget the child whose "I" emerges within the "we" of the family and some larger community. The differentiation of the individual from others emerges from interpersonal relations. This much supports Heidegger's claim that *mitsein* is a primordial fact of human existence. However, capacities, as initially orientations toward an indeterminate range of ends, are malleable characteristics of individuals. While the "we" shapes such capacities and initially directs their probable line of development, the capacities themselves have a logical priority over such formation by social conditions. Without the marble, the sculptor would have nothing to shape. This much supports the claim that individuals are also primordial facts. But the meaning of "individual" here is hardly more differentiated than the simple negation: "I am not you."[161]

In more technical language, Heidegger wrote of several basic or "equiprimordial" (*gleichursprünglich*) characteristics of human existence. Perhaps if we understand them as correlative terms, "individual" and "institution" refer to such characteristics; however, there are other ways of describing their relations. Usually when we talk carefully of cause and effect, we are saying there is an intelligible relation of dependency of the latter on the former. But capacities depend on institutions for their actual formation, and institutions depend on individuals-with-capacities for their emergence and maintenance. "Interdependence" and "reciprocal causality" are descriptive terms for expressing an understanding of how both are related. Put in the form of a proportion – as prior integrations (e.g. habits) are to our current choices so institutions are to us as individuals.[162] Using the terminology of the *Primer*, we can formulate an implication of this proportion: the second terms can stand to the first as both receptivity and activity (*et motus et movens*). That is, the causal relations between the terms are reversible. For example, actual choices can modify prior integrations (habits); individuals can reform as well as corrupt institutions. In short, persons produce institutions, institutions produce persons, and both types of products can act back on their producers.

In contrast, the first view of political institutions is non-dialectical. It assumes that individuals are the basic realities while political rela-

---

161   Readers may be familiar with Hegel's *Phenomenology of Spirit* and the first stage of the Master-Servant Dialectic. There the first understanding of "self" is relational but purely negative.
162   To suggest an analogy: as the orientations of individuals become the determinate or habitual ways they live so new institutions gradually can become the habitual patterns of social interactions among individuals. To think of institutions as the "habits of the group" opens up the discussion of how the latter effectively demand that individuals acquire new habits, skills and virtues if they are to fill their roles. In the language of the dialectical viewpoint: the product acts back on the producer.

tions are secondary phenomena. This assumption seems at odds with the findings of contemporary psychology and sociology. One attempt to reconcile those findings with this assumption already appeared. If we distinguish between social and political institutions, we might suppose the former type, e.g. family life, is equiprimordial with the individual, and so both are basic realities. However, political institutions arising from contractual arrangements among citizens are artificial and secondary constructs.[163] This maneuver seems plausible since family life usually comes first as a determinant of an individual's development. However, should we assume that the political relations of a larger society do not shape family life? Are families somehow immune from, i.e. surprisingly independent of, the political orders in which they function? Are political institutions an exception to the usual dialectical relation between persons and other institutions? These questions may go unnoticed if dialectical thinking is not part of one's analysis.

What if we understand individuals and at least some types of institutions as equiprimordial correlates?[164] One implication would be that correlates in such a dialectical relation are distinguishable but not separable; rather, the reality of each historically takes on determinate content only through its relation to the other. If we try to understand either correlate as an independent entity, then we understand it abstractly or partially. But then any subsequent analysis of the isolated correlate risks losing touch with a more complex reality.[165]

Given the contrasts between these first two views of institutions, perhaps it has become apparent why the second chapter's discussion of organisms and their ecosystems preceded this chapter. The question about the multiple forms of dependency organisms have in relation to their

---

163   As noted earlier, some may even hold that political orders are not real, only their members exist.

164   To return to the preceding chapter, multiple types of organisms emerge and survive in a hierarchical order within an ecosystem, but they also interact with other components and so sustain the functioning whole, the ecosystem. Eliminate either general term in such a relationship and the other perishes. In Section IV of this chapter, a similar argument will appear based on how explanatory insights require both terms and relations.

165   Perhaps this is the reason many anarchist proposals, and those of their contemporary libertarian heirs, prove so feckless. While principled arguments appealing to general concepts of autonomy and heteronomy may be logically valid, they overlook how such conceptual contraries are in fact real correlates of human living. The concluding section of Chapter Four in *A Theory of Ordered Liberty* criticized an example of a logically valid but unsound argument and detected its hidden dependence on an old but still durable conceptualist tradition. The argument begins by juxtaposing concepts of autonomy and heteronomy, works out the implications of each term and produces a logically valid argument to the effect that it is self-contradictory to hold autonomous persons ever have a duty to obey, i.e. to assume a heteronomous position in relation to, political authority. The further question goes beyond word definitions: Are persons in fact both autonomous and heteronomous?

environments is a subject of intense research. Current research suggests it is no longer tenable to understand an organism as something separable from its interactions with other components of some ecosystem, for organisms are nothing without the niches in which they emerge, endure for a time and pass away. Can the same be said of persons? Discounting feral children, can we adequately understand persons apart from a web of relations to institutions ranging from a shared language and social etiquette to political structures and economic practices? A strict analogy between ecosystems and institutions is not something a third view defends.[166] What it defends is an analogy between the relation of individuals to institutions and the relation of organisms to ecosystems. Thus, the third view (1) explores how biological things are related to processes that are not themselves things and (2) asks if insights from biology are relevant to understanding how persons are related to institutions, e.g. might the latter be patterns of relations and not themselves things?

Recall three of the characteristics of ecosystems mentioned in the preceding chapter: (1) they exhibit dynamic relations among their hierarchically arranged components that (2) mutually condition one another and so (3) operate as open systems, i.e. there are flexible and non-deterministic relations among both components and subsystems such that variations in both are possible.[167] Recall, as well, the question in land art about the possibility of creating an ecosystem. Affirmative answers gave way to negative responses because of insights into the complexity and indeterminacy of natural ecosystems. A terrarium provides an artificial environment isolated from interfering variables, but then, it supplies a poor substitute for the dynamic relations found in non-artificial, open environments and so is a quite limited "specimen" for ecological inquiry.[168]

Now critics of the first view of institutions might suspect that talk of individuals as temporally and morally prior to institutions reflects a "terrarium" view of the former's relation to the latter. Their suspicion

---

166   The appropriate analogy is not between institutions and ecosystems but between the relation of individuals to institutions and the relation of organisms to ecosystems.

167   To provide a descriptive example, flexibility appears in what urban raccoons have for dinner and where they go to eat; non-deterministic outcomes occur because, no matter what food sources are close at hand, humans are inconsistent in what they discard. Variations appear when new restaurants open up and their trash provides a richer source of garbage than was previously available, so the raccoons can become healthier, live longer and have more offspring. What of any systematic element? Raccoons must routinely eat and mate; what and where they eat and with whom they mate are indeterminate. In other words, systematic patterns are dependent on conditions that are met in accord with probability.

168   The faux Prada store near Marfa, Texas, implies a similar critique of commercial institutions and the market for luxury goods. The terrarium is severed from a more complex botanical niche and so is "artificial" and simplistic. The Marfa installation stands in isolation from the marketplace that would otherwise sustain it and so appears misplaced and detached.

may be premature. Critics first need to consider a methodological question: What is the basic unit of study in sociology or political theory? This question already appeared in the history of ecological studies. What is the basic unit of study there? The earliest studies focused on individual organisms as specimens of kinds or classes. Later studies assumed populations were the appropriate unit of study. Eventually some consensus appeared that certain types of relatively stable systems were more appropriate candidates for this function. In time the understanding of ecosystems (with the three characteristics cited above) became a basic unit of study.

Is there any similar pattern found in sociological studies? Comte offered his facile division of the three ages of humankind and the types of persons belonging to each. He thought himself a representative of the positivist age and so a specimen of the scientifically mature type of person in the nineteenth century. Population statistics later became important in both ecological and sociological research. Talcott Parsons advanced an alternative basic unit of study. A commentator on his work linked his notion of a social "system of expectations" to A. I. Oparin's work on biological systems.[169] Both writers understood a system to be "boundary maintaining" in the sense that, relative to variations in and among its components, "it maintains certain constancies of pattern, whether this constancy be static or moving...."[170]

Reaching for a serious concept of institutions can begin with this first approximation to the meaning of "institution," namely, a boundary maintaining system with a relative constancy in pattern. Familiar examples are the U.S. Presidency and the local Starbucks. Presidents come and go, but the office and its constitutional functions have flexible boundaries within which individuals carry out routine operations. At Starbucks, a modern ship of Theseus, specific managers, employees and customers come and go, but the commercial enterprise with its assigned roles and routine operations endures. What are the "constancies in pattern" amid such turnovers in populations? Empirical research would reveal cyclic routines. For example, an account of the presidency and its functions would include references to voting by the Electoral College, the administering of the oath of office, the forming of a cabinet, compiling and submitting a budget to Congress, signing and vetoing legislation. A complication quickly appears. Just as the study of ecosystems revealed hierarchies among subsystems so study of the presidential "system" uncovers

---

169   Philip McShane. *Randomness, Statistics and Emergence* (Dublin: Gill and MacMillan, 1970), 225.
170   Parsons quoted in ibid. 225.

a web of relations among other institutions, e.g. the Electoral College, the Congress, the Judiciary.[171]

Such complications require a second approximation to the meaning of institution. To move toward one, advocates of a third view ask how multiple forms of organization can operate together as some type of complex functioning unity. Descriptive examples are easily within reach. Hospitals continue to operate because of the routine functioning of internal and external offices. Internally they rely on billing departments, janitorial services, legal departments, surgical scheduling offices and so on. Externally they rely on accrediting agencies, governmental medical benefits programs, insurance companies, medical supply companies, local utility departments. Both lists are far from exhaustive, but they suggest how the routine operations of a single enterprise depend on a complex web of relations among organizations.

If inquirers remain in a picture world and try to imagine such interdependent functions, they probably would speak of kinds of workers staffing the various offices: accountants, janitors, lawyers, nurses, physicians, electricians and so on. In such a model, imagined employees are pictured inside something else, for example offices. The relation is one of containment. However, problems then multiply. Such workers, like presidents, are not the institutions. Perhaps the roles they fill are what deserve emphasis.[172] That would be an improvement, but inquirers might still be thinking about imaginable individuals doing types of jobs and so would not break free of the first type of realism and its association of the real with the imaginable.[173] To exemplify the problem, someone can conceive of communities as aggregates of individuals in proximity to one another ("neighbors" in a literal sense), but someone else may ask what makes them communities? As most urban apartment dwellers know, proximity will not suffice as an answer. Most neighbors remain anonymous.

---

171   The legislative and judicial branches in the U.S. system of checks and balances might be considered equals of the presidency and so not part of a hierarchy among systems. However, talk in the last century of "an imperial presidency" is symptomatic of historical variations in the relations among systems. Might, then, the Constitution be thought of as boundary maintaining, i.e. as setting flexible limits on what variations can occur and still be legal?

172   Kenneth Boulding suggested as much: "The unit of such systems is not perhaps the person – the individual human as such – but the 'role' – that part of the person which is concerned with the organization or situation in question, and it is tempting to define social organizations, or almost any social system, as a set of roles tied together with channels of communication." Quoted in Joseph E. Pluta. "Kenneth Boulding's Skeleton of Science and Contemporary General Systems Theory," in Wilfred Dolfsma and Stefan Kesting (eds.) *Interdisciplinary Economics: Kenneth E. Bouding's Engagement in the Sciences* (London: Routledge, 2013), 11.

173   Appearing in the next section, an objection to the first view of institutions as aggregations or collections of individuals is precisely this hold of the imagination on thinking, i.e. the assumption that to be real is to be something perceived or imaginable "out there."

To offer a further example, ecologists know that counting specimens in an ecosystem and arriving at population numbers will not answer their questions about mutual dependencies, the emergence of variations and system-wide fluctuations. It seems that explaining both natural and social systems demands what is beyond the capacity of picture thinking to supply.[174]

Perhaps the impasse central to this chapter is now clear. If inquirers picture individuals as the real constitutive elements of institutions and insist that institutions, if they are to be considered real, must be equally imaginable, then they will likely side with the first view; namely, persons exist but not institutions.[175] Does the dialectical view offer a way beyond this impasse? Its emphasis on relations of interdependency is arguably an improvement over the first view of institutions since relations are not imaginable. Still, the question remains of how advocates of the dialectical view should conceive of equiprimordial institutions? Are they realities and, if so, of what kind? Is existence to be said of them in the same way that it is said of persons?

The third view of institutions and the holistic view of ecosystems in Chapter Two suggest ways to handle these questions. Regarding the latter, ecosystems exhibit "emergent properties" that cannot be reduced to their constitutive components. The same is arguably true of institutions. If defenders of the second, dialectical view think of them as patterns of relatively constant relations among human "specimens" and if they do not identify reality with what is imaginable, then they might conclude that both persons and institutions exist.

But do they use "exist" in the same way when talking of persons and institutions? One option is to distinguish within *esse reale* between *esse intentionale* and *esse naturale*. Geneticists studying fruit flies (*esse naturale*) accept that the insects are part of the natural order, but no one believes that acquiring knowledge of them means the geneticists have fruit flies in their heads. To comprehend what makes something what it is means that one knows it intentionally (*esse intentionale*). Put another way, since explanatory knowledge is by way of identity, to have a correct, albeit incomplete, understanding of what makes fruit flies what they are is to

---

174   This is another implication of remarks in the preceding chapter about insights not being reducible to the puzzling images that prompt questions leading to insights. An adequate understanding of institutions begins with descriptions of persons filling various roles, but further why-questions will gradually demand leaving behind such initial pictures.

175   The two earlier books in this series explicitly defended a notion of reality as whatever can be intelligently conceived and reasonably affirmed in response to questions. Left behind was the viewpoint of Hegel's Sense-certainty and its identification of the real with whatever is given in sensation.

know something of their "deep structure" or actual nature. Then one is no longer describing but instead explaining what makes something what it is.

How well does this distinction work for the question about the existence of persons and institutions? An initial reservation is that the latter are not natural but artificial set-ups. Nonetheless, supporters of the third view can argue that organisms and ecosystems, persons and institutions as explanatorily understood are all, at least initially, intentional beings.[176] Note the wording, "explanatorily understood." No mention here of the person across from you in the room as a visible object "over there." What then is that person if not an object-in-sight? The same type of question already appeared about institutions once we got past the brick-and-mortar viewpoint. Might the answers to both questions be about what is invisible?[177]

To develop this line of thought (a product of H3) requires a shift into H2. A preliminary step is to identify basic categories serving as the terms in correlations belonging to an explanatory account of institutions. Lonergan produced a diagram identifying what he considered key variables in understanding the emergence, functioning and reform of institutions. Suppose we modify the original diagram, add descriptive examples of each variable and finally suggest how some of them are related to one another. The eventual goal is to flesh out a third view of institutions that (1) exploits the earlier distinction between intentional being and natural being and (2) formulates an explanatory understanding of institutions. We begin with the diagram.[178]

INDIVIDUAL		SOCIAL	ENDS
capacity, demand	operation	cooperation	particular good
plasticity	development, skill	institution, role, task	good of order
liberty	orientation, displacement	personal relations	terminal goods

---

176   A distinction between *ordo cognoscendi* and *ordo essendi*, introduced below, will follow up on this claim.
177   In keeping with the second type of realism, readers will not have a problem with an affirmative reply. The meanings of the ink marks they have been reading are quite invisible and are instances of "intentional entities." *Method in Theology*, 159.
178   This is an amended version of a diagram found in ibid. 48.

Clues to understanding this diagram appeared in the *Primer* with its extended remarks on correlations between structured operations in inquiry and what those operations intend, i.e. their "proper ends." While questions of judgment ask what is the case and so intend "facts," questions for deliberation ask what can be the case and so intend possibilities that may be turned into realities. The first category, <u>capacity</u>, refers to an understanding of how persons spontaneously intend various goods and can act in various ways to procure them. They ask questions about what problems they face and possible ways of solving them. An easy example is someone shivering in the cold, wanting warmth and being able to build a fire. The fire is a means, and warmth is the end or good that meets a human need or <u>demand</u>. Here is a clear instance of attention focused on or intending a <u>particular</u> <u>good</u> as its end. Next we can reflect on the history of human mastery of fire and other forms of energy as means of survival. The demands are recurrent, but the means for responding to them have changed. The <u>operations</u> or actions that expressed human capacity and produced heat for cave dwellers required modest <u>skills</u> but also <u>cooperation</u> among clan members. Whose role is it to gather the wood? Who builds and tends the fire? Who is responsible for preserving the embers to start tomorrow's fire? Over time both operations and skills became far more complex. The flexibility or <u>plasticity</u> of human capacities permits development of new means (skills) for understanding and controlling sources of energy. Among the gradually developed means are <u>institutions</u> that now routinely supply energy on demand to paying customers. For example, city utility departments are humanly designed orders for delivering basic services (particular goods) so that customers have heating in the winter and air conditioning in the summer.

Reliable access to such services is possible only because of the ongoing cooperation among persons who fill certain roles and competently carry out assigned <u>tasks</u> with the required skills. The cooperative relations may be among anonymous parties, e.g. the persons who produce and those who consume energy from public utilities. Such anonymous relations link consumers as bill payers to utility plant employees, repair crews, managers of city departments and their staffs.

If all the related roles are predictably to yield energy for consumers, they must form a relatively stable order that people at least partially understand and repeatedly decide to maintain by carrying out their tasks in ongoing set-ups or institutions. Such patterned operations in turn belong to more complex forms of social organization. Institutions that distribute energy are dependent on other organizations supplying energy that continue to do so as long as there are other organizations exploring for new energy resources, and all of the preceding require the recurrent functioning of financial institutions.

Particular goods will keep flowing as a result of such a complex good of order composed of so many diverse interactions within and among institutions. But this order acts back on its creators. Institutional roles and tasks require certain types of skills, and this demand on human capacities favors the emergence and development of some operations over others. For example, businesses demand that what in the child is a capacity for counting become professional accounting practices. The child's capacity for social interaction and the adolescent's social skills will, in corporate settings, become the procedures of personnel departments. Even the child's capacity for daydreaming can, given the right market demands, become the skills used in making predictions about consumption rates and labor costs.[179]

In review: operations express capacities and respond to demands; human plasticity makes possible the emergence of new skills, and institutional roles and tasks both presuppose those skills and evoke new ones. But what of the terms in the third row of the diagram? Its categories portend both individual and institutional transformations.

The social orders that result from institutional networks sustained by the deliberate cooperation of largely anonymous persons are far from static arrangements. In the short run, institutions may seem unchanging, even inert, but their existence is rarely secure or stable. As is the case with ecosystems, initial conditions make possible the emergence of institutions and, if sufficiently altered, can threaten their survival. So there will be requisite skill-levels in an available workforce, but it experiences turnovers, and any replacements may be far less skilled. Investor confidence may launch an enterprise only later to vanish in a market panic. Consumer demand may expand and create new business opportunities, but it also may contract and leave some ventures high and dry. Besides cooperation in the workplace, there are the animosities that fuel office feuds and strikes. And then there are the external threats of political rivals, economic competitors and natural disasters, any of which can undermine the original conditions under which an institution first

---

179   To anticipate judgments about any good of order, consider how the commercial markets that encourage the development of new skills may also manipulate very young populations into becoming the next generation of thoughtless consumers. "Children have become conduits from the consumer marketplace into the household, the link between advertisers and the family purse." Juliet B. Schor. *Born to Buy: The Commercialized Child and the New Consumer Culture* (New York: Scribner, 2004), 11.

appeared and flourished.

So challenges to the survival of institutions and even to the survival of social orders are numerous. Institutions and more complex social orders owe their emergence to individuals asking questions, devising intelligent plans and deciding to cooperate. If they owe their survival to the routine recurrence of such intentional acts, why are the acts recurrent? Threats to their recurrence may prove enlightening. If external natural disasters can disrupt institutional functions, systemic corruption and personal malfeasance can disrupt them internally as betrayals of trust. One difference here is that natural disasters do not proceed from intentional acts, but betrayals do. We assume people are at <u>liberty</u> to choose means and ends. They can cooperate for what they perceive to be the "common good," but they can also compete solely to advance private goods. However, whether they pursue common or private goods is not the decisive issue; rather, the question is whether what they routinely seek and actually produce is not what seems good but what is good. In the latter case, they will, regardless of their intentions, be contributing to a good of order that provides particular goods that are in fact good.[180] Thus, while a particular institution may function poorly so that its effects on a broader social order are largely negative, the offsetting benefits of other institutions within that more complex good of order may preserve the poorly performing member well past its useful lifespan.

There is no shortage of persons using liberty irresponsibly and of institutional practices harming human goods. Suppose a CEO is primarily intent on earning salary bonuses and amassing stock options larger than any rival's compensation package. Leveraged buy-outs and accounting practices that inflate the company's annual earnings may be the means selected to gain these ends. Whether the company's artificial "growth" is sustainable and whether employees' retirement funds and stockholders' investments are at risk are of little concern to the CEO whose focus has narrowed to gaining personal benefits and avoiding personal costs. But then the decisions that follow will undermine personal relations since they ignore the legitimate expectations of others for honesty and fair returns on their labor and investments. Instead of the good of <u>personal relations</u>, the CEO sees employees and investors simply as resources to be manipulated in pursuing private ends and particular goods.

---

180   The question of intention here is subordinated to the question of what actually results from one's actions. Actual goods may follow from self-interested pursuits; at least this is the popular reading of Adam Smith's hidden-hand argument. For a critical account of the limits of this version of what Smith meant, see Jerry Z. Muller's *Adam Smith in His Time and Ours* (New York: The Free Press, 1996).

Fortunately there are leaders who run private and public institutions differently and avoid such abuses of trust. They consistently make responsible uses of their capacities and skills. Executives and employees understand how their cooperative efforts produce both personal and communal goods. Feelings of loyalty to the institution, its personnel and customers guide choices. Despite occasional disagreements, they believe that what they are doing as a group is worthwhile, and so they sacrifice time, energy and private interest to sustain their common enterprise. Why do they do this? Presumably they are in agreement that some goods are worth the effort, i.e. are <u>terminal</u> <u>goods</u> worth promoting. These may be popularly labeled as the "values" of financial security for employees' families, the solid reputation of the firm and the professional integrity of its officers. Behind such talk are shared judgments about the goods of family life, of corporate responsibility to larger communities and of the ethical standards of a profession. When routine actions follow upon such judgments, the actors' decisions "complete" their best judgments about what is good to do. Operations, then, have as their correlates objectives that are actually good.

This correlation of personal decisions and their objectives is a step toward understanding the categories <u>orientation</u> and <u>displacement</u> as they occur in the diagram. If a person's orientation is toward understanding and doing what is good, then efforts to make moral decisions become a pattern or habit that witnesses few lapses. The old maxim was "the good is what good people do." On the other hand, if a person's orientation toward what is good is haphazard and episodic, decisions are inconsistent. Moments of clear moral resolve occur infrequently during longer periods of inattention to what one is making of a life. A momentary thought that one could be doing better by oneself and by others is met not so much with indifference as by a preference for comfortable routines in thinking and acting. The tension between envisioned growth and a reluctance to shed old habits becomes a test of a person's liberty: "Will I move forward or rest where I am?" The test is personal and existential: "What am I to make of my life?" While no one presumably can take away my responsibility for how I answer, others are part of the test since the question is also, "What are we to make of our community?"

The category "displacement" refers to an understanding of how persons sometimes dramatically reverse their habitual orientations. Addicts may reverse self-destructive patterns of living; a new parent may reverse a narcissistic focus on personal convenience and decide to take more responsibility for parenting; an insider's loyalty to some group may become subordinate to new concerns for the effects that group is having on outsiders. Still, what comes first are the established orientations, and so the question is how persons are ever "displaced" from such prior integrations of thinking and acting. St. Augustine offered a succinct response: "*Incipit exire qui incipit amare.*"[181] Finding someone or something worthy of one's love offers a powerful antidote to the fears and rationalizations that sustain inadequately developed orientations. But that is just a beginning, and a new "film clip" ideally will record new integrations of emotions and decisions yielding new orientations toward what is actually worth doing with one's life. Absent these new orientations, one wavers between moments of firm resolve and drifting along old paths.

The preceding has been a descriptive exposition of the terms and relations suggested in the diagram. There was a promise to offer an explanatory account of a limited number of those terms. Again, the guiding questions are what do we mean by "institution" and how are individuals related to it? To move toward an explanatory set of answers, consider how acts of meaning ground and sustain institutions. The following comments proceed from H3 and move toward H2.

Presumably institutions represent shared integrations of prior intentional acts, i.e. the common meanings groups of persons have understood and agreed upon in living together.[182] These are their "habits" or institutionalized orientations toward handling a range of shared problems in a given environment. Thus, it is more probable that such groups will first adopt tried-and-true responses to new problems than that they will rely on untested experiments. Institutionalized orientations are analogous to neuropsychological demands for continuity and stability.[183] Taken together they are integrations of neuropsychological processes and psychosocial meanings that become conventional guides to planning, deciding

---

181   "One begins to leave who begins to love." Quoted in Eric Voegelin, "Eternal Being in Time," in *Anamnesis* (Columbia: University of Missouri Press, 1990), 140.

182   The explicit grounding of institutions in intentional acts is, these authors argue, an advance over some of the usual descriptive definitions of institutions. Pluta lists several of the latter. "Evolutionary economists define institutions as groupings of people with common behavior patterns. Institutions include habits of thought (like custom and tradition), established social practices (like human behavior and family life), and forms of organization (like markets, business firms large and small, banks, governments, and a legal system). Institutions are also considered to be established forms of ceremonial behavior." 12.

183   Institutions tend to privilege stability over experimentation. "Traditional disciplines themselves are institutions. They are often static in their methods, past binding, resistant to change, authoritative (even dictatorial), ceremonial, and past-glorifying. They may even slow the speed with which new technical knowledge is introduced and human progress is achieved. Mainstream economics has certainly done this with its continued embrace of such dubious concepts as the invisible hand, consumer rationality, equilibrium, the marginal productivity theory, the inevitability of diminishing returns, and the fiction of pure competition." Ibid.

and acting. Still, institutions offer a flexible range of possible intentional responses to problems. Human "plasticity" provides evidence that flexibility remains a possibility in institutional settings both because human agents remain malleable and because novel conditions evoke adaptations if persons and their integrated meanings are to survive.

The neuropsychological and intentional patterns traditionally called "virtues" offer a further analog to institutional routines. Suppose that a capacity for performance becomes actual performance and, with repetition, becomes habitual performance. When actual performance is consistently one of morally sound judgments and decisions, then actual virtues become patterns of recurrent normative intentional acts in doing what is good. In other words, established neuropsychological and intentional patterns make it more likely that a person will respond to highly variable situations with morally appropriate judgments and decisions consistent with past ones. Suppose, then, that institutionalized routines are likewise a flexible range of responses to variable problems. The "range" has relative limits set by the "boundary maintaining" routines; it amounts to a relatively stable pattern of responses that are available for meeting new challenges. In some institutions this may mean there is a shared "culture" of creative and morally responsible ways of responding to new situations. Past decisions created and sustained the culture and so increased the probability that future decisions will be morally sound ones.

Of course, there can be institutionalized routines that systemically undermine a variety of human goods. Then the flexible range of responses will form a relatively stable pattern of morally defective judgments and decisions. In either case, responses to new problems are more likely to "fit" the established patterns and fall within the range of routine solutions to similar problems. When morally defective judgments and decisions have become routine within institutional settings, we can still speak of a "good of order." For example, a corporate culture of "closing the deal" no matter what it takes will form its own patterns of operations. Routine practices will "shade" the truth about a company's products, will ignore the legitimate interests of customers, will sacrifice personal relations within and outside the firm to monthly sales quotas, will use the most effective high-pressure sales techniques and will encourage intense and often humiliating competition among subordinates for upper-management's approval. All of this may contribute to a good of order, but it will produce a flow of particular goods to some and a flow of avoidable and unjustifiable harms to many others.

Here we can return to the question above about the third row in the diagram. How can liberty, displacement and personal relations disrupt such flawed orders? The category "displacement" refers to an understanding that persons sometimes radically reverse even well entrenched orientations. How this is possible? There is no obvious answer since "radical reversal" amounts to the occurrence of the improbable. That is, determinate orientations are habitual responses to the psychoneural demand for continuity and stability both in personal living and, by way of analogy, in institutional performance. Minor departures from habitual patterns in thinking and acting are not uncommon. For example, people change jobs, abandon old acquaintances for new ones, respond to mid-life crises with plastic surgery, changes in diet or home remodeling. But <u>radical</u> departures or displacements amount not to revision but reversal; they are discontinuous with previous patterns of thinking and acting. They go contrary to the psychoneural demand for continuity and stability.

These remarks on discontinuities prepare for the move into an explanatory context and a refinement of the third view. An earlier study of evolutionary ecology left clues on how to proceed. Philip McShane uses Lonergan's notion of schemes of recurrence to understand organisms and their conditioning of and by ecosystems. He claims that this notion is key to understanding both ecosystems and institutions.[184] Some descriptive examples of schemes in nature follow.

> If a dog chases the rabbit it will run into a burrow, [sic] and come out later when all is clear. Here we have a single instance of a scheme. This scheme has a range-the notion parallels Darwin's idea of range of temperature-endurance of plants, etc.-the range includes the number of available burrows, etc. Again the rabbit has a reproductive scheme, a feeding scheme, etc. There is a circle of such schemes within which the rabbit lives, but the circle is flexible-having escaped the dog the rabbit [can move on to feed or sleep].[185]

---

184   Regarding ecosystems and schemes of recurrence, see *Randomness*, 223. The claim about institutions and schemes of recurrence occurs in McShane's definition of the former as "flexible patterns of schemes of recurrence." "One Hundred and One Damnations," *FuSe* 14, 2 (philipmcshane.ca).
185   *Randomness*, 224. Further on McShane adds: "But there is [...] a large variety of schemes and systems within the organism, ranging from the biochemical cycles within individual cells to the larger schemes such as blood circulation. Moreover these larger inner schemes are usually interlocked with schemes which go beyond the organism. Thus, the vascular circulation

Before turning to institutional examples of such recurrence schemes, we should qualify talk of cycles, circles and flexibility. The use of "cycles" is conventional but still metaphorical since no exact repetition or retracing of steps occurs, "except perhaps in such things as clocks and orbits."[186] In addition, since the interdependent schemes of recurrence within and outside an organism are multiple, talk of "circles" is less accurate than talk of "ranges" of schemes. That is, organisms do not move in lockstep from one scheme to the next in a fixed sequence but can move toward a number of options within their ranges. For example, after feeding an animal can enter a sleep cycle, but it also may play or investigate new surroundings. Such optionality justifies talk of "flexibility" within such ranges of schemes.

> [Having eluded the dog,] the rabbit can move into any of several other schemes of operation. Thus we speak of a flexible circle of schemes. Again, each scheme in which the animal functions has an inner flexibility [...such that] the rabbit has no determinate mate, nor has it a determinate burrow to run to, nor has its diet the fixity of a medical prescription. But regularly it eats, mates and runs for cover.[187]

A final qualifying remark: talk of schemes presupposes components or things that survive in and through such relatively stable schemes or patterns.[188] The specific actions of organisms are unique occurrences that depend on and contribute to schemes. The organisms themselves may undergo dramatic changes without necessarily changing external

---

depends on the digestive system which depends in turn on the schemes of recurrence by which the organism wins sustenance from the environment." 234.

186   Ibid. 227. In the same place McShane offers examples of variability in recurrence. "Pulse rates vary with stair-climbing and chemical reactions with the temperature. In the case of carbon or nitrogen cycles, the flow of the elements in nature is completely lacking in uniformity so that the best one can do is to consider the period of circulation to be some type of statistical average for each cycle, and, further, [an] average over a period of cycles."

187   Ibid.

188   The difficult question of the unity of organisms or of persons as things (traditionally referred to as "substances") is beyond the scope of this chapter. The most we attempt here is to ask how things as unities are related to the schemes of recurrence that are enduring features of their emergence and survival. Our minimal claim is that ecosystems and institutions are not "stage settings" for organisms and individuals since (1) in an explanatory context both are understood via their intelligible relations forming schemes of recurrence; and (2) those schemes are intertwined with the functioning of both. For explicit discussions of the unity of things and an application of comparative interpretation to contrasting views in those discussions, see "The Unity and the Meaning of Being," Chapter Six in the second book in this series and Chapter Seven in this book.

schemes; even when individual organisms mature and later die, the external schemes continue.[189]

These qualifying comments have been preparatory to identifying a second approximation to the meaning of "institution." McShane, following Lonergan, writes of institutions as "flexible patterns of schemes of recurrence." In keeping with the preceding qualifying remarks, we might amend this new version to "flexible ranges of social schemes of recurrence." This is an advance over the first approximation with its talk of systems that are "boundary maintaining with a relative constancy in pattern." Consider how groups design defensive schemes of recurrence such as legal aid clinics, emergency services agencies, early warning systems, insurance companies and centers for disease control. Through intentional acts of understanding, planning, deciding and agreeing, an institutional set-up emerges as commonly understood and agreed upon ways of employing resources, exercising capacities and developing skills for sustaining flows of goods, flows dependent on (1) the ongoing cooperation of persons filling their roles in the agreed upon ways and (2) the recurrence of the intentional acts sustaining the whole set-up. Consider how flexible such defensive schemes and the required skills and roles can be. Emergency service agencies experience internal emergencies. When trained personnel are not available, other staff members "rise to the occasion" and temporarily fill new roles. Centers for disease control cannot anticipate where and what types of epidemics will suddenly appear, but they stockpile resources in strategic locations and develop contingency plans for deploying them in response to crises.

In a roundabout way, the preceding pages have been setting the conditions for the third view's answer to the main question of this chapter: What is the ontological status of institutions? The second approximation drew upon evidence of ecological schemes to suggest how we might understand social schemes. How legitimate is this analogical approach? The test lies in what it contributes to answering the main question. Institutions belong to a world mediated and constituted by meaning. They are not objects for inquiry by *Naturwissenschaften* but by *Geisteswissenschaften*. Unless the latter are studies of what is unreal, their practices presuppose a division of *esse reale* into natural and intentional beings. This distinction is supplemented by a further distinction. The medievals talked of the *ordo cognoscendi* and the *ordo essendi*. In doing so

---

189   Again, the Presidency survives any temporary office holder. The durability of ecosystems and institutions, in contrast to the transiency of individuals, is part of the puzzle about whether "existence" is ascribed to both in the same sense.

they were following Aristotle who asked about the priority of real objects in relation to the cognitive acts that led to knowledge of them. In the order of understanding, the cognitive (intentional) acts precede knowledge of real objects. However, in the order of being the object of investigation precedes those acts. Without something to puzzle over no questions get asked. All the same, not all answers are correct and so may not be about real objects in the *ordo essendi*.

How does this further distinction supplement the differentiation of natural and intentional beings? Natural phenomena, as yet-to-be-known objects, presuppose the constructive or synthetic functions of intellect if they are actually to be known. Put bluntly, to understand the former first requires they be "invented" by the latter.[190] But the point of is-questions and of acts of judging is to settle whether what has been invented or hypothesized is in fact what is the case. Sometimes inquirers find that their bright ideas are actually discoveries about what is the case. Then, in regard to actually known natural phenomena, the claim is that they exist independently of any intentional acts. The same is not true of intentional beings. Again, understanding what institutions are, how they emerge and survive requires constructive or synthetic acts of intellect. However, to judge that understanding to be correct is not to claim that the institutions exist independently of intentional acts. They are dependent on minds (1) in their origins, (2) in their survival and (3) in their being understood.[191]

But there was a further question: Are institutions more than their ingredients, their members? Answering this question requires an excursus into questions about how more complex realities might emerge from and be sustained by less complex realities. These questions already appeared in Chapter Two where there was mention of the "emergent properties" of ecosystems. Can the latter exhibit intelligible functions over and above their constitutive organisms? While in Chapter Two there was mention of Lonergan's notion of emergent probability as relevant to understanding how more complex organisms and patterns of relations might emerge from less complex ones, the details were initially left unexplored. The current questions about the ontological status of

---

190   This general insight anticipates provocative suggestions in Chapter Six that neurons discovered and even "invented" themselves.

191   The distinction between beings that are mind dependent and those that are mind independent is not uncommon. However, a common-sense realism may misplace the basis for the distinction by locating it in some objectively given x rather than in an understanding of distinct intentional acts and their proper objects. Common-sense realism draws a distinction between that which is mind dependent and that which is mind independent, but it fails to concede in a higher-order way that the difference between mind dependency and mind independency is itself mind dependent.

institutions and how individuals are related to them return us to this question of emergence. To begin with a simple example, no one designs or controls modern market economies. Thousands upon thousands of individuals unknown to each other make choices, and the results are functioning markets. In turn, the results of so many fragmented choices act back on those individuals in the form of price fluctuations, varying employment rates, trade imbalances, obsolescence of old industries and their replacement by new technologies. How are we to understand the genesis of complex webs of such relations arising from uncoordinated choices and producing consequences for so many individuals?

Emergent probability offers one option for answering this question. While Lonergan focused on emergent probability as an answer to questions about the intelligible order of the natural world, we can ask whether his account is relevant to understanding the emergence and survival of institutional orders. First, we need to summarize what he meant by emergent probability, i.e. how it was a solution to a set of puzzles. Second, we need to decide whether a solution to puzzles about natural phenomena is relevant both to understanding institutions as "flexible ranges of social schemes of recurrence" and to moving toward a third approximation of their meaning.

What were the problems that Lonergan thought emergent probability solved? An understanding of evolutionary processes as aggregations of mutations is inadequate in explaining how more complex organisms appear over time. Variations occur, but they do not merely pile up like rocks in a quarry. Instead, they lead to novel and more complex forms of life. How does this happen? The general answer of emergent probability rests on an acknowledgement that (1) organisms exist in and through schemes of recurrence, (2) variations occur because of changes in relations organisms have to schemes within and outside themselves, and (3) both organisms and their relevant schemes are conditioned phenomena. Regarding the last claim, the routine functioning of organisms and ecosystems depends upon the recurrent fulfillment of antecedent conditions. For example, the growth of plant species depends upon rainfall and sunlight, i.e. hydrological and planetary schemes; the survival of herbivores, in turn, depends upon all three types of conditions being met within an adequate range. Similar descriptive examples of such conditionality and interdependence are plentiful. Lonergan pushes beyond them to explain how such intelligible relations among objects and events are only partly accounted for by laws formulated in physics, chemistry and biology.

The fact that new species appear and more complex ecosystems develop over time finds a general explanation in the conditionality of such laws. For example, immunology tests presuppose that whenever chemical agents of certain types are applied to human skin, their interactions with T-cells at the chosen sites will produce indicators (e.g. rashes) in patients who have different kinds of allergies. However, false negatives can occur because the chemical laws presupposed by the procedure are "abstract." That is, they take into account a limited number of variables and formulate an understanding of how such variables interact, but they do not "capture" all the variables that may interact in specific cases. For instance, the efficacy of chemical agents may be compromised by improper storage or skin reactions may not occur because T-cells are not adequately distributed at the chosen site for the test. In short, a series of conditions have to be met before results predicted by the abstract laws actually appear. By themselves the laws are insufficient to determine specific outcomes; they must be supplemented by a range of other conditions that may not always be met.[192]

The abstractness of what Lonergan called "classical laws" was the key insight that led to his understanding of emergent probability. While actual outcomes may conform to such laws, they do so as a matter of probability, not of necessity.[193] Probability, therefore, governs the actual functioning of organisms and their relevant schemes of recurrence. Now just as qualifiers were noted earlier in talking of "circles" of schemes, so talk of variability among antecedent conditions requires qualifiers. Such variability does not necessitate that schemes break down or that organisms or ecosystems undergo dramatic changes. Defensive schemes can allow organisms to function under changed conditions. For example, sharp drops in average rainfall and a decline in plant growth may evoke migratory responses from herbivores. Disrupted schemes and population losses within an ecosystem may recover when previously met conditions are again being fulfilled. Because a newly dominant species in a local food chain may be replaced or its numbers sufficiently diminished by the reappearance of a previously dominant rival, populations and ecosystems that had nearly disappeared may be restored.[194] Again, the range of possible conditions that may be satisfied is much larger than the series of conditions actually being satisfied. Those possibilities include unexploited

---

192   *Insight*, 70-71.
193   Ibid. 141-142.
194   Recent reports about the effects on Yellowstone National Park of returning wolves to the area dramatize how earlier ecosystems and populations can rebound. New conditions, e.g. a new class of predators, can spell doom for some species and some ecosystems but can also mean reforestation, more stable river flows, increased bird populations and so on.

conditions that classical laws cannot anticipate in their entirety. Thus, variations in species and in ecosystems with their hierarchical orderings of species are ever possible.

Now to transition from talk of ecosystems to talk of institutions, advocates of the third view can begin with descriptive examples of persons desiring certain goods, cooperating with others to obtain them and in the process acquiring skills and forming relationships that over time become routine ways of cooperating and distributing new roles and responsibilities so as to allow a flow of desired goods to continue under variable conditions. Subsequent talk of schemes of recurrence assumes that ongoing intentional acts are what create and sustain such patterns or schemes of relationships. Talk of "emergent properties" in institutions that are not reducible to their members becomes more plausible if such schemes (1) emerge from a range of possible intentional acts, that (2) establish initial distributions of roles and responsibilities (3) enduring beyond those founding acts and (4) forming intelligible patterns of relationships that subsequent generations at least initially accept as normative, "objectivated realities" for their own social living. Legal systems in which "no one is above the law" are strong candidates for being instances of institutions having emergent properties and conditioning the thinking and acting of later generations.

What is the relevance of the preceding for formulating a third approximation to the meaning of institution? The distinction between natural being and intentional being permits talk of "real relations" as constituted by acts of meaning. Thus, common sense accepts marriages as realities; they are not legal fictions. An understanding of emergent probability offers an explanation of how institutions with emergent properties are irreducible to their individual members. As well, it adds to an understanding of the flexibility of institutional arrangements in responding to changing conditions.[195] As insights into new puzzles occur as a matter of probability, so intelligent responses to new conditions may allow institutions to survive dramatic changes in, for example, business environments. Defensive schemes anticipate such challenges and are instances of human "plasticity" and the flexibility of humanly constituted schemes.

Finally, to formulate a <u>third</u> <u>approximation</u> to the meaning of institution, let an institution be understood as a range of conditioned

---

195   Talk of the emergence and flexibility of schemes of recurrence is one way of accounting for the survival of very old institutions despite major changes in the conditions under which they first appeared. Examples that easily come to mind are the Eastern Orthodox and Roman churches, the British Houses of Parliament, the Icelandic Althing.

series of social schemes of recurrence emerging from and sustained by ongoing intentional acts that in recurring can develop or correct those schemes and so respond to changes in the conditions they initially satisfied.

To summarize the movements among viewpoints in this section, the first view of institutions was wedded to the picture thinking manifest in the narrative of Classical Liberalism. The second, dialectical view moved beyond that narrative with its imaginable individuals engaged in contract negotiations and evaded the either-or impasse of asking if individuals or institutions had priority. As well, it qualified a wholly instrumentalist view of institutions since relations of dependency between correlates are poorly grasped when one term is viewed as always the cause (*movens*) of the other (*motus*). Finally, the third view mixed insights from ecology with those from sociology but did not propose an analogy between ecosystems and institutions. That is, the analogy is not between parts and wholes, between atomistic particulars and organic unities, as has been the case in previous debates about the relation of individuals to institutional orders. Rather, the analogy was one of proportion: as organisms are to ecosystems so individuals are to institutions. Both terms in each relation are mutually conditioning. This much is present in the dialectical understanding of institutions. What the third view adds to the second are the insights that intentional acts condition the emergence and survival of institutions while the latter demand both the recurrence of those acts and their flexibility in adapting to changing conditions. In short, institutions originate in the raising and answering of questions, but, once set up, social schemes demand new questions and answers making them both *motus et movens*.

III. Two Sequences of Views

The first view of institutions focuses on their "ingredients," e.g. a society is equal to its members and exists only as an aggregation of those members. This view is plausible since it seems quite concrete. Individuals, or perhaps small groups, are the basic imaginable units of a society or state. Since they are distinct entities, to talk of them as parts of some organic whole is either to abuse language or to use shorthand in saying that they are in proximity to one another and have, by design or by accident, become secondarily related to one another.

To make the subsequent relations or any unity among them objective realities is to mistake "ideas" for reality. No one perceives ideas. When asked to say exactly what one perceives in talking about institutions or states, a clear-headed response would produce descriptions of particular individuals, their behaviors and locales. Lists of such descriptions may lead to talk of communities, nations and institutions, but these will be abstract terms. Their empirical base will remain their ingredients. The latter exist as concrete particulars, but an idea is an abstraction. To hold otherwise is to lapse into some form of idealism or, perhaps, to use ordinary language carelessly.

The second view of institutions employs a different ontology, adopts a different type of realism. Things, whether persons or organisms, exist in relation to one another. They thrive in and through their relationships. The contexts for the latter may be natural ecosystems or social patterns of relations commonly referred to as institutions. An understanding of dialectical or reciprocal causality permits evasion of the question of priority. While open to claims that institutions are "objectivated realities," the second view is not specific on how such human products are realities and in what sense existence is attributed to them.

The third view is more explicit in handling the question of the ontological status of such human products. The distinction between intentional being and natural being is relevant to claiming that both things and their schemes are real. Although schemes of recurrence or patterns of relations are not things, things are not explainable without reference to how they depend upon internal and external schemes. Recall the earlier note that explaining anything, whether fruit flies or legal systems, was a matter of first attending to some puzzling experience, asking questions, making guesses about what something might be and then checking any guess or meaning to determine whether it was correct. Next, recall how affirming a guess as correct follows upon an invisible act of judging an invisible meaning to the effect that it is what actually is the case. To have an incomplete but correct understanding of fruit flies or of legal systems is not to clutter one's brain with insects or legal documents. Whether natural or social phenomena, both are intelligible and reasonably affirmable types of beings. The ontological difference is that natural phenomena are not constituted by acts of meaning whereas institutions are so constituted. The former are known by such acts, but in judgment are known to exist independently of those acts. Dinosaurs did not await human inquiry before coming into being. However, courts of law and businesses only emerge and continue through such acts.

How might specialists in FS3 arrange these three views in some sort of developmental sequence? Presumably different sequences might reflect the background differences between two types of realism and two types of knowing. Thus, one sequence might favor the first view of institutions over the other two because it evades the "idealism" lurking in talk of institutions as distinct realities. Since the dialectical view is less explicit than the third view in asserting the existence of real relations, it may seem a middle stance in the sequence. Thus, a first sequence would arrange the views, proceeding from the least developed to the most developed, as $3 \rightarrow 2 \rightarrow 1$.

In contrast, a different specialist in FS3 might favor the third view because its talk of real relations, some of which are constituted by acts of meaning, seems justifiable. The questions are whether one accepts that institutions fall under the category of "intentional being" and are both intelligible patterns of relations distinct but not separable from their "terms" and affirmable as having emergent properties, i.e. ones not identical with either of their terms?[196] To answer positively is to depart from the first view and so to favor a different sequencing of the views. The likely outcome, again moving from least to most developed, would be to reverse the first ordering to read: $1 \rightarrow 2 \rightarrow 3$. The dialectical view's superiority over the first will plausibly be its recognition of the mutual dependency or conditioning of individuals and institutions.

IV. Doing FS4

As with the previous case studies in this series, the application of FS4 amounts to a comparison of genetic sequences of viewpoints to UV.[197] Thus, a series of familiar questions organize this final section of the chapter: (1) What major differences are there among the three views

---

196   For example, a legal system is constituted and sustained by ongoing acts of meaning and so falls under the heading of "intentional being." It functions as a complex series of schemes of recurrence that are intelligible patterns of relations among assigned roles and procedural rules. Individuals deciding to fill the roles and to follow the rules are necessary conditions for the continuance of the system but are not the same as the system. Given the historical and "objectivated" status of an institution for new generations, it will not be identical to the individuals either temporarily filling assigned roles or currently deciding to affirm its legitimacy.

197   As noted previously, the comparative work of the future will draw upon the results of GS and so be able to evaluate competing views to an acquis or conventionally accepted developmental ordering of views on a common issue.

of institutions? (2) Which differences can be traced back to explicit or implicit stances on questions about RKO? (3) Which of these stances are compatible with these authors' understanding of the meanings of RKO? (4) What might be brought forward from any of the less developed views?

The first two questions can be answered together. The major difference between the first and the other two views is the former's implicit model of reality as whatever is imaginable. The familiar narrative of Classical Liberalism and the explicit claim that individuals exist but not society suggest this model is operative in the background. Imaginable individuals as members of a society exist "out there;" they can be observed. But relations are not out there to be observed. Social or political relations, whether consensual or inherited, are not visible, just as all meanings are invisible. Since no relations are already out there to be sensed, they must be human constructs or ideas. Admittedly this conclusion causes problems in talking about marriages, families, businesses and political systems; still, ordinary language should not be in charge. Careful tracing of names and general terms to any empirical referents may help to disabuse us of sloppy linguistic practices.[198]

In contrast, both the second and third views affirm real relations such that changes in either the "terms" or their relations may alter their reality. A business that goes under alters its workers' roles; a spouse that assents to a divorce alters both partners' roles; market collapses bankrupt corporations and families; flows of ocean waters engineered to be part of cooling systems for nuclear power stations can become tsunamis destroying lives and businesses. In other words, the realities are the terms-with-relations and the relations-with-terms such that significant changes in terms or relations alter the realities. In an explanatory context, organisms are understood in relation to ecosystems, and individuals are understood in relation to social schemes. In neither pairing are the terms explained without relations to one another. To explain either term is to implicate the other. The terms are distinct, but their reality includes their relations.[199]

As distinct from the first view of institutions, both the dialectical view and the ontology of the third view affirm real relations. Can this major difference be traced back to implicit assumptions about RKO? Readers of the two previous texts will anticipate the answer. As already noted, the implicit picture model of reality is arguably behind the first view's denials that society exists and that invisible relations are real.

---

198   For a critique of the implicit view of linguistic reference here, see Chapter Four of the *Primer*.
199   *Insight*, 520.

A contrasting notion of reality as whatever can be understood and reasonably affirmed does not require such denials. Relations constituted and sustained by invisible acts of promising, trusting, deciding and agreeing are not visible but intelligible; as well, they generate commonly understood roles in adult living at home, in the workplace and in sociopolitical organizations.

If knowing what is real requires an empirical reference point for any truth-claims and if "empirical" is coextensive with "observable" or, more broadly, with "sensible," then the denials above will seem defensible. Institutions as mediated and constituted by acts of meaning elude detection by eyes and ears alone. However, if by "knowing" one means correctly understanding something experienced and if "experience" expands to include invisible acts of meaning and the relations they constitute, then one may affirm institutions as both real and knowable.

Finally, if one's understanding of objectivity is whatever is empirically given, i.e. a property of sensible objects or events, then the givenness of concrete persons seems solidly reassuring, but the vagueness of relations is suspect. Perhaps, if by objectivity one means public consensus that something is real, then laws and contracts, churches and businesses can be tolerated as "objectivated realities." The dialectical view is thus an acceptable intermediate position in the first sequence since this secondary meaning of objectivity may be tolerable. However, it remains an ambiguous stance regarding objectivity. Is something objectively real because a public agrees it is or does a public agree because it is objectively real?

A more complex, four-part notion of objectivity appeared earlier in this book series as part of UV.[200] Without repeating the details, we can align the second sequence of views with those differentiated meanings of objectivity. When the first view emphasizes the "ingredients" of social orders and finds relations suspect, it reflects the notion of empirical objectivity as whatever arouses attention and evokes questioning. The dialectical view of institutions is compatible with the second, normative notion of objectivity. Whatever procedures intelligently guide inquiry and deciding may be inventions of previous generations of inquirers. As methods are inherited patterns of inquiry, so institutional routines are what are in place to guide a new generation's patterns of activity.

The third view of institutions[201] is compatible with the first two

---

200   *Primer*, Chapter Three, 101-105.

201   To repeat the third approximation: "an institution is a range of conditioned series of social schemes of recurrence emerging from and sustained by ongoing intentional acts that in recurring can develop or correct those schemes and so respond to changes in the conditions

notions of objectivity. What of the third notion, "terminal objectivity," and the fourth, "contextualized objectivity"? Are the relevant conditions met for affirming the reality of both social schemes through which children are raised and educated and the ongoing intentional acts that adapt those schemes to changing conditions, e.g. new forms of family life and of educational technologies? Schools teaching dyslexic students to use specially designed computer-based reading lessons are not an illusion. They both fit the third approximation to the meaning of institution and are verifiable as innovative patterns in teaching and learning.

The fourth notion refers to an understanding of expertise both as a personal achievement and as a collective possession, i.e. the "lore" of some group. Insights accumulate, judgments discriminate and collaboration shares the results. Individuals inducted into the group are expected to internalize such results if they are play their roles and sustain the common enterprise. The latter is a series of schemes through which persons function, but when they do so the enterprise then demands they acquire new skills and develop new virtues. The habits of the group (e.g. punctuality, loyalty, cooperation) are to become part of the orientations of its new members. In short, the schemes that emerge and survive because of the intentional acts of persons, in turn, change them. What begin as external relations may in time become internal relations.[202]

The answer to the question of compatibility of the two sequences with these authors' positions regarding the meanings of RKO comes as no surprise. The opening question about the ontological status of institutions eventually became a question of whether persons are real and institutions are just ideas or publicly shared meanings.

If by "reality" one means anything "already out there" that sometimes is given to sensibility, then, since relations are invisible, they do not fit this model of reality.[203] Perhaps some kind of social consensus on invisible meanings can qualify as a mark of objectivity, but even then the terms and their relations would have to be separate kinds of entities.

they initially satisfied."

202   External relations leave either "term" unchanged whether they are present or absent. Internal relations are part of the intrinsic meaning of the "terms" such that their absence alters the understanding of the "terms." (*Insight*, 517.) To exemplify the former: which employees ride the same subway train to work is incidental to understanding them or their roles at work. To exemplify internal relations, the meaning of an impartial judicial system would dramatically change if the same judge were allowed to fill the functions of judge, jury and final arbiter of all appeals in a case. Such a conflation of roles would alter both the judicial schemes in place and what it means to be a judge.

203   "On the basic counterposition, there is simply no meaning to talk about real relations. The real is a subdivision of the 'already out there now.' That is simply given. All relations arise only through the activities of our understanding. Therefore, no relations are 'already out there now,' and so none are real." (Ibid. 519.)

This is the best outcome the first view of institutions can tolerate. Thus, the first sequence placed the dialectical view in an intermediate position since it allowed for contractual agreements without insisting that they be more than Nozick's "bit of the real world."

Lonergan articulated a rationale for the second sequence and its ranking of viewpoints.

> On the position, the real is being; it is whatever is to be grasped intelligently and affirmed reasonably. Now within the limits of proportionate being, whatever is grasped intelligently is never a term without relations or a relation without terms. To express an insight, one needs several terms and relations, with the terms fixing the relations and the relations fixing the terms. To suppose that there are any terms without relations or any relations without terms is to suppose an oversight.[204]

With this position these authors agree. Within being it is possible to distinguish between natural beings and intentional beings. Institutions belong to the latter class. Their "grounding reality" is the ongoing occurrence of intentional acts by which persons understand, agree and decide to fulfill roles within schemes. In turn, as intelligently designed solutions to previous problems, these enduring schemes demand participants anticipate and creatively respond to new problems.

There still, however, is the question of what can be brought forward from the first sequence. Worth preserving is the intermediate position it accords the dialectical view. Insofar as *mitsein* is an equiprimordial feature of human living, this stance is defensible, even if it falls short in explaining how displacements from socially entrenched beliefs and practices are possible. What may come forward from the first view of institutions? Within the narrative of Classical Liberalism there is recognition that acts of promising, trusting and agreeing can be constitutive of, can be the foundations of political institutions. While this chapter has not concerned itself with questions of political legitimacy, it obviously agrees with a constructivist view of institutions as deriving from intentional acts.

---

204   Ibid. 520.

CHAPTER FOUR:
ECONOMIC REALISM AND SELF-INTEREST

The preceding chapter reached for an explanatory understanding of institutions. One implication of the third approximation to that goal was that individuals cannot be explained independently of their social relations. This conclusion has further implications for contemporary debates about economic realism and a dominant view of rational agency as acting out of self-interest. Section I highlights key issues in the debates while Section II investigates the history of the psychology and language of self-interest. Insofar as readers are comfortable with this language and its implicit view of rational decision-making, this genealogy may reveal some surprises. Why have these words and this view become so entrenched in economic discourse? They once were novelties, and a historical account may provide some critical distance from these now established features of common sense, at least as it appears within popular discussions of economics. Section III offers details about competing views of economic realism. Section IV orders these views as genetic sequences, and the next section applies FS4 to the sequences first by tracing some of their differences to basic stances on RKO and then by evaluating those stances in terms of UV. Section VI links the findings of this chapter and the preceding one to the question of the meaning of environment.

I. Issues under Debate

The first book in this series raised the question of whether communication was possible among persons operating in different horizons.[205] The initial answer was that, whatever communication occurred, misunderstanding was likely. Examples are not scarce. For audiences confined to a practical pattern of experience, talk of human spirituality will seem

---

205   *The New Comparative Interpretation: A Primer*, Chapter Two.

vague unless one translates it into talk of the psychological consolation religion can provide or of the moral training it can supply to a new generation. Beyond these purported practical benefits, chatter about formal theology or anaphatic mysticism will seem quite pointless to such audiences and so not worthy of their attention. Similarly, for political realists convinced that politics is fundamentally a power game played among rival interest groups, ethical questions will seem secondary concerns that deserve attention only if misconduct risks bad publicity.

In response to this question of communication between different horizons, this book series has defended a three-part thesis: (1) between persons at home in different horizons miscommunication is likely when insights belonging to one horizon are missing in persons operating with less developed viewpoints; (2) the problem is not resolvable by simply relying on arguments to produce the missing insights;[206] (3) any resolution of the problem requires at least a minor, and sometimes a major, displacement in one party's viewpoint. As noted previously, major displacements are the occurrence of the improbable. This is not the place to repeat how such departures from previous viewpoints are possible.[207] However, this chapter reviews issues often debated by persons operating in different horizons. Both they and their audiences often presume disagreements arise because of explicit ideological differences. However, the origins of some of the differences may be far more basic and implicit.

As an example of a debate reflecting differences in horizons, consider the following two versions of economic realism. The first represents a psychology of persons moved by self-interest and exhibiting their rationality by choosing effective means to their ends. The second version operates with much broader views of human motivation and rationality.

In an interview Milton Friedman was asked whether he defined "self-interest" as whatever the individual wants. He replied:

> Yes, self-interest is what the individual wants. Mother Teresa, to take one example, operated on a completely self-interested basis. Self-interest does not mean narrow self-interest. Self-interest does not mean monetary self-interest. Self-interest means pursuing those things that are valuable to you but which you can also per-

---

206   Chapter One of the *Primer* offered a lengthy defense of this conclusion. Speakers and audiences may use the same words but may understand them quite differently. Differences in development are reflected more in the absence of insights and less in the mastery of vocabulary or skills in argumentation.

207   The conditions for such possibilities were a topic in Chapter Four of the *Primer*.

suade others to value. Such things very often go beyond immediate material interest.[208]

In contrast, Amartya Sen criticized a view of self-interested economic actors for ignoring evidence that persons routinely rise above an ethic of self-interest in their economic and political decisions. In doing so, they must be irrational according to the views of rational agency adopted by the classical liberal view. Sen is blunt in his assessment: "The purely economic man is indeed close to being a social moron. Economic theory has been much preoccupied with this rational fool decked in the glory of his one all-purpose preference ordering," i.e. advancing his self-interest.[209]

What are readers to make of these competing views? Who is the realist here? The Friedman interview expands the meaning of self-interest to include all motives, even the apparently self-less care for impoverished and socially unproductive populations. Here a student of logic could fault Friedman for committing the fallacy of vacuous contrast. His basic category means nothing or everything. On the other hand, Sen would seem to have some empirical evidence on his side. Single-issue voters have their "causes," but their campaigns often have only tenuous links to personal advantage. Furthermore, an experiment indicated that first-year graduate students in economics fared poorly in games that, while requiring cooperation to maximize group benefits, also rewarded them individually for refusing to cooperate.[210] An additional study found that, while students of economics behaved like "anti-social reincarnations of Ebenezer Scrooge," most test subjects, contrary to "the core model of behavior in economics," cooperated "far more frequently than the postulates of self-interested rational calculation" predicted.[211]

While Sen disparaged the "rational fool" and any single "all-purpose preference ordering," readers might wonder why many economists would reduce something so obviously complex as human motives to a single category. They cannot be unaware of depth psychology.[212] They

---

208   "*Free to Choose:* A Conversation with Milton Friedman" in *Imprimis*, Vol.35, No.7 (Hillsdale, MI: July, 2006), 7.

209   "Rational Fools: A Critique of the Behavioral Foundations of Economic Theory" in *Philosophy and Public Affairs*. 6(1977), 336.

210   "The research found, in a dry but cutting phrase, that the economics students 'performed significantly more in accord with the self-interest model' than did the non-economists." Ormerod, 34.

211   Ibid. 35.

212   That awareness was not missing in other fields outside psychology. Wittgenstein remarked that in the interpretation of dreams one never knew when one had reached the bottom, i.e. never knew when layers of disguise had been entirely removed. Kissinger, in a far different context,

are not fools, at least not in any greater numbers than members of other professions. Might it be that the appeal to self-interest has little to do with empirical research and far more to do with limited horizons? This suspicion has ancient roots. In his *Gorgias* Plato was quite explicit in distinguishing between self-interest and perceived self-interest. Archelaus of Macedonia was a powerful individual in his day. He could act with impunity. However, Socrates asked whether his power to do whatever he wanted meant that he was advancing his real interests. Plato's judgment was succinct. Without wisdom a powerful tyrant can pursue perceived self-interest yet in fact be harming himself. Did Plato's horizon include what the rational fool's horizon is missing, namely, a normative understanding of what ends are actually in one's interest to pursue?

This first section offers no more than an introduction to basic issues. Still, these authors are ready to acknowledge two suppositions. First, the category of self-interest today serves a methodological purpose. Nineteenth-century utilitarians searched for a quantitative measure of happiness in order to put their science of ethical acts on firm ground and so do for ethics what Newton had done for natural acts or motions. They failed. The category of self-interest has, in lieu of any better candidate for the elusive function, become a "place holder," an empty or all-inclusive category, masking the deficit. As such it may reassure some that economists can reliably predict behavior.

Second, the implied understanding of rational agency suffers from its own deficit. While Plato could distinguish between perceived self-interest and actual self-interest, many thinkers in the West today hesitate to identify what good ends rational persons as such should pursue. "Rational" has become for them practical or instrumental rationality, i.e. choosing effective means to preferred ends, whatever those ends may be.[213] Substituting "self-interest" for "preferred ends" reveals the second deficit. Being rational becomes a matter of choosing means not ends. If views of the normative ends for human living have proved too disparate and contentious, a practical solution is to focus on procedural goods. Secondary debates ensue, but their origins often remain hidden. For example, long-running arguments about substantive (positive) rights and formal (negative) rights have been with us for a few centuries. For Hobbes, liberty meant the absence of constraint, and eventually liberty, as a basic right, meant persons should be able to pursue their own "life

---

quipped that speculation on motives was an endless path.
213   For a lengthy discussion of this cultural change in the meaning of rationality, see *Cracking the Case*, Chapter Four, Section III.

plans" with the fewest number of external constraints. This stance is part of the picture thinking of Classical Liberalism and its narrative of the origins of the state. But an infrequently asked question is why anyone should esteem such liberty, especially since so many persons abuse their discretion. In the extreme, lack of a normative notion of liberty leads some to confess they are unable to explain how persons-at-liberty could ever waste their lives.

Perhaps readers of Chapter Three begin to recognize why its discussion of a good of order and especially of the terms in the third row of the diagram of an institutional matrix preceded this chapter. The category "liberty" was the first term in that line followed by "orientation," "personal relations" and "terminal values." While common sense may treat each term in isolation from the others (e.g. liberty as simply the absence of constraint), explanatory understanding treats terms in relation to one another. Again, the terms fix the relations, and the relations fix the meanings of the terms. At least an effort was made to do that in the previous chapter. The third section of this chapter will make use of these four terms in presenting an alternate view of economic realism.

To conclude this first section, it may help to state some difficult questions one can ask about the first version of economic realism and its language and psychology of self-interest.

> 1. Are perceived self-interests identical with rationally chosen ends such that pursuit of the former is what we mean by rational decision-making?

> 2. In lieu of agreement on normative ends, can agreement on procedural goods be a sufficient condition for the survival of a good economic order?

> 3. In acknowledging diverse and sometimes incompatible interests or ends, does reliance on "side constraints," i.e. individual rights, and their legal protection provide adequate checks on abuses of discretion?

As a final note, all economic realists expect conflicts of interest, violations of side constraints and criminal infractions; they do not expect virtuous behavior to be universal. However, they have at least a latent hope that most persons will identify their self-interest with maintaining a given economic order. The rationale for entering into the social contract assumes as much. Consent derives from the expectation of a flow of goods made possible by cooperation and respect for law. Cooperation sustains the flow, and laws penalize threats to both. However, does the appeal to self-interest do justice to the amount of cooperation and respect for law that persons routinely manifest? Might an implicit act of faith, even for the staunch realist, be that not too many will be "social morons"?

II. The Language and Psychology of Self-Interest

What preceded modern talk of persons free to pursue their interests in ideally open markets? What preceded talk of rational agency as practical intelligence choosing effective means to whatever one's preferred ends? Chapter Four in the second book of this series answered the latter question. It summarized Eric Voegelin's account of the originating insights behind talk of reason (*nous*) among Classical Greek philosophers. Without repeating that summary, we can cite a central feature that sets up a contrast between earlier and later psychologies of human activity. Plato and Aristotle conceived of the good life as one orientated toward good ends, toward the acquisition of virtues. The medievals agreed with them. For example, prudence was the acquired habit of judging what was good to do; its end was practical wisdom.[214] Fortitude was the acquired habit of being able to conform the will to one's best judgments despite resistance from oneself or others. Temperance was the deliberate cultivation of moral character able to withstand competing desires that would thwart prudential judgments and their aims. To the degree that a theory of virtues was specific and was the basis for talking about a good life, rational agency had identifiable normative ends. Part of the study of human psychology, then, was inquiry into how persons and their actions reflected orientations toward good ends.[215]

Today agreement on normative ends is often in short supply. One symptom of the shortage lies in a modern psychology of human action

---

214   Today even this traditional understanding of the primary "natural" virtue is contested or is just one of a number of ways of talking about prudence. "Prudence can be defined as a trait, virtue, norm, skill, mode of reasoning, and form of character." Robert Hariman, "Prudence in the Twenty-First Century," in *Prudence: Classical Virtue, Postmodern Practice*. Robert Hariman (ed.) (University Park: The Pennsylvania State University Press, 2003), 293.

215   It is only "part" of the study of human psychology because persons can and do lead disordered lives, vices contend with virtues, self-control and ordered liberty are precarious achievements.

that substitutes a language of motives for the earlier language of orientation toward moral ends. What moves or motivates persons? A dis-
tinctively modern response to the question employs the vocabulary of
"interests." One author gave the following account for the change:

> The term 'interest' was selected by liberalism so that pub-
> lic discourse about politics and economics might avoid
> the limitations associated with the term 'opinion,' which
> the Enlightenment made synonymous with religious
> beliefs (read: fanatical superstitions) about the common
> good, and with the term 'passions,' which also carries a
> connotation of arbitrariness. The implication of the term
> 'interest' is that pursuing one's interest is more in accord
> with the public interest than acting in the name of the
> common good.[216]

Since modern writers recognized that interests could be narrow or
broad, they spoke of "enlightened self-interest" as a goal their writings
on economic liberty were to promote. But their purpose was not to elab-
orate a theory of virtues and moral development.[217] Instead, their focus
was on understanding how, under certain institutional arrangements
(e.g. open markets), the pursuit of self-interest could yield unintended
social benefits. In short, the promise was that one could have good
outcomes without necessarily having virtuous persons.[218] Enlightened
self-interest would recognize and cooperate with institutional set-ups
that made this possible.

These remarks, however, are limited to changes apparent in the
eighteenth century. What was happening much earlier? How did religious beliefs come to seem "fanatical superstitions" and so bring into
disrepute talk of a "common good"? Voegelin's analysis reaches back

---

216   Fred Lawrence, "Editors' Introduction" in Bernard Lonergan. *Macroeconomic Dynamics,*
CW 15 (Toronto: University of Toronto Press, 1999), lxx.
217   The notion of moral development presupposes some end or ends, movement toward
which constitutes "change for the better." In the absence of agreement on ends, defenders of
the first type of economic realism are unlikely to make use of the phrase "moral development."
218   By extension, it was thus possible to collapse Plato's distinction between perceived and
actual self-interests. If an institutional order could turn acts aimed at either type of self-interest into socially beneficial outcomes, the distinction was less important. Especially if agreement
on normative ends for individual living was lacking, agreement on socially beneficial outcomes
might nevertheless occur. Still, most writers recognized that open markets did encourage individuals to acquire a limited range of virtues, e.g. self-control (delayed gratification for the sake of
capital formation?), reliability, honesty and reciprocity. Of course, critics worried that the practical rationales for acquiring these limited virtues left self-interested actors content at a fairly basic
level of moral development and indifferent to what further growth was possible.

to the Stoics and what he calls the "deformation of symbols."[219] Some of the symbols or verbal formulations that Classical Greek philosophers used to stabilize insights into their spiritual experiences, e.g. *nous*, *psyche*, *methexis*, eventually passed into common usage. But in the mouths of less spiritually developed persons, the terms could be used without personal experience of their originating insights. Just as a political party has its slogans the repetition of which shows one's adherence to the group, so later generations could repeat the words of major thinkers without any serious understanding of them. The repeated phrases signaled a disciple's loyalty, but their original meanings were unknown to all but a few. Such has been the fate of great thinkers across the ages.

The decline from an earlier level of insight involved more than nominal understanding of public words. The same words, as noted before, can convey different meanings depending on the development of audiences. When Christian philosophers and theologians made use of terms from Classical Greek philosophy to expand their understanding of the Scriptures, the same variability in meaning was inevitable. Additionally, when imperial politics and doctrinal debates became entangled, more than misunderstanding followed. What Voegelin labels "*dogmato-machies*" became a pattern extending across the following centuries.[220] Many who were ignorant of the complex meanings of traditional phrases in creedal statements were still bent on proving their orthodoxy, and the proof was thought to lie in repeating those phrases even if doing so was devoid of understanding. Subsequent wars of religion accelerated the decline from spiritual insights to verbal partisanship.

To onlookers, often themselves unfamiliar with the originating experiences and insights, the contentious parties with their slogans seemed fanatical espousers of empty phrases. Worse yet, though they proclaimed themselves representatives of revealed truths and doers of God's will, they clearly behaved in ways contrary to explicit teachings about love of neighbor and the ultimate mysteriousness of the divine. Little wonder, then, that onlookers saw all the religious factions and their deadly squabbles as dangerous superstitions. Again, because of the ongoing deformation of symbols and the primacy accorded creedal formulations, even fewer people preserved the originating insights that once grounded spiritual faith and talk of reason. For all sides the slaughter was obvious, and, while the disputed formulations were familiar, in increasing numbers those disgusted by the strife found the latter to be so much bewildering nonsense.

---

219   *The Ecumenic Age* (Baton Rouge: Louisiana State University Press, 1980), 33-48.
220   Ibid. 48-57.

The seventeenth century witnessed searches for political remedies to the religious conflicts and for intellectual alternatives to the religious dogmatomachies. Thomas Hobbes contributed to both. For our purposes his shaping of a new psychology of motivation is his primary contribution to the emergence of a new common sense in the West. If agreement on the *summum bonum* proved elusive and fraught with danger, perhaps one could order society and understand human behavior by the study of what was much lower. If pride-filled individuals could be checked by fear of death, the *summum malum*, a theory of the passions might reveal other "reasons" persons acted or refrained from acting. Emerging here is an inversion of a classical psychology of orientation toward normative ends and of an understanding of politics as the art of "soul-making."[221] The Leviathan exercised a monopoly on the legitimate power to execute malefactors, and fear of death was the motive for signing a contract, surrendering natural liberties, respecting the terms of the contract and restraining one's other unruly passions.

Locke and Classical Liberalism presented a more positive version of the motives of the contracting parties. Cooperation under the terms of the contract provided security from external and internal threats, but it also provided a more efficient way of satisfying human needs, of pursuing varied interests. The shaping of a new common sense and a new understanding of political and economic institutions was going forward. Both types of institutions were instruments for satisfying human needs while allowing diverse interests free play with "side constraints."[222] The best instruments would be those maximizing the satisfaction of needs; in reality, since "the enemy of the good is the best," persons should settle for political and economic orders that, more than any other available options, produce satisfaction of the needs and interests of the greatest number of people.

Obviously indebted to Voegelin, the preceding remarks have briefly sketched the emergence of a modern common sense and its offspring, the first version of economic realism. It suggested a historical rationale for both the language of self-interest and the acceptance of the outcomes of market economies. That rationale presupposed widespread disagreement on the proper ends rational persons as such should pursue and so employed "self-interest" as the empty (or all-inclusive) category for whatever ends persons happen to pursue. It assumed that market economies

---

221   Eric Voegelin. *From Enlightenment to Revolution* (Durham: Duke University Press, 1975), 69.

222   The preceding chapter criticized the limits of this view of institutions.

have historically lessened conditions of scarcity far better than any of their rivals. Thus, it seemed realistic to endorse them as actual solutions to problems of acquiring, protecting and distributing wealth. Fantasies of the utopian socialists and others might remain attractive but only for those unschooled in reality.

Nonetheless, a competing narrative about markets and liberty was also part of the eighteenth century. Rousseau posed his question of how to turn so many egoists into citizens. The former doggedly sought personal advantages at the expense of society while the latter were ready to sacrifice in order to preserve their social orders. Troubled by what today we call the "tragedy of the commons," Rousseau wondered how the pursuit of self-interest might be checked, not by Leviathan but by the education of liberty. In this inquiry he was not alone. Adam Smith was intensely interested in how natural liberty could be educated to moral ends. Many popular readings of Smith emphasize his hidden-hand argument and skip over his questions about character formation and the ordering of liberty. Regarding both he gave a traditional response. Institutions–family, church, school and even government–were necessary means to these ends.[223] Far from trusting in free markets to yield good results without virtuous people, he anticipated that the ongoing cultivation of good character was a precondition to the survival of liberal institutions, both political and economic.[224] In this he stood apart from later generations who often invoked his name in defending their own views of individuals-at-liberty pursuing varied ends. Furthermore, he rejected the view that individuals were real but that society and institutions were mere ideas or incidental "bits of the real world." The formation of character was not a secondary issue, and the means by which it was achievable were not incidental.

---

223   "Adam Smith is best known as an advocate of 'natural liberty.' But the understanding of what liberty means and of why it is worth having has changed radically from his day to ours. If Smith's association of liberty with institutionally fostered self-control sounds strange to us, it is because we have adopted the assumption that the most 'authentic' self is the self that is least inhibited by external standards, and so many have come to identify liberty with the absence of legal constraint, social constraint, and even self-restraint – with unbounded will and unconstrained desire; and imagine that Adam Smith offered the ultimate rationale for 'doing as one likes.'" Jerry Z. Muller, 2-3.

224   To trust in free markets as some type of *fatum* is easier than facing the difficult task of understanding how the education of liberty could be achieved by large numbers of persons. However, difficulty in understanding is not a criterion of whether something is true or even possible. All the same, it is easier to believe that, given the right institutional set-up, even "social morons" would not need to change. There is some irony in recognizing that this belief was one of the basic flaws in Marx's writings beginning with the 1860 manuscripts. Prior to them he had struggled with the question of whether revolutionary change first required better people or better institutions. Later he focused solely on institutional change as the way forward.

Of course, one could gloss over difficult questions here by say-ing that "enlightened self-interest" is really what Smith and other eighteenth-century thinkers were advocating. If this means that persons can be taught to promote the interests of others as a means of advancing their own, the practical insights involved hardly require extensive labor by either teachers or students. Presumably Smith meant more when he wrote of the importance of character formation.

This second narrative about markets and the education of liberty was a reflection of an older tradition of *paideia* and the self-control expected of rational persons. This is not surprising. Some remnants of an earlier common sense, one that endured for at least two thousand years in the West, were likely to survive in any replacement. All the same, the dominant version of economic realism today uses the language of self-in-terest and relies on a psychology of motivation to understand rational decision-making in the marketplace.

III. Competing Views of Economic Realism and Rationality

A question about economic liberty appeared above: why do persons esteem liberty? Premodern answers cited mastery over the passions and the acquisition of virtues as the ends of liberty. The situation today is that agreement on specific normative ends is elusive. As already noted, one symptom is a modern psychology of human action that substitutes a language of interests for the earlier language of moral virtues. Eigh-teenth-century writers sought to understand how, under certain institu-tional orders, self-interest might produce unintended social benefits.

What are some consequences of limiting the "ends" of economic liberty to talk of interests, enlightened or otherwise? First, voluntary eco-nomic exchanges do not secure all human goods, something that is es-pecially apparent for at-risk populations unable to compete successfully in the marketplace.[225] What are the options for securing these further goods? Some argue that free markets do a better job than any other arrangement in increasing the aggregate wealth of a society and so in enlarging the pool of resources for protecting at-risk populations.[226]

225   There is a further debate we are not engaging here; namely, regardless of whether exchanges are voluntary or not, are there some human goods that should never be available for sale?
226   For many holding this position, protection of these at-risk populations was the responsi-

Opponents cite the problems of maldistribution of resources under market conditions and argue that universal access to basic goods is more likely through the regulation of some economic activities by state agencies. The first group defends a type of laissez-faire option that ideally will produce good results without requiring that persons be virtuous, i.e. without the development of liberty beyond concern for advancing personal interest.[227] Their opponents rely on state agencies but then assume: (1) those regulating economic activities will reflect ordered liberty in their own lives; (2) they will routinely overcome interference from competing desires, i.e. they will exhibit enduring benevolence as guardians of a common good; and (3) a social order guided by them can flourish even if the vast majority of its citizens do not manifest a similar ordered liberty.

Arguments are available for defending each option and for attacking its contrary. The contending parties all claim to be realists. Perhaps the debate should shift to a study of historical outcomes produced by diverse types of economic orders. Then the questions are what difference has it made when persons have enjoyed great discretion in ordering their own lives and what difference has it made when such discretion was absent? This shift in focus anticipates finding pragmatic reasons for esteeming liberty. The expectation is that economic history provides a reliable guide to political and economic policy making.

Some pragmatic answers are quite familiar. J.S. Mill provided the best known rationale for liberty as noninterference. The free circulation of ideas in open forums will eventually reveal the beneficial ones and unmask the injurious. As a result, societies progress when individuals, free of unnecessary constraints, can speak their minds, access competing opinions and make their own decisions as to what opinions to adopt and what ends to pursue.

Lonergan offered his own version of this pragmatic argument. Improvements in local situations require insights into local conditions; the relevant insights tend to occur to the persons "on the scene;" therefore, those persons should be left largely at liberty to diagnose and to decide what their variable circumstances require.[228] To impose policies from the "top down" without close attention to local conditions: (1) is to assume that generalities, abstracted from local variables, are a sufficient

---

bility of charitable individuals or institutions. They assumed that greater aggregate wealth would make benevolence in the form of philanthropic giving more probable. Coercive means of redistribution (e.g. progressive income taxes) were not an envisioned or acceptable solution.

227   A further claim is that the welfare state obstructs the maximization of wealth and opportunity and so leads to greater numbers of the impoverished.

228   *For a New Political Economy. CW* 21. Philip J. McShane (ed.) (Toronto: University of Toronto Press, 1998), 34-35.

basis for sound decisions, and (2) is to overlook the diagnosis problem that requires insight into local conditions. If physicians proceeded to apply their medical generalities and skipped diagnosing individual patients, funeral homes would be much busier.

Richard Rorty had a further version of the pragmatic rationale for liberty. He disparaged "foundationalist" efforts to justify the language of human rights and the liberal practices consistent with such rights. Instead, he offered a pragmatic-historical defense of both. If a particular society finds that advocating universal human rights and supporting institutions that promoted their protection "work" to its benefit, then that is sufficient justification for that language and those practices until someone provides adequate reasons for changing either of them.[229]

Critics cite at least three problems with pragmatic arguments that appeal to the durability of a belief or a practice as reason enough to sustain either of them. The least serious of the three is that even the most durable practices rarely win universal acceptance. Economic policies distribute benefits and burdens unevenly. While they may "work" for many or even for most, they usually "cost" some parties what they otherwise would not "pay." The rationales for the practices may be durable, but their defense may consist of dismissals of both the complaints of some injured parties and of alternatives as "impractical" because they are not what persons are accustomed to doing. In effect, pragmatic arguments tend to be surprisingly conservative and dismissive of fantasy and experimentation.

A second problem is specifically relevant to defenses of economic liberty within the laissez-faire option. What are the limits of this liberty? For competent adults, the usual answer is that the liberty of the other person sets the limit, the side-constraint, on one's own. Hence, forbearance rights usually have priority over substantive rights. But here even the staunchest libertarian seems to acknowledge an intersubjective world has some primacy in the minimal sense that other persons are legitimate inhibitors of liberty. Nevertheless, in times of peace and prosperity, a social order can tolerate wide variations in how citizens choose to exercise their liberty. The very stability and economic success of the society supply evidence for the pragmatic defense of economic liberty. However, in times of political turmoil and economic distress, the same pragmatic calculus may reverse priorities. Restoring social order and prosperity may

---

229   A standard complaint against Rorty's stance was that his version appeals to "local" practices to justify a rhetoric that is universal in its claims. That is, the language of human rights applies to all locales, but his pragmatic argument amounts to an appeal to what has been successful locally.

seem to require curtailment of liberty. In effect, if liberty is praised only because of its pragmatic benefits, its durability may be wholly at the mercy of *Fortuna* and the accidents of marketplaces and battlefields.[230]

Perhaps the pragmatic response to such problems is only a negative defense of political and economic liberties; namely, we have seen how societies work under tyrants or elites exercising central control over public and private affairs. The historical evidence is that such social orders are not successful in distributing adequate benefits to most of their members. Thus, we assume political arrangements favoring the diffusion of liberty will work better.

This pragmatic response can go on to defend its lack of any more comprehensive rationale for praising economic liberty. After witnessing the horrors of the last century, many blamed those who dreamt of human perfectibility and believed that a temporary coercion of recalcitrant liberty could fulfill their dreams. From the monstrous misdeeds of totalitarian regimes, these critics concluded that persons are not perfectible and that efforts to coerce perfection will reveal not what is best in us but what is worst. What then is to be done? If the Leviathan is a failed option, tolerance may by default become the leading political and economic virtue. As a rationale for the default, a pragmatic stance may assign liberty as noninterference and specific forbearance rights first place in the ranking of social goods. Individuals, within limits, should enjoy maximum discretion in their choices of means and ends, whether ordered or disordered lives result.

Given the previous section's genealogy of modern economic realism, one could conclude that praise of economic liberty reflects a pragmatic, historical compromise that has produced definite benefits (e.g. fewer wars over ultimate ends) but at a cost. First, it employs a psychology of motivation that assumes the pursuit of self-interest or personal satisfaction is the motive of all human actions. This assumption is the basis for substituting *homo economicus* as a rational calculator of personal utility for older accounts of moral agents as capable of pursuing moral ends beyond their rudimentary wants and desires. Again, this change promises and may deliver at least a temporary peace. But this may be because traditional institutions are still in place and for a time continue to "form" or to educate persons so that they learn to desire moral goods beyond personal satisfaction. A durable cultural tradition emphasizing the goods of family unity, civic responsibility, charitable acts and patriotism

---

230   Today one might add "and at the mercy of perceived terrorist threats and how nervous populations respond to them."

may check potential abuses of a liberty no longer explicitly linked to high moral ideals. But the "cultural capital" built up over centuries and invested in institutional set-ups may be draining away as new generations repeatedly hear that the good we cherish most is allowing individuals to pursue their own satisfaction.

Allaying such a worry at first was faith in the automatism of a marketplace that would, under non-monopolistic conditions, offset expected abuses of liberty through competition among different interest groups. That faith reinforced the assumption that persons did not need to develop beyond the condition of rational calculators of their own interests for a social order to prosper. Presumably after the financial crises and disclosed abuses of recent years, that faith has faded for many people; in turn, perhaps its assumption about rational calculators is now more questionable. When promised solutions come up short, the drawing board is not a bad place to be.

There is yet a further objection raised against almost every pragmatic argument. Someone may ask why a particular practice, technique or law works. This further why-question is not adequately answered by simply saying, "It just does." The question anticipates an explanation, and asserting a matter-of-fact is no explanation. Amateur bakers may follow recipes successfully without expertise in thermal conduction and dynamics. Citing their reliable outcomes is no answer to the question of why the recipes "work."

Historically a number of defenses of liberty offered explanations. Teleological theories argued that the moral ends persons-at-liberty might pursue could justify political and economic orders that offered opportunities for them to do so. If a virtuous life could not be imposed on persons, then social orders that fostered the pursuit of virtues and that trusted individuals to undertake the pursuit in their own ways were an attractive option. Talk of inalienable rights to liberty and the pursuit of happiness presumed such trust in persons and disbelief in coercion as an effective way of making persons virtuous, i.e. forcing them to pursue their proper ends.

Theological defenses of liberty follow the same pattern. If the proper ends of human living are reached by spiritual purgation and growth, coercion might contribute to the former but not to the latter. Therefore, liberty is a necessary (though not a sufficient) condition for spiritual development, and as such it is to be esteemed.

Both types of teleological explanations evoke new problems. Historically theories of virtues have had metaphysical and theological roots that engendered endless debates. Overt appeals to theological assumptions in talking about the ends of human living have generated little consensus. Penalties for actions inconsistent with such theological stances have generated strife and even war. Thus, the language of "interests" and the psychology of rational calculation made their historical entrances as alternatives to a normative hierarchy of goods. For purposes of contrast with what follows, let this first view of economic realism be labeled "a realism of historical compromise."

A second view of economic realism draws upon one of these authors' earlier book, *A Theory of Ordered Liberty*. It formulated a normative notion of liberty as distinct from procedural tolerance: "liberty is the capacity to respond to the mediated demand of the principle of completion in ways that develop or correct the antecedent integrations that initially condition its exercise."

What implications does this normative notion of liberty have for working out a second view of economic realism? To answer this question, we need to locate this notion of liberty within the broader explanatory framework of the "structure of the good." In particular, we need to relate it to the other categories in row three of the diagram: "orientation," "displacement," "personal relations" and "terminal values."

The relations among the categories appeared in the earlier books in this series that defended an understanding of decision-making as a distinct type of intentional act in a structured process of wondering that tends toward completion. The act of deciding occurs within a scheme of recurrence among intentional acts responsive to demands of distinct types, i.e. demands for images, feelings, insights, facts, options and worthwhile objectives. The capacity to respond becomes determinate, becomes a concrete orientation, through actual operations that, interacting with prior integrations, establish the historicity of the person making decisions.[231] Three basic insights specified a minimally adequate moral orientation.[232] To this minimum was added a general

---

231   To cite the earlier text: "Suppose decision-making is first an indeterminate capacity for choosing ends and means. Its correlate will be a field of possible ends and means. The empirical possibility of different ends and courses of action is one basis for the indeterminacy of the capacity. But actual decisions are eventually made from among the possibilities, and these add determinations to the capacity. The latter may be the impersonal determinants resulting from choices made by anonymous others, e.g. the cultural patterns new generations find already in place so that they uncritically believe that burning witches cures plagues or executing persons is a way of reducing violent crimes. They may be the personal determinants resulting from choices which, with repetition, become habits or established orientations." *A Theory of Ordered Liberty*, 170-171.
232   The hypothesis was that being moral in decision-making is, at a minimum, a matter of being careful (1) in distinguishing between what is good and what merely seems good, (2) in distinguishing between personal goods and the well being of others, (3) in giving some consideration before making a decision to its effects on others.

account of a "virtuous orientation."[233] Talk of "virtues" became talk of "flexible ranges of schemes of recurrent normative intentional acts." For example, a virtue such as prudence can be understood as a determinate orientation to make morally appropriate judgments and decisions such that highly variable situations requiring choices are routinely met by a patterned capacity (a determinate orientation) to respond with a high probability of morally appropriate choices.

Earlier talk of "displacements" suggested that some types of orientations were instances of determinate capacities that were more developed than others because they more readily met the mediated demand of the principle of completion. For instance, a type of intellectual displacement is evident when a person moves beyond "picture-thinking" about institutions in terms of imaginable actors doing their jobs in imaginable edifices and, instead, understands that invisible acts of meaning create and sustain ongoing institutional activities. The visible activities in a grocery store recur because of the invisible and recurrent acts of understanding, promising, trusting, deciding and hoping occurring among suppliers, shoppers, employees, managers and so on. Asking what makes any business an ongoing enterprise, an enduring reality, will eventually lead to talk of such invisible acts of meaning and their recurrence, assuming, of course, the questioner is responsive to the demand for more complete understanding and so moves beyond descriptive answers. With further insights into what sustains cooperation and the good of order, the questioner may be better able, more "at liberty," to revise or to develop any inherited views on what persons are to make of themselves and their personal relations.

A type of moral displacement can occur when the questioning expands beyond consideration of effects on "me and mine" and takes into account the effects on "outsiders." A further development is evident when the questioning focuses on whether anyone would be justified in doing such-and-such a thing under similar circumstances. A more "complete" orientation in moral reflection is at work in this third form of questioning

---

233 "Suppose that virtues are habits that result when indeterminate capacities for acting (1) gain determinate direction through prior experiences and (2) are 'completed' by gaining such direction. For example, a realized virtue of prudence presupposes (1) a capacity for judging and deciding, (2) a person's actual history of acts of judging and deciding, and (3) a preponderance of those acts being morally sound judgments and decisions. Within populations such established patterns of operation, or virtues of prudence, make sound moral judgments and choices more probable in the future. The analogy to skillful performance in a sport is apt. A capacity for performance becomes actual performance and, with repetition, can become skilled operation such that one habitually displays a high level of competence. Now suppose the performance is that of moral decision-making. Then the 'skill' is a determinate orientation in choosing, a relatively stable pattern in how one arrives at morally responsible choices." *A Theory of Ordered Liberty*, 176.

since one's understanding of *mitsein* has expanded to include any person whatsoever. One does not have to be, for example, among a population of undocumented immigrants to empathize with their fears of deportation and anger at workplace discrimination. From this enlarged perspective, a questioner will more readily grasp the incompleteness of the view that talks of the discrete individual-at-liberty as a basic category in talking of economic exchanges.[234] From this perspective, the realism of Classical Liberalism appears out of touch with reality.

Actual responses to questions about what is genuinely good to do are decisions, and affective responses to possible courses of action are crucial in decision-making. The cultivation and refinement of affects is often part of personal relations. How might such refinement occur in response to the mediated demand of the principle of completion? Consider how personal relations may make a difference in what stance one takes in the usual debates about the merits of a free-market system.

One claim is that free markets promote ingenious solutions to problems, spur economic innovations and give rise to an improved standard of living in the aggregate. Since intellectual talents and psychological aptitudes for making innovations are randomly distributed within a population,[235] a market system that provides equality of opportunity is a practical means for promoting economic goods. Critics of this set of claims commonly hold that voluntary economic exchanges do not provide or protect all human goods. They cite the legitimate interests of at-risk populations unable to compete in the marketplace, e.g. the very young, the incapacitated and the aged who lack adequate financial resources.[236]

One resulting question is what, if anything, can and should be done to offset the ill effects of the marketplace on such populations. Two options seem incompatible with the normative notion of liberty. The first option advances a traditional laissez-faire argument that (1) individuals pursuing their self-interest will produce unintended social benefits and (2) in doing so will benefit more people in the long run than if we were to allow the moral agendas of political reformers to intrude on market decisions. One assumption here is that liberty in decision-making need

---

234   At least this was one hoped-for outcome of the preceding chapter.

235   Here we have in mind both the intellectual gifts of inventors and the psychological aptitudes of entrepreneurs who bring the formers' discoveries to markets. Schumpeter's distinction between the two is worth recalling.

236   Examples of unintended harms or "third-party effects" on such populations are not difficult to find. Infants can go without adequate neonatal care because of the downsizing of parents' jobs. The disabled can lack access to private businesses because owners find it too expensive to retrofit older buildings. The elderly on fixed incomes can lose their homes because of rising property values and taxes in areas being "gentrified."

not develop beyond an understanding and consideration of one's self-interest, at least when the questions are about economic exchanges with non-family members. Further questions about what range of relevant considerations should be part of our prospective economic judgments are left aside.

The second incompatible option is to rely on political power, exercised through bureaucracies, to direct economic activities toward some envisioned end. The end is usually some reduction or elimination of social problems, but the price tag is the reduction or elimination of liberty.

Why precisely are these options at odds with the normative notion of liberty? The laissez-faire stance appeals to an impersonal "mechanism" of the marketplace almost as a type of *fatum*.[237] In other words, progress will occur unintentionally and even despite widespread, defective schemes of normative intentional acts. Socially beneficial outcomes will occur even if the moral development of most persons is minimal. But, then, the demands of the critical and normative operators are presumably irrelevant to the making of a better history. Replacing a normative understanding of liberty is a psychology of self-interest passing for a complete account of human operation and cooperation. However, smuggled into the account are acts of faith that (1) an impersonal economic order will produce virtuous results without virtuous actors and (2) competing interest groups will ultimately check inevitable abuses by their rivals. But these acts of faith are usually left implicit while reliance on private charity is explicit as the remedy for those who fail to compete successfully.[238]

The second option makes a different act of faith. In relying on technicians to design programs to remedy the ill effects of a market economy, it trusts that such experts will themselves have adequately responded to the mediated demand of the principle of completion for thoroughly understanding problems, creatively imagining remedies and correctly judging which are best and how best to implement them. Even if the

---

237   The frequent use of "mechanism" in discussions of macroeconomics is open to criticisms voiced in earlier books in this series. Machines have imaginable parts comprising imaginable wholes. But are institutions and the intentional acts sustaining them at all comparable to machines? Has anyone ever seen an institution or an act of deciding? In the background of the mechanical analogy is an eighteenth-century worldview dismissive of moral issues as alien to science. Lonergan replied: "when physicists can think on the basis of indeterminacy, economists can think on the basis of freedom and acknowledge the relevance of morality." *Macroeconomic Dynamics*, 105-106.

238   As an alternative to a positive defense of the laissez-faire option, a negative defense cites the failures of "directed" economies and compares their results in raising average standards of living with the results achieved in market economies. This line of defense assumes a complete disjunction between market and directed economies and ignores empirical evidence of mixed economies achieving significantly higher average standards of living. Still, the issue for the second realism is not merging the two options but imagining a third one.

trust is warranted on occasion, the technician model assumes that such responsiveness is a routine occurrence within a population of experts whose personal integrations are not liable to regular interference from competing demands. Even if such integrations were commonplace among economic technicians, most members of a society need not meet the demand of the principle. The message to them is: "Trust the experts who do the planning; you do not need to understand what is going on but just be compliant." In other words, pursuing a more complete understanding of what is good to do and then actually following through and doing it is not a task for the many but for the few. On this account CEOs make the best politicians; the rich must be virtuous; the huddled masses need to lower their expectations to match their abilities. Still, the main criticism of this second option is that it assumes the determinate orientations of these few are as well developed as their plans.[239]

Is there another option, another version of economic realism, that is an alternative to either a *fatum* or dependence on an economically educated elite? Suppose it is the slow "education of liberty." What might this mean? Adam Smith was not unaware of this option. He cited the importance of traditional institutions in shaping "natural liberty," i.e. in forming moral character. *A Theory of Ordered Liberty* located the primary issue in how individuals responded to both inner and outer demands. In response to inner demands, natural liberty takes on determinate form in acts of selective attention, in questions of diagnosis about specific situations, in judgments about the adequacy of diagnoses, in creative fantasies about improving situations, in careful evaluations of options and in decisions about what is best to do. Ideally a series of intentional acts develops and comes to a relative "completion" in an act of deciding, the quality of which depends upon how well previous intentional acts have responded to the varied inner demands. But how much education and what displacements will it take to make adequate responses to these demands commonplace within large populations?

What faith in an impersonal market mechanism or in an economic elite promises is a shortcut. One does not have to wait for any widespread growth toward ordered liberty. Instead, the advocates of automatic market remedies settle for underdeveloped notions of liberty and rationality,

---

239   Another way of criticizing the second option is that it is a non-dialectical reading of the tensions between integrations and operations. Insofar as the economic plans of technicians are efforts to maintain a given order, they are responses to the demands of a principle of assimilation. But the demands of the principle of completion are what spur innovative departures from prior integrations. In contrast, bureaucracies are good at routine tasks, but their failures to anticipate and to respond creatively to novel situations are notorious.

ones subordinated to the demands of sensibility for personal satisfaction. Insofar as the pursuit of particular goods in open markets is thought inevitably to maximize aggregated social benefits, individuals need not "grow" beyond or experience displacement from an initial orientation of self-interest. In contrast, defenders of command economies acknowledge more developed notions of liberty and moral responsibility. However, they tend to assume that only a few persons will operate in ways consistent with these notions. They assume most people are incapable of intelligently and morally administering their own economic affairs. As a result, a few are to be free; the rest are to be regimented.

Trust in the impersonal "mechanism" of the marketplace or in the enduring benevolence and intelligence of economic planners is open to criticisms directly based on a normative notion of liberty. Again, liberty is the capacity to respond to the mediated demand of the principle of completion in ways that develop or correct the antecedent integrations that initially condition its exercise. In practice, acts-at-liberty may fail to meet this mediated demand but instead may yield to other demands for maintaining or retreating to some less developed set of integrations.[240] Normatively, however, acts-at-liberty responding to the mediated demand of the principle of completion should meet the challenge of improving prior integrations. Such acts are then consistent with and complete the demands of the operators of intentional acts for reaching their objectives.

How are persons to recognize such immanent demands in themselves and their relevance to economic decision-making? The proposed answer in terms of the "education of liberty" promises neither shortcuts nor detailed plans.[241] However, some audiences may be eager to hear of any alternative to the intellectual and practical impasse of contemporary economic options. Alisdair MacIntyre has described the impasse:

> On the one side there appear the self-defined protagonists of individual liberty, on the other, the self-defined protagonists of planning and regulation, of the goods which are available through bureaucratic organisation. But in fact what is crucial is that on which the contending

---

240 "Maintaining" occurs, for example, when a resolution to break a bad habit or to adopt a policy that would mitigate "structural evils" is not acted upon. Instead, a prior pattern of operations remains in place. "Retreat" occurs when in times of social upheaval previously cooperative members of a distressed society withdraw to an ethic of personal survival promoting private goods above all others.

241 This is not to say plans would never be available. Designing them is not part of FS4. The division of labor within FS identifies distinct specialties that focus on formulating policies (FS6), developing plans (FS7) and implementing them (FS8).

parties agree, namely that there are only two alternative modes of social life open to us, one in which the free and arbitrary choices of individuals are sovereign and one in which the bureaucracy is sovereign, precisely so that it might limit the free and arbitrary choices of individuals. Given this deep cultural agreement, it is unsurprising that the politics of modern societies oscillate between a freedom which is nothing but a lack of regulation of individual behaviour and forms of collectivist control destined only to limit the anarchy of self-interest.[242]

Lonergan was trying to find a third way around this very impasse when he wrote of a need for new "rules" to guide persons in their economic decision-making. Political economists of a previous century had provided "a rule of *laissez faire* for governments and a rule of thrift and enterprise for individuals."[243] For a time faith in the automatic adjustments of the marketplace held these rules to be sufficient. If the Depression of the 1930s left that faith shaken, what new rules were individuals to follow? Lonergan formulated the stark options:

> Without [new and more satisfactory rules] human liberty will perish. For either men learn rules to guide them individually in the use of the economic machine, or else they surrender their liberty to be ruled along with the machine by a central planning board.[244]

If faith in the automatic adjustments of the marketplace and trust in an impersonal *fatum* are lost, then the question is what type of intelligent direction of the economy we will have.

> Is it to be absolutist from above downwards? Is it to be democratic from below upwards? Plainly it can be democratic only in the measure in which economic science succeeds in uttering not counsel to rulers but precepts to mankind, not specific remedies and plans to increase the power

---

242   *After Virtue: A Study in Moral Virtue* (Notre Dame: University of Notre Dame Press, 1981), 34.
243   *For a New Political Economy*, 110.
244   Ibid.

of bureaucracies, but universal laws which men themselves administrate in the personal conduct of their lives.[245]

But how plausible is any alternative that requires widespread understanding of how a market economy works and widespread consent to act according to new precepts drawn from that understanding? Some realists will despair of the chances of success because they doubt large numbers of people will ever rise above an ethic of self-interest. They may also question whether large numbers of citizens could ever acquire the needed understanding of economics. However, a realist advocating the envisioned education is not expecting everyone to become a professional economist, just as educating people about health care does not aim at making everyone a physician. Instead, just as most persons can learn which activities threaten their health and which benefit it, so most people can learn to recognize which activities threaten economic growth and which promote it.

Someone may quickly object by pointing out that large numbers of people ignore health warnings and avoid activities known to produce health benefits. Such, however, is the result of leaving people at liberty. The principle of completion makes its demand, but inertia, human folly and accidents will always play roles in the human drama. The last century proved that the curtailment of liberty by a top-down direction of command economies produced neither a good order nor morally responsible uses of liberty. A more promising option appears to be some type of education of free individuals in the workings of a market economy and in what kinds of activities are compatible with its functioning as a genuine good of order.[246]

What are the obstacles the education of liberty faces? This author's previous writings have identified some of them.[247] No detailed summary of them is possible here nor is one possible in regard to what Lonergan called the "pure cycle" in the rhythms of a market economy, i.e.

---

245   Ibid.

246   A caveat is perhaps unnecessary regarding this educational option. An eighteenth-century dream of an enlightened age assumed that ignorance was the primary barrier to progress. As the previous texts in this series have noted, there are multiple limits on liberty, including irrational acts that constitute moral failures. They have also remarked on various displacements as prerequisites to a more comprehensive understanding and better practices. Those displacements require more than overcoming ignorance and so underscore the limits of the eighteenth-century dream. For expanded comments on these further displacements, see Lonergan's "Healing and Creating in History" in *A Third Collection* (New York: Paulist Press, 1985), 100-109.

247   Section IV of Chapter Six in *A Theory of Ordered Liberty* (320-334) offers the most detailed account. A shorter account appeared in "Obstacles to a Basic Expansion" in *The Lonergan Review*. Vol. II, no. 1 (Spring 2010), 121-129.

its steady state, surplus expansion and basic expansion. Suffice it to say with Schumpeter that dynamic market economies experience a cycle beginning with "steady states," i.e. ones lacking major innovations, then entering "expansionary states" exploiting major innovations that then ideally come to completion when the aggregate standard of living reaches a higher plateau than before the expansion.

In his analysis of the pure economic cycle, Lonergan suggested three points where completion of the cycle (in a basic expansion and a rise in the aggregate standard of living at a "higher plateau") could break down. They are: (1) what Thorstein Veblen called a culture of conspicuous consumption that encourages excessive spending in the consumer market during a surplus expansion; (2) a politics of envy that censures and would diminish the nonegalitarian results of a surplus expansion; (3) a narrow but widely accepted psychology of motivation that assumes "rationality" in the marketplace is equivalent to the pursuit of perceived self-interest and so has no room for a principle of benevolence outside of close associations.

Avoiding these pitfalls presents a number of challenges to the education of liberty. Since the appeal is for voluntary and intelligent cooperation in effecting the transitions among stages in the cycle, one challenge (as already noted) includes widespread literacy in market dynamics. Are the educational tasks impossible? Consider how modern societies experience flows of traffic on their highways. First of all, most drivers know the difference between competent and incompetent performance behind the wheel. Because some are incompetent and others drive irresponsibly, regulations and the threat of penalties remain parts of social order. Still, most drivers go about their business without top-down supervision and without being motivated solely by threats. Presumably they understand what kinds of driving are required to maintain the good of order that is a traffic flow. They use their liberty to play their part in maintaining it while still driving defensively because they understand not everyone will cooperate in sustaining this common good. Social morons do show up. The analogy suggests that realists might find a similar middle way between the options of an anarchic liberty in the marketplace and a regimentation of its participants.

To understand is one thing, to do is another; so we can ask: How probable is it that large numbers of economically literate persons will voluntarily adapt their economic decisions to the rhythms of a market economy? In particular, what forms will resistance to a basic expansion take?

First, current practices will have their defenders who see themselves as realists. For them: (1) market economies depend on ever-escalating rates of consumption to absorb ever-expanding rates of production, and so conspicuous consumption is a necessary evil; (2) politics is always competition among interest groups, and so the politics of envy is simply one more ploy in the game of power politics; (3) the profit motive is what drives innovation and economic expansion, and so, while moral rhetoric is what a public may expect from leaders, it is not to be taken seriously as describing what actually occurs in marketplaces. These economic, political and psychological "realisms" are not refutable by formal arguments. The slow climb to an alternative realism and to new economic practices requires that various displacements become a topic of serious conversation.

What might those displacements be? Schumpeter expected economic accelerations to give way to contractions, but he envisioned results that would leave the aggregate standard of living at a plateau above the starting point of the expansion.[248] In contrast, a severe recession or depression amounts to a retreat below such a starting point. For Lonergan such an outcome is a failure of creative intelligence. The challenge is to find ways to bring about the basic expansion and thereby to exploit the benefits made possible by the prior surplus expansion, but to do so without high inflation, significant unemployment, and a loss of confidence among investors and consumers.[249] How did he think it was possible to meet this complex challenge?

In summary form, Lonergan took a normative position[250] based on his understanding of the rhythms of the productive process. The purpose of a substantial surplus expansion is to produce a major basic expansion. While the former initially generates nonegalitarian results (e.g. unusually high financial rewards flowing to investors and entrepreneurs "behind" the economic take-off), eventually there should be a more egalitarian distribution of opportunities and benefits through a major basic expansion.[251] How did he think this was possible? He first distinguished between normal and surplus profits. "Normal" profits are income needed to maintain one's enterprise and to provide a reasonable standard of living for one's family. "Surplus" profits are income beyond what is required to maintain the enterprise and a reasonable standard of living.[252]

---

248   "The Analysis of Economic Change" in *Essays of J. A. Schumpeter* (Port Washington, N.Y.: Kennikat Press, 1969), 134-142.
249   *Macroeconomic Dynamics*, 80.
250   For this usage of "normative," see Fred Lawrence. "Editors' Introduction" to ibid. lv-lvi.
251   Ibid. 139.
252   But who decides what is "reasonable"? To understand reason in terms of the demand of the critical operator for answering is-questions is a step toward answering this question. Then there are further questions about displacements, their multiple forms and implications.

The shift to a basic expansion faces its first challenge in how people respond to a surplus expansion. Ideally those initially benefiting from it do not spend their surplus profits on the consumer level because they understand that doing so leads to high inflation and a draining of investment monies needed to sustain the surplus expansion. Similarly, those who are not initially benefiting from the expansion and who witness the nonegalitarian distribution of its rewards will ideally accept those early results and some inflationary pressures as preludes to a more egalitarian basic expansion. Those are the ideal responses; they presuppose that large numbers of persons understand the rhythms of the economy and consent to play their roles in eventually providing a higher aggregate standard of living.

Similar understanding and consent will ideally be present as a surplus expansion slows. In Lonergan's terms, people need to treat surplus profits as a "social dividend." What does this mean? The precept for promoting a surplus expansion is "thrift and enterprise," i.e. accumulate savings and invest them in credible innovations. For a basic expansion the precept is "benevolence and enterprise," i.e. use the same ingenuity and enterprise that produced the surplus expansion to devise innovative ways of allowing more consumers to participate in its benefits. Possible means are private and public investment in retraining those left behind by technological innovations, so that they may enter higher-paying jobs; investing in community projects such as new parks or the restoration of historical landmarks; shortening the average work week, thereby increasing the number of wage-earners; launching low-tech industries to employ the unskilled. A practical objective of such innovations is to broaden the consumer base so as to absorb the increased production of the surplus expansion.[253] This practical purpose is compatible with the moral purposes of the precept of benevolence and enterprise, namely, human flourishing and solidarity.

How are the three obstacles to a basic expansion linked to the education of liberty?[254] If most people assume ever-escalating incomes and the conspicuous consumption they make possible are the criteria

---

253   An obvious but neglected insight here is that consumer societies do not suffer from lack of production capacity but from "ineffective demand" by consumers.

254   "Now to change one's standard of living in any notable fashion is to live in a different fashion. It presupposes a grasp of new ideas. If the ideas are to be above the level of currently successful advertising, serious education must be undertaken. Finally, coming to grasp what serious education really is and, nonetheless, coming to accept the challenge constitutes [sic] the greatest challenge to the modern economy. We have had the great surplus expansion of the industrial and scientific revolutions. But we have yet to master the basic expansion." *Macroeconomic Dynamics*, 119.

of personal success, then they will resist efforts to complete the cycle with a basic expansion. Such assumptions lead to excessive spending in consumer markets during a surplus expansion and so exacerbating inflationary trends that threaten those on fixed incomes. But these public displays of wealth and inflationary threats will provoke the politics of envy. Subsequent calls for taxes on windfall profits or for renegotiating labor contracts to increase wages could unintentionally erode further financing of the surplus expansion. Finally, proposing that surplus income be treated as a social dividend will seem at odds with a prevailing sense of economic realism.[255] What this realism dictates is preservation of the high incomes, profit margins and savings enjoyed during a surplus expansion. When the surplus expansion slows and the earlier high incomes decline, if cutting the wage bill fails, then realists will think the smart thing to do is to invest in safe securities (e.g. government bonds) that guarantee fixed returns.[256] In the meantime the government probably will embark on deficit-spending programs as a way of stimulating economic activity and, in doing so, will be draining the economy of monies needed for the next surplus expansion.

The fantasy of the education of liberty is that there is another alternative consistent with the rhythms of a market economy: large numbers of persons are able to learn about these rhythms, are able to make informed decisions about how to act and will adopt a moral stance of solidarity, i.e. not each individual pursuing a narrow self-interest but intelligent subjects freely choosing to maintain and to develop their social order and its flows of goods.[257]

Realizing this fantasy will not be easy or occur soon.[258] First, there is the challenge of having large, economically literate populations. Then a prosperous segment of that population must know not to spend excessively on the consumer level during a surplus expansion but, instead, to invest

---

255   A political rationale will also be ready-to-hand in terms of the inviolability of legitimately acquired private property. What many people adopting this rationale fear are confiscatory taxes; what the education of liberty envisions is the fantasy of persons intelligently and voluntarily "spending down" their surplus income in innovative and benevolent ways.

256   A "smart" alternative may be to find new financial instruments promising high returns equal to what investors enjoyed during the surplus expansion. One can read the disastrous fantasies of "derivatives" and bundled home mortgages as reflecting such fantasies.

257   Again, the preceding chapter's affirmation of institutions and social orders as intentional realities is worth recalling. Are we being realists if we deny they exist and affirm that only particular individuals exist? Are we being realists if we think of economic institutions not as intentional realities but as impersonal processes independent of intentional acts?

258   Lonergan supposedly quipped: "This [economic theory] will take a hundred years to catch on." The writers of this book series could make a similar prediction regarding how soon FS4 will become part of conventional scholarly practice. Fantasizing about better economic and scholarly practices should not require any apology assuming, of course, there is room for improvement.

and so fund further expansion.[259] Of course, economic literacy is only half the battle. There is also a need for affect-laden counterweights to a social psychology of conspicuous consumption and its encouragement of extravagant purchases on the consumer level. Especially liable to this pathology will be those benefiting the most during a surplus expansion and eager to retain their profit margins and high incomes. But the issue is not simply one of educating and persuading those initially benefiting from a surplus expansion. There are also psychological obstacles to confront in populations not directly participating in a surplus expansion. As already noted, during a surplus expansion the nonegalitarian financial returns to investors and entrepreneurs may elicit the "politics of envy" in some and result in calls for imposing taxes on windfall profits or for renegotiating labor contracts. This is especially likely since those living on relatively stable incomes will feel threatened by the inevitable inflationary pressures of a surplus expansion.

Both of these psychological patterns can interfere with the two types of expansions. If wages keep pace with inflation during a surplus expansion when no new goods or services are yet entering consumer markets, then inflationary pressures will grow worse. Taxes on what are alleged to be windfall profits may drain monies otherwise going to further investments supporting a surplus expansion. Persons enthralled with conspicuous consumption will resist calls both to distinguish between normal and surplus profits and to treat the latter as a social dividend. They may defend their resistance by appealing to a narrow but widely held view of rational agency in marketplaces. They may believe that the pursuit of personal profit supplies both the motive and the criterion for how one ought to behave in economic activities. As "realists" they may assert that, while norms beyond the pursuit of self-interest may be praiseworthy, they have no standing in a realistic account of economic behavior. In addition, the realists can cite how stock markets react to declining corporate profits, how boards of directors may become unhappy with managers who do not maximize profits, how foolish executives may look to those directors if they voice moral concerns that seem at odds with attaining impressive quarterly reports. The fears are real, but psychological, moral and intellectual displacements are possible. Absent them, the pattern continues of failing to complete the pure cycle with a basic expansion raising the aggregate standard of living to a new plateau.

---

259   Precedents for meeting this part of the challenge can be found in the widespread investment in war bonds by private citizens during World War II. Cf. Lonergan. "Savings Certificates and Catholic Action" in *Shorter Papers. CW* 20 (Toronto: University of Toronto Press, 2007), 68-73.

The consequences of such a failure are predictable. The first stage will yield a new population of multimillionaires living lavishly and publicly alongside a larger population experiencing no such improvement in their standard of living; and, for those whose jobs were exported or rendered obsolete, the visible prosperity of the newly enriched will seem to have been achieved at their expense. Desperate people will seek out villains when the real source of the difficulties has been a failure to understand how an economy works.[260] Political instability may soon follow upon economic difficulties, but at a minimum the surplus expansion will have ended without Schumpeter's lift to a new plateau. Is this all any realist should expect, not tomorrow but in a hundred years?

IV. Genetic Sequences of Views

A. Summary of the Views

The first view of economic realism represents a historical compromise. Its language of self-interest and its psychology of motivation reflect an inversion of the common sense that had prevailed in the West for at least two thousand years. Traditional views of rationality and of a psychology of orientation had presupposed normative ends for rational living. While many did not pursue virtuous lives, major thinkers still distinguished between well-ordered lives and disordered ones. Given this distinction, they knew that natural liberty was not enough to ensure the lives of individuals or societies would be well ordered.

However, once the earlier understanding of normative ends was no longer widespread, a new emphasis on procedural goods and a new understanding of rationality as pragmatic intelligence began to emerge.

---

260   "The fact…is that no difficulty is experienced in financing the surplus expansion. It is the first step towards increasing the standard of living of the whole society, and there seems to be little evidence that entrepreneurs, financiers, engineers, workers commonly are hesitant about taking that step. The difficulty emerges in the second step, the basic expansion. In equity it should be directed to raising the standard of living of the whole society. It does not. And the reason why it does not is not the reason on which simple-minded moralists insist. They blame greed. But the prime cause is ignorance. The dynamics of surplus and basic production, surplus and basic expansions, surplus and basic incomes are not understood, not formulated, not taught. When people do not understand what is happening and why, they cannot be expected to act intelligently. When intelligence is a blank, the first law of nature takes over: self-preservation. It is not primarily greed but frantic efforts at self-preservation that turn the recession into a depression, and the depression into a crash." *Macroeconomic Dynamics*, 82.

The language of self-interest masked the absence of agreement on ends appropriate for rational beings, and their rationality seemed best identified with choosing means to whatever ends they preferred. The plausibility of this new common sense was strongest for populations increasingly repulsed by religious quarrels and confined in their thinking to a practical pattern of living.

The second version of economic realism carries the label "the education of liberty." Parts of this version were present in the eighteenth-century narrative competing with a new common-sense view of self-interested individuals pursuing their diverse ends in the marketplace. As a remnant of the much older common sense in the West, this narrative spoke of character formation, the ordering of natural liberty and the importance of institutions in achieving both.

In the preceding section only a brief reference to the specifics of character formation appeared. Three basic insights represented a minimal development of moral character. They mark the beginning of a virtuous orientation, one cooperating with others to build personal relations based on love of genuinely good ends.[261]

Further contrasts between these two viewpoints appeared in how each would answer a basic question: why should anyone esteem liberty? The pursuit of self-interest in voluntary economic exchanges has third-party effects, some of which are quite damaging to at-risk populations unable to compete in the marketplace. Those effects have fueled the debates between advocates of laissez-faire policies and proponents of regulatory interventions in open markets. As MacIntyre noted, those debates continue today, and actual policies oscillate between the two options. In practice, contemporary market economies are themselves compromises between the contending parties while on the fringes the purists continue their debates. Most persons, however, are reluctant to place their unqualified faith in either option, unregulated markets or benevolent elites.

The preceding section sketched arguments for and against each option. The historical compromise of the first view of economic realism rests on a pragmatic argument. Allowing individuals maximum discretion in the pursuit of diverse interests, albeit with some "side-constraints," has to date been the best way of increasing and distributing economic benefits while at the same time avoiding the horrors accompanying efforts to mandate good ends that all should pursue. For all its limitations, the

---

261   Augustine's definition of community comes to mind here: "A group of rational persons in agreement on the things they love."

historical compromise promises "to keep the peace." For this pragmatic reason, realists should esteem liberty.

The second version of economic realism has ties to older teleological and theological stances. An orientation to a good life marked by virtues is part of human capacity. In theological terms, persons are called to spiritual growth in both understanding and loving what is ultimately good. Since compulsion cannot make competent adults virtuous or loving, it is good to allow them discretion in how they develop that capacity and in how they choose to grow. Since liberty is a necessary condition for such growth, realists should esteem it. Still, it is not natural liberty as such that wins trust; rather, it is the capacity of persons to develop into morally responsible adults manifesting ordered liberty that deserves esteem.

The cited obstacles to the education of liberty specified several displacements in thinking and acting if ordered liberty is to be common among actors in the marketplace. Describing them may evoke criticism from defenders of the first view of economic realism. However, before such criticism ever occurs, the "education of liberty" must gain a wide audience, and that has yet to occur.

B. Two Sequences

Suppose historian A believes that the historical compromise represented by version one, while not describing morally ideal behavior in the marketplace, does reflect what actually occurs there. This stance need not reflect moral resignation to human failings; it may be more an acknowledgement of the limits of human knowing. Consider the following line of reasoning adapted from an often reprinted article by Milton Friedman.[262]

Stockholders expect corporate officers to pursue strategies that eventually will return profits on their investments. Strategies that spend corporate funds but enhance a firm's reputation for being "community-minded" and a "good citizen" are acceptable if they build brand loyalty among consumers and morale among employees. However, corporate largesse that funds projects dear to a CEO or board of directors without such results amounts to theft from stockholders. Individual corporate officials may be as generous as they wish with their own funds, but in their corporate roles they are responsible for advancing the interests of stockholders. Since the presumption is that the latter invest expecting profits, corporate leaders

---

262   "The Social Responsibility of Business Is to Increase Its Profits." *The New York Times Magazine* (September 13, 1970).

have a first duty to satisfy this known type of interest. Whatever other interests shareholders may pursue, they are likely to be a range of diverse ends, many of which are unknown to corporate officers.

Given these two constraints, the duty to seek profits for shareholders and ignorance of the other diverse interests they might all share, historian A believes the first version of economic realism is superior to the second. Admittedly the latter may seem to enjoy a rhetorical advantage because of the former's language of self-interest and neglect of "higher" moral objectives. Still, the diversity of ends persons actually pursue, the absence of a common understanding of what ends they all should pursue and the miseries attending past efforts to compel universal assent to a single set of ends are all reasons for preferring the historical compromise.

Suppose historian B is aware of all three reasons for favoring the first version. All the same, remnants of an earlier common sense are part of the horizon of historian B. While persons pursue diverse ends, some ordering or ranking of those ends survives in talk of virtues and vices, of well-ordered lives and those marked by drift, of persons of good character and those of base character. How are any of these distinctions still justifiable? If one's understanding of reason or rationality proceeds from one's experiences in raising and answering questions, then reason concretely may mean raising and answering is-questions. There are questions for practical intelligence, e.g. is something likely to be an effective solution to a problem? But there are also further questions about what is good to do. Would anyone in similar circumstances be justified in doing what I am about to do? Will these actions build personal relations and the trust that future cooperation and friendship will require?

Historian B need not be familiar with the third horizon and GEM. It may be enough to have puzzled over the tough decisions whistleblowers with families face, the risks first-responders take in rescuing strangers, the efforts business executives make to avoid laying off employees in hard economic times. Historian B will be familiar with persons turning a blind eye to corrupt practices or rationalizing downsizing as a normal and untroubling business practice. However, the horizon of historian B includes questions about how persons find it within themselves to act courageously and at great personal risk to help others. The concrete cases are admirable, and, without calling them examples of ordered liberty and rationality, historian B may think they reflect what realistically is best in persons.

Such courage and eclipsing of self-interest are not products of external compulsion. Instead, they reflect the orientations of persons-at-liberty toward more than personal satisfaction. While many may not routinely exhibit such orientations, the capacity to do so is why liberty is worthy of esteem. How to turn natural liberty into ordered liberty is the challenge the second version aspires to meet. Insofar as one does not despair of meeting the challenge, i.e. to the degree one believes it is a real possibility, the second version of economic realism will seem more developed than the first.

V. Doing FS4

FS4 stands to the three previous specialties as decision-making stands to operations of attending to data, interpreting the data and judging which interpretive accounts are more developed than others. The two sequences of views of economic realism express the judgments of two hypothetical practitioners of FS3. They admittedly are very thin accounts of what historians in that specialty will someday produce in far greater detail.[263] Still, for the purposes of this chapter and book, the elementary sequences supply materials, no matter how modest, for experimenting with the new comparative interpretation.

So which sequence of views have these writers decided is more developed? The reader will have already anticipated the answer. However, the reasons for it are worth spelling out. As usual, the first question is what major differences set the two sequences apart? A general answer is that they differ in which version of realism they rank as more developed. But what are specific differences between the two versions?

If "self-interest" means nothing or everything, then we need to restrict its use. Its conventional identification with self-regarding motivation is not an arbitrary restriction. Next, if we understand a psychology of motivation as giving priority to self-regarding motives for acting, then a major difference emerges. In contrast to the first version of economic realism, the second version (1) affirms some good ends are worthy of pursuit independently of personal benefit and (2) subscribes to an older psychology of orientation that understands rational decision-making in

---

263   Recall the temporal distinction in talking about FS4. At present GS is in its infancy. In the future an inherited acquis of developmentally ordered interpretations of some issue will be the basis for comparing and evaluating new views relevant to that issue.

terms of such ends.[264] This major difference probably reflects different answers to the question of whether persons can know what genuinely good ends rational persons should seek. To adopt a skeptical stance in relation to any positive answers is to favor the first version of economic realism. To affirm that persons can come to know what ends are proper to rational beings is to favor the second. Of course, the meaning of "rational" is also under debate and so identifies a second major difference.

As already noted, Voegelin traced the devolution of the meaning of *nous* to that of pragmatic intelligence. His strategy of anamnesis was explicitly an effort to avoid having his genealogy treated as a "doxographic relic" in the history of ideas. Even if his attempt fails with some readers, the practice of GEM can acquaint a few of them with a non-controversial and empirical meaning of rationality. We all routinely raise and answer is-questions. With a little self-attention we can note not all of our questions arise within a practical horizon. While some few may want to extend their skepticism about universally good ends to include every answer to an is-question, any defense they offer for either version of economic realism will be an instance of performative contradiction. To argue for either version will be to make truth-claims. Advocates of both versions will presumably evade this intellectual dead end, but proponents of the second version still bear the burden of proving that persons ever develop beyond the demands of human sensibility for personal satisfaction. Examples of courageous risk-taking on behalf of strangers offer some support.[265]

The second version faces an even tougher challenge. The education of liberty envisages large numbers of citizens embodying ordered liberty in their marketplace decisions and so moving past an ethic of self-interest. One precondition is that they become sufficiently informed about how market economies function to be able to make intelligent decisions. Clearly this understanding is not yet widespread. Here then is a third major major difference between the two realisms. Specifically, what stands do they take in regard to historical progress? McShane has phrased the question directly: "Do you view humanity as possibly maturing-in some serious way-or just messing along between good and evil, whatever you think they are?"[266]

---

264   One can read as ironic Aristotle's argument that, since benevolence is a virtue, egoists who want the best for themselves will want to be benevolent.

265   Are ad hoc arguments that translate such examples into instances of self-interest indirectly acknowledging evidence contrary to the first realism?

266   *The Everlasting Joy of Being Human* (Vancouver: Axial Publishing, 2013), 77. In one formulation of this question, McShane added: "Do you view yourself and humanity as possibly maturing...?" This version increases the emphasis on taking a personal stand. How many readers will

So the two versions of economic realism reflect at least three major differences: (1) in how they answer the question of whether we can know what ends rational persons should pursue; (2) in how they understand rationality; and (3) in how they are likely to answer McShane's question about the maturation of humanity.

In applying FS4, the next question is whether any of these differences originate in basic stances regarding the meanings of reality, knowing and objectivity. These authors' positions were explicit in earlier chapters. Rather than repeat them here, let's turn to the question of what stances might be implicit in both versions of economic realism.

To affirm that self-interest is the motive for decisions by rational agents in the marketplace is probably an extension of the view of individuals-at-liberty as the primary realities in economic exchanges. Consumers and sellers are imaginable figures in economic transactions. The preceding chapter on the ontological status of institutions criticized this view. Just as species of plants and animals are inexplicable apart from their ecosystems, so persons are inexplicable apart from the webs of relationships constituting *mitsein*. Further, if the category of self-interest is a linguistic marker for the beliefs that (1) so many diverse individuals have highly diverse ends, and (2) no one can know how to rank those ends normatively, then the best we can achieve is allowing persons-at-liberty to pursue their diverse ends with limited "side constraints."

The fact of diversity among individuals and their interests is not under debate or in doubt. What is in question is whether we can know if some diverse ends are superior to others. The first version appears to adopt a skeptical stance in regard to this question; the second version does not. The education of liberty presupposes that persons in large numbers will one day learn how a market economy functions and will then conform their market decisions to that understanding, thereby exhibiting ordered liberty. The eighteenth-century narrative associated with Adam Smith made similar assumptions about potential development in understanding and moral acting. His emphasis on the role of institutions in forming moral character, in directing the development of natural liberty, not only surpassed talk of the discrete individual, it also affirmed the possibility of knowing normative differences among ends.

Are these assumptions about intellectual and moral development plausible? The third row of the earlier diagram suggests one pattern of

deny the possibility of their own growth? To generalize: do they believe in the possibility of adult growth or, like Proust's aristocrats, do they expect to arrive at old age but much faded versions of their young selves? *Remembrance of Things Past*. Vol. 2 (New York: Random House, 1981), 1042.

development. It begins with persons-at-liberty and then makes the question of their orientations central to their further development as potential critics of whatever institutional orders they are part of. A basic displacement from sensibility to intelligence is part of an initial shift in orientation. Personal relations are in most cases affect-laden inducements to transcend a narrow self-regarding orientation. That is, association with virtuous people can transform earlier patterns of thinking and acting; continued association with them can sustain and develop new patterns. In short, one's models-for-living are instances of "incarnate meaning" and can invite one to grow with them.

What is the envisioned growth? Consistent cooperation with the demands of the intellectual, critical and normative operators for knowing and doing what is good form the determinate orientations or habits of virtuous people. They thereby become "contexts" for making more reliable judgments and moral decisions in the future. Recall the meaning of "contextualized objectivity."[267] The measure of objectivity of judgments, moral and otherwise, is not something "out there" to be sensed and is not public consensus; it is the cumulative effect of repeatedly meeting the inner demands of intentional operators. To have searched elsewhere for that measure and to have failed in the search can lead to skepticism about positive judgments regarding moral ends. The historical compromise represented by the first version reflects such a mistaken and failed search. Lack of cultural consensus on normative ends is evidence of diversity but not of the impossibility of correct judgments about the proper ends for rational living. Again, even if it does offer psychological reassurance when present, public consensus is a faulty measure of objectivity in knowing. Thus, the first major difference probably originates in conflicting views of objectivity.

What of the second major difference, i.e. divergences in the understanding of rationality? The shift from the original meaning of *nous* to reason as practical intelligence occurred slowly. The genealogical sketch in Section II cited a number of reasons for the shift. One thesis was that the language of self-interest served as a placeholder for earlier talk of virtues and of the normative ends of rational living. Dismissal of those traditional terms left a vacuum that had to be filled. To make a tautological observation, purposeful activities must have ends. If many no longer agree on the highest ends, a linguistic formula to mask that deficit may prove useful. One result is to narrow talk of rational decision-making to choosing effective means and then to use the terminology of self-interest

---

267   See Chapter Three of the *Primer*.

to classify whatever diverse ends persons happen to pursue.

But rationality as the capacity to raise and answer is-questions is more fundamental than any historical shift in concepts. Thus, the basic issue is whether persons ever correctly answer such questions. A negative response is incoherent. However, could is-questions about moral ends be an exception? Someone may argue that they really are questions about "subjective" preferences and that, given human diversity, no one should be surprised by the diversity and even incommensurability of answers. Again, diversity is not in doubt, but a key question is whether judgments affirming preferred ends are always arbitrary. We return, then, to the question of whether persons ever answer is-questions correctly but this time in relation to preferred ends. To differentiate between virtues and vices or to acknowledge cases of development in moral understanding and acting is to presuppose that non-arbitrary judgments about means and ends do occur. Further, to make reasonable judgment the criterion of knowing whether ends are good or not is compatible with the position on knowing formulated in UV. In contrast, the first version limits the meaning of rationality to choosing means and adopts a skeptical stance toward knowing moral ends. Thus, the second major difference seemingly originates in opposed views of knowing and its limits.

What of the third difference regarding McShane's question about humanity's maturation? Recent history seems to support a negative response. Dreams of progress on any grand scale had a bad time of it in the last, most disappointing century. The new millennium is not off to a better start. What are the chances of doing better in this millennium? Solving the problem of the transition from a surplus expansion to a basic expansion requires a serious educational effort and widespread cooperation with its findings. FS4 offers no detailed educational agenda or specific policy proposals. That is a task for other functional specialties. It does reject both the illusion that impersonal market forces will eventually solve our problems and the equally illusory stance that a benevolently minded elite will succeed in imposing the required solutions. There are no substitutes for the educated liberty of persons who have experienced personal displacements transforming them and, with the cooperation of likeminded persons, potentially transforming economic practices.

The preceding endorsement of the second version of economic realism (and so of the sequence of historian B) is not a complete rejection of the first version. The historical compromise that the latter represents has served and continues to serve some practical purposes. It, however, reflects a response to cultural problems arising at particular periods in

Western history. To claim that its views are alone realistic assessments of human potential is to call a premature halt to developing that potential. Just as market economies are dynamic realities and ideally move toward "higher plateaus," so too the rational beings that create and sustain those realities can develop further. The language of self-interest and the psychology of motivation seem to deny the latter possibility. The prospects of the education of liberty may take a long time to realize, but economic realism must include the demand of the deliberative operator expressed in questions about better options. To answer those questions with "This is all we can realistically hope for now and in the future" is to call a premature halt to inquiry. It is also to overlook how persons and their economies are parts of a dynamic universe requiring long periods of time and large numbers to realize any significant advances.

VI. In Retrospect

What has this excursus on economic realism contributed to answering the primary question of this book? In keeping with earlier insights into how initial conditions provide the grounds for the emergence and survival of organisms and ecosystems, this chapter has described some of the historical conditions that favored the relatively recent emergence of reason as practical intelligence and of the language of self-interest. The contrasts between two types of economic realism further suggested how from a range of prior conditions different integrations or meanings are possible. For example, some conditions in contemporary economic environments are unfavorable to any widespread acceptance of the second economic realism. To mention three: most consumers understand little about the rhythms of a market economy; conspicuous consumption seems normal to many; picturing discrete buyers and sellers as the basic units of an economy seems commonsensical. However, conditions change. In a small way this inquiry into the meaning of environment may contribute to changing at least the last of the three unfavorable conditions.

Chapter Three made use of an analogy of proportion: individuals are to institutions as organisms are to ecosystems. Answering the question of the ontological status of the latter terms in each pairing left behind picture thinking. The affirmed position was that reasonable judgment was both the measure of and what gave meaning to the term "real."

142

That was the basis for affirming real relations as intrinsic to the intelligibility of individuals and organisms. To affirm such intelligible relations is to move beyond the earliest views of environment as a setting or container for imaginable entities. But an economic realism that assumes discrete individuals are the basic units of the marketplace is probably still wedded to this descriptive view of an environment. That is, the marketplace is the setting for the totality of buyers and sellers engaged in economic exchanges. As well, stances asserting that self-interest alone moves those individual actors in the marketplace probably operate with the same assumption and view. However, in an explanatory context, buyers and sellers vanish along with simplistic notions of what causes ("pushes and pulls") them to move.[268] Talk of discrete, imaginable individuals and organisms gives way to talk of flexible ranges of schemes of recurrence among functionally related roles in institutions and ecosystems.

What, then, is the elusive meaning of environment if we no longer think of it as containing imaginable objects? All sorts of negative responses have appeared so far.[269] A positive response will appear in Chapter Seven. The movement toward that response next passes through surveys of how environmental historians have thought about the object of their inquiries.

---

268   Chapter Five offers an alternative in talking about how multiple variables interact to produce ecological changes.

269   To summarize some of those negative responses: an environment is not an independent entity; it is not a thing; common-sense speaking notwithstanding, it may not be something we can create or harm; it "exceeds" any ecosystem or "entirety" of ecosystems; it is not a whole with parts; it is not adequately understood simply by referring to energy exchanges. Accepting these negative conclusions does not solve the problem of saying something positive about the meaning of environment. Any "saying" must resist the habits of ordinary language and common-sense thinking. Consider how tempting it remains to think of objects in an environment. That simple preposition "in" seems so innocuous, and yet it conflicts with a number of the preceding negative responses.

CHAPTER FIVE:
DEVELOPMENTS IN ENVIRONMENTAL HISTORY

The preceding chapters have provided a background for the following study of environmental history. Insights into ecosystems, institutions and economic exchanges are relevant in understanding the multiple ways historians have thought about environments. In their studies of diverse environments over the past forty years, historians have operated with different assumptions about what exactly they were studying. In identifying some of these assumptions, this chapter will be asking the leading question of FS3, namely, what was going forward in environmental history during these decades? As well, different answers to this question will provide materials for doing FS4. The practical test of this book series again appears: How useful is the new comparative interpretation for understanding and perhaps resolving debates in scholarly fields?

I. Overview

Environmental history emerged in the 1960s and 1970s. It attracted interest primarily because of simultaneously appearing signs of environmental degradation. The theme issue of *History and Theory* in 2003 presented a series of essays reflecting scholarly inquiries in the relatively new field.[270] The lead article by J.R. McNeill offered an overview of developments in the field over the previous twenty-five years.[271] As a member of an early generation of practitioners of environmental history, he tracked various developments in understanding environments and ended his article by identifying yet-to-be-explored areas within the field. Ten years later Paul S. Sutter conducted a similar review of more recent developments in the field, what old problems

---

270   *History and Theory*, "Theme Issue 42: Environment and History," 4 (2003).
271   Ibid. "Observations on the Nature and Culture of Environmental History," 5-43.

practitioners had resolved and what new puzzles they were facing.[272] Within this relatively brief ten-year period there were noticeable changes in how historians conceived of the relations between society and nature; in particular, the meaning of "environment" had become more complex. The second chapter on art and ecology has already offered an initial tracking of shifts in the meaning of environment from the 1960s to the early 1980s. This chapter will focus on the field of environmental history and track other shifts during the next three decades. Competing views of relations between environments and humankind will provide the intellectual controversies to which we will apply FS3 and FS4. We begin with McNeill's essay from 2003.

II. Competing Views of Environments

McNeill defines environmental history as the "history of the mutual relations between humankind and the rest of nature." He accounts for the rapid growth of the field in terms of worries that the former has "acquired the power and the numbers to become a rogue mammal, exerting ever increasing influence upon earthly ecosystems."[273] In recording how others have diagnosed human effects on the environment, he notes that one of the most contentious issues in the field arose in the 1990s because of claims that "the Judeo-Christian West developed a rapacious culture that contrasts poorly with [other cultures]."[274] McNeill is not persuaded of this because environmental harms have occurred far beyond the reach of a single culture and have more likely been due to technologies, population numbers, control over labor forces and uses of animals. He then adds a crucial insight into what harms people of a particular culture actually had on their environments: "the liability and resilience of their ecosystems had a great deal to do with what impacts their actions had, and how durable they were."[275] Presumably human actions are

---

272   "The World with Us: The State of American Environmental History" in *Journal of American History*, Vol.100, 1(June 2013), 94-119.

273   McNeill, 6.

274   "It is invidiously compared, typically, with East Asian traditions informed by Buddhism and Taoism, but also with the culture of indigenous peoples, in the Americas, Oceania, or Africa." McNeill also cites a more localized diagnosis blaming an "'American culture of capitalism'" for producing significant harm. (Ibid. 7.) He later notes that in the 1970s and 1980s Latin American historians, "usually adopting the general framework of *raubwirtschaft*," assumed colonialism and capitalism jointly produced a plundering of the environment. (24)

275   He further separates himself from an opposing view that weights culture as a primary source of environmental degradation. "[My] position, I hasten to add, is not shared by quite a number of environmental historians, who prefer a more Hegelian position: behavior is

not the sole determinants of environmental decline, a fairly obvious point to survivors of natural disasters, but one worth stating as will be clear below when more recent debates over "hybridity" appear.

Among the signs that environmental history was maturing at the close of the last century, McNeill cites its increasing acceptance as a subdiscipline within the profession and its fluid relations with other specialties such as climate history, disease history, agrarian history, urban history and so on. However, in recounting the prehistory of the environmental subdiscipline, he traces a series of slowly emerging insights that suggest a more basic rationale for claims to maturation. First, ancient historians clearly recognized that geography shaped a local population's character, but slower to gain acceptance was the idea of mutual dependency, i.e. environments changed peoples who in turn changed environments, and those altered environments subsequently changed those peoples. Nineteenth-century German historians largely focused on the written text, not on dirt, forest and water, and so they concentrated largely on political and intellectual history. Early twentieth-century French historians, e.g. Lucien Febvre and Marc Bloch, broadened the field of inquiry to include animals, forests and diseases. But McNeill's judgment is that they, and perhaps the most famous member of their *Annales* movement, Fernand Braudel, were predecessors of rather than explicit practitioners of the environmental studies they later inspired.[276]

In the U.S., historians of the western frontier (Frederick Jackson Turner) and the Great Plains (Walter Prescott Webb and James Malin) were sources of inspiration for future generations intent on understanding the interactions between societies and environments. As already remarked, the primary motivator for focusing on such interactions was rising public concerns in the 1960s and 1970s about environmental degradation.[277]

> Together with almost everyone else, historians came to see new sets of problems. Many felt a desire to help find solutions, and saw a chance for moral engagement, a chance to serve humankind by providing a usable past. Historians could hope to help by uncovering the origins and history of a given problem, for example. Or they might point the way to a better future by revealing

---

fundamentally conditioned by ideas and culture." Ibid. 7-8. Here we see a difference in emphasis on mutual dependencies among environments, ideas, technologies, population numbers and animals. Noting such differences among historians is one of the tasks in doing FS4.
276   Ibid. 13-14.
277   In China the motivation was later in arriving. By the late 1990s there was inescapable evidence of "conspicuous ongoing environmental deterioration in China and…increased contact with American, European, and Australian historians." Ibid. 28.

the existence of societies in the past that had managed their relations with the environment more successfully, perhaps even sustainably.[278]

Responses to this call for "moral engagement" included some missteps and overgeneralizations, e.g. blaming the problems on a single culture, on patriarchal social orders, on soulless capitalism or imagining indigenous populations living in harmony with nature in some pristine wilderness.[279] Even if the causal analyses were simplistic, insights into mutual dependency were becoming explicit, if only in an alarming way. Environments had shaped humans who in turn were changing those environments and in doing so were risking their own extinction. The professional and non-specialist readers of Rachel Carson could not neglect the alarm bell she sounded.

McNeill cites as another misstep the exaggerated emphasis in the 1990s on the social construction of reality, both social and natural. While noting that most of his colleagues were more favorable, he found "the emphasis upon social construction unenlightening compared to the old cultural/intellectual environmental history of the 1970s." His explicit stance reveals something about his implicit views of reality and knowing and so is worth quoting here and returning to in Section IV.

> I think the cultural construction of nature just isn't all that important compared to what has happened and is happening to real nature, and how nature has affected and still affects us (there is some reality out there independent of our perception!).[280]

In concluding his survey of ever broadening inquiries by U.S. environmental historians, McNeill complains of how slowly his peers were responding to earlier calls to internationalize those inquiries. That is, most studies

---

278   Ibid. 15.
279   McNeill comments on such imagined harmony: "Native Americans, despite the limitations of their technologies and their numbers, engaged in large-scale environmental manipulation, mainly through fire. So did Australian aborigines. Polynesians brought about animal extinctions on the islands they settled. [...] Ecological angels, the environmentalists' equivalent of the Noble Savage, proved hard to find if tempting to imagine. These were disappointing results for those intent on finding in the past the antidote for the present." Ibid. 16. Later in his essay McNeill reviewed environmental historians in India and found they had their own angels in a precolonial age of "ecological harmony." He predicted: "it is likely that, as in the Americas and Africa, further research will do much to undermine the blissful image of the precolonial past." (21-22.) He is also critical of ecofeminism and its claim that "women are especially close to nature and endowed with a special capacity to appreciate and live harmoniously with it...." (38) Implied in this criticism is a rejection of patriarchy as the source of environmental degradation.
280   Ibid. 17.

stopped at the U.S. borders as if pollution, animals, diseases and ecosystems respected such political boundaries.[281] He does identify why such "macro-level" studies were few. "Given the interconnectedness of all parts of the planet in matters ecological, it makes excellent sense to study environmental history on the global scale. But any form of history on that scale is a daunting prospect, and runs counter to the conditioned reflexes (acquired in graduate school) of most historians."[282] However, by the next decade several historians (Radkau and Hoyles in history and Chew, de Vries and Goudsblom in sociology) were beginning to do environmental history on a global scale.[283]

Less inchoate and more successful were regional studies that crossed borders in doing environmental history. McNeill cites such studies in China and Southeast Asia. The key development was that environmental historians expanded their inquiries beyond the borders of nation states and so beyond what McNeill called, "the wrong scale on which to operate [in doing environmental history]."[284] This seems to be an advance since, again, pollution, diseases, animals and ecosystems, with perhaps the exception of island countries, rarely stay within political borders.

A repeated criticism of early environmental histories was that they were "relentlessly depressing accounts of environmental destruction: just one damn decline after another." McNeill thought the complaint "misplaced" since, just as military histories could be well written and exciting, so environmental histories could produce compelling narratives. This is especially likely if their focus is on environmental success stories, for example, on access to "clean drinking water and sanitation for several hundred million people since 1880...."[285] All the same, McNeill worries that the "moral engagement" of earlier practitioners motivated by environmental destruction has waned. He is unsure why this has occurred but surmises that it might be a sign that "as environmental history has grown more scientifically sophisticated it has grown more neutral in tone."[286]

This surmise is relevant to another criticism of environmental history. Readers have often complained that concrete persons disappear or are reduced to abstractions in studies in which "climate, or viruses, or technology hog the spotlight." There have been exceptions, but McNeill responds to the complaint by identifying the real issue as one of "scale." On a small scale, such as the history of an urban area, specific human

281   Ibid. 17-18.
282   Ibid. 31.
283   Ibid. 31-32.
284   Ibid. 35.
285   Ibid.
286   Ibid. 34.

actors may well take center stage. However, "macro-scale environmental history tends to emphasize the processes and forces, both cultural and natural, rather than the doings and fates of individuals."[287] The earlier surmise was that as environmental history has grown more scientific it has had fewer explicit moral and political agendas. Might this also extend to macro-scale inquiries? That is, to the degree that such inquiries pursue explanatory understanding, they will abstract from particular persons and events and concentrate on patterns of relations among classes of persons and events.

As noted multiple times in this book series, the transition from descriptive to explanatory understanding, from the first horizon to the second, marks a development within a scholarly field of inquiry. But McNeill observes: "Historians in general are thin on theory...[and very] few environmental historians have explicitly tried to build theories."[288] He notes that Immanuel Wallerstein's world-systems theory has been influential in the social sciences and has its followers among environmental historians. However, his judgment is that it is a model "derived exclusively from non-environmental history," from, for example, economic rhythms "that are hard to square with the rhythms and patterns of nature." He concludes, "environmental history has too much chaos in it to accommodate comfortably the prescribed rhythms of world-systems theory."[289]

Still, exchanges between historians and scientists have been central to the growth McNeill tracks. Perhaps "it is in biology and what is now called earth system science that environmental history" is most at home. For example, genetic testing now allows for tracking ancient population movements and the intermingling of migratory and established populations. The same type of testing can reveal the history of diseases and their presence or absence in populations.[290] Climatology has aided the expansion of environmental history. The influence of weather patterns

---

287   Ibid. 36.
288   Ibid. 36-37.
289   Ibid. 38. In the same place McNeill adds: "Ecology involves complex overlapping systems that evolve, and affect human affairs, on their own schedules." In his summary of John Soluri's *Banana Cultures: Agriculture, Consumption, and Environmental Change in Honduras and the United States* (Austin: University of Texas Press, 2005), Sutter mentions the "agroecological instabilities" detailed by Soluri that lead him to suggest: "Once environmental historians appreciate these instabilities...they see the geopolitical, economic, labor, and consumer histories of the banana as necessarily more contingent than can be contained by grand theoretical frameworks." (Sutter, 109.) Materials in previous chapters on flexible ranges of series of schemes of recurrence and on a "pure economic cycle" as distinct from actual economic rhythms might be useful in diagnosing the seriousness of these objections to a theoretical framing of environmental narratives. Such a diagnostic project is beyond the limits of this chapter.
290   Ibid. 39.

(e.g. El Niño) on political events (e.g. the French Revolution), of ozone depletion, climate change and coal production on agriculture have all been of interest to historians. Refined techniques in archeology have permitted historians to understand past events where "textual evidence is nil or slim…."[291] Similarly useful in the absence of textual evidence has been the

> study of strontium/calcium ratios in human teeth, a method developed since the early 1980s, [that] allows reconstruction of diets among past populations…[and can] indicate the ages at which children were weaned, allowing inferences about birth spacing and fertility rates. In favorable circumstances it can even indicate migration patterns among a given population….[292]

Relevant to future developments in environmental history is McNeill's list of "unexplored frontiers": soils history (e.g. the effects of farming on soil fertility), mining (e.g. its effects on local ecosystems), human migrations (e.g. the transfer of agricultural practices from one continent to another), seas and oceans (e.g. the effects of fishing and pollution on aquatic ecosystems).[293] Future developments involving exchanges between the natural sciences and environmental history will ensure that the latter continues to be an important specialty within the discipline of history.[294]

Ten years after McNeill's survey of the international scene, Paul S. Sutter narrowed the focus and assessed the current state of environmental history in the United States. His reading of the output of the national profession is that it "has grown like kudzu on a hot July day." Consistent with what worried McNeill, he observed that many within the second generation of environmental historians were less explicitly concerned with the first generation's moral agenda, i.e. drawing from the study of the past "lessons" useful in avoiding or undoing environmental decline. Instead, the second generation seemed to be suspicious of hidden "personal assumptions and values" in previous environmental studies and more eager to adopt a critical (read: value-neutral) approach in their inquiries.[295]

---

291   Ibid. 40.
292   Ibid. 41.
293   Ibid. 42. This expansion of interacting variables relevant to understanding changes in ecological systems leaves behind simplistic notions of causality and of imaginable agents effecting those changes.
294   McNeill concludes his survey of twenty-five years by observing that environmental history has expanded "to the point where no mortal can keep pace with it." (Ibid.) This book series, of course recommends FS as a way of responding to such growth in any field.
295   Sutter, 95.

This critical approach appeared in their reflections on "nature" as a basic category in environmental history. Was it at all clear what historians meant by nature or environment?[296] At first they operated with the traditionally bifurcated pairings of nature and culture, natural environments and social environments. These separations permitted the overgeneralizations about pristine wildernesses and a rogue type of mammal that despoiled them. According to Sutter, a third generation of environmental historians is now embracing a view of "all environments as interweaving the natural and cultural in complex ways." He phrases this new viewpoint succinctly: "all environments are hybrid." While a first generation of specialists had perceived human domination of nature (e.g. damming a river) as destroying a natural system and a second generation saw such manipulation of nature as creating a "second nature" or artificial system controlling energy flows, the new generation was moving beyond what its predecessors had assumed; namely, there was a pre-existing ahistorical nature that human actions later modified.[297]

Hybridity replaces this assumption, but it cuts both ways. That is, in rejecting the strict separation of nature and society, it implies both that natural environments already bear a human imprint and that societies "cannot be easily isolated from environmental forces and circumstances." Natural systems as hybrids and cultures as hybrids reflect historical alterations originating in the interactions between both.[298] The new generalization understands "environments as necessarily historical, produced by forces of change, human or not, over time."[299] In other words, the earth as we know it is not in some fallen state, as if Eden had once existed; instead, both nature and society are correlates in a dynamic pattern of relations in which human activity is one of many variables.

Sutter acknowledges this shift in understanding as an advance in the field, but he suggests that hybridity is transitional. While the category helps evade a "good versus evil" reading of environmental and human interactions, it remains too undifferentiated. Much like Dilthey's category *Leben*, too many complex differences are left unsorted for the term to offer any analytical clarity. Sutter raises further practical questions. "What

---

296   Raymond Williams' thesis that there is nothing natural about nature (cf. Nisbet, 4) underscores the generality that every concept has a history. A central question of these chapters is whether there have been advances in understanding nature, environment and ecosystems.
297   Sutter, 96.
298   "Evolutionary history shows not only how humans have steered the evolution of other species through breeding, hybridization, and direct genetic manipulation but also how human actions have produced unintended evolutionary consequences, such as pesticide resistance, and meaningful coevolution of humans and other species." Ibid. 109.
299   Ibid.

counts as damage in hybrid environments? Are some hybridities better than others? If so, what makes them better? [...] How do we make sense of environmental causation in a hybrid world?"[300] One might add: How do we make sense of human causation in a hybrid world? Both forms of the question presuppose some notion of "agency," and Sutter takes up this puzzle.

It is one thing to talk of environmental or human "causation;" it is another to understand relations of dependency. As the *Primer* worked through the early stages in Hegel's dialectic of consciousness, a first meaning of agency or cause appeared in the imaginable "push and pull" of the child's experiences with toys in motion. A more adequate notion of causation involved thinking about relations of intelligible dependency, i.e. one event would be inexplicable without understanding its relation to another. Sutter recounts how historians have puzzled over related issues and have "grown rightly uneasy" in speaking of nature as having "agency." He approves of this hesitancy, and in explaining why he detects a further problematical term, namely, "nature."[301] It too is an undifferentiated category, and "environmental historians have profited by breaking down nature into more supple causal taxonomies and models of hybrid causation." In effect, they have begun to differentiate classes of interacting variables: "animals, energy, climate, evolution, or human-environmental interfaces [e.g. technologies and industries] without necessarily invoking an overarching nature that acts in history." These distinctions may seem part of the "fragmentation" of the field of environmental history into further subspecialties, but it may also be a sign of maturation, i.e. the discipline that McNeill thought short on theory is beginning to puzzle out the basic categories it employs and the ways it "frames" its inquiries.[302]

Inquiry into the meaning of "agency" may be one such sign. Applied to both human and natural interactions, the term is too undifferentiated and more likely to obscure than to clarify matters. As Sutter remarks, "coal seams or fertile soils in particular places [have] certainly mattered to human history, but to talk of coal or soils as having agency

---

300   Ibid. 97.
301   Sutter comments on Mart A. Stewart's study of rice cultivation along the Georgia coast in "If John Muir Had Been an Agrarian: Environmental History West and South," in *Environment and History*, 11(May 2005). "Environmental actors and forces take many forms in Stewart's study, from the power of the tides that planters and slaves harnessed to the forces of disorder such as hurricanes, freshets, weeds, and bobolinks that threatened to undo rice culture. There is no 'unitary' nature in Stewart's analysis, but many discrete human and nonhuman actors arrayed in and around a tenuous system of production defined by energy flows." Ibid. 107.
302   Ibid. In the same place Sutter remarks in passing on the discipline's use of "the encompassing and surprisingly undertheorized term 'environment.'"

seems a stretch."[303] Natural disasters, microbes and insects have shaped the course of human lives, but to speak of them as agents departs from ordinary language usage. Sutter calls for moving beyond this undifferentiated term for a further reason. Traditionally environmental historians employed "agency" only in regard to human actors as part of their separation from nature and its nonhuman forces. However, the turn to hybridity seems to require a new language, one that is not yet available, or at least not in common use.[304] To invent this new vocabulary is no simple task. Words express insights; significant shifts in terms usually presuppose significant new insights. For example, it may seem easy to disassociate "agency" from natural processes, e.g. earthquakes seem mindless events and not actors. It is much harder to delete its use in regard to imaginable human actors. Any attempt to do so runs counter to a common-sense view of human subjects as the makers of history, the *dramatis personae* within narratives about nature and human affairs.[305] Sutter sees environmental history as in need of new ways of talking about "historical causation that not only disaggregate the grand category of nature but that also break down distinctions between human action and the larger material world in which humans operate."[306] However, this challenge still remains unmet.[307]

A second major challenge for environmental historians is not simply to describe how historical acts and events have affected environments but to identify negative consequences, i.e. to make normative judgments about such changes. From the beginning what motivated many historians to enter this subdiscipline was concern for environmental decline. Yet, as McNeill observed in 2003, the moral advocacy of the first generation waned in the second. Sutter notes the same shift and offers a diagnosis. First, later practitioners found that the environmental sciences did not operate with a normative view of natural processes, one that might have provided historians with a basis for their judgments about decline.[308] Second, those

---

303   Ibid. 98.
304   The next chapter will identify a similar problem with terminology in the neurosciences.
305   Chapter Three formulated correlations between organisms and ecosystems and between individuals and institutions such that to operate with insight into such relations is to deny primacy to either term as the sole agent or "mover." Sutter's comments on evolutionary history are compatible with this conclusion. He quotes Edmund Russell on replacement of a "'master-breeder narrative' – that breeding has been an imposition of human will on inert biological material – with a "'bidirectional view' that emphasizes how culture and biology influence each other through evolutionary processes." Put succinctly, Russell suggests "'the possibility that organisms domesticated humans as well as vice versa.'" Sutter, 109.
306   Ibid. 98.
307   The language of schemes of recurrence, useful in explaining patterns of relations among organisms and ecosystems and between individuals and institutions, may help in meeting this challenge. Section IV will explore this possibility.
308   Reluctance to advance a normative view in the sciences has a complex history. The

later practitioners criticized the moral narratives of their predecessors for championing preservation policies that "masked social and cultural agendas that often structured or reinforced social inequalities."[309] As a result, a second generation became more reluctant to engage in advocacy and, instead, investigated how the earlier narratives were "constructs" based on implicit (and so suspect) moral and aesthetic commitments.[310]

Sutter agrees with McNeill that the shift from moral advocacy was a sign of a maturing field; however, he does not voice the latter's criticism of the constructivist views so prevalent in the second generation of environmental historians. He does, all the same, detect some resurgence of the earlier interest in moral engagement. This time the hybrid view of nature includes human and nonhuman exchanges that modify both, and, while no longer assuming the eventual mastery of nature by the human species, historians can identify what changes negatively affect this one species, and, using its well being as a criterion, can make defensible moral judgments about those changes.[311]

Such judgments seem to be unavoidable and defensible in historical studies of disease and health. Sutter mentions a number of environmental works comprising a "new literature" on how, for example, "settlers assessed new lands not only in terms of their fertility and resource richness, but also in relation to how settler bodies responded to their air, water, soil, and vegetation."[312] Another example of that literature is Gregg Mitman's history of allergies and asthma.[313] With the nineteenth-century

---

theological underpinnings of a natural law tradition had allowed the Stoics and medievals a basis for believing that nature taught moral lessons, but it has been some time since scientists operated with such metaphysical and theological commitments. The fact-value distinction of the late nineteenth-century remains widely in use. Hume's "naturalistic fallacy" continues to present an obstacle to anyone wanting to argue from descriptive conclusions to normative claims.

309   Sutter, 99. As examples, Sutter cites "how the creation of national parks dispossessed native peoples; how national forests enclosed commons resources and displaced farming communities; how state and federal policies to protect fisheries and wildlife privileged recreational hunters and fishers and functioned to control immigrants, African Americans, Native Americans, and others with marginal access to state power...." (101)

310   While Sutter does not mention Hayden White's influential work, *Metahistory: The Historical Imagination in Nineteenth-Century Europe* (Baltimore: The Johns Hopkins University Press, 1973), it is plausible that White's uncovering of such variable commitments preoccupied historians for a number of years.

311   Such moral judgments appear in Marsha Weisiger's *Dreaming of Sheep in Navajo Country* (Seattle: University of Washington Press, 2009). Sutter reviews her very balanced assessment of state-management policy of the 1930s regarding grazing on Navajo lands. (Sutter, 102-103). He admires Brian Donahue's *The Great Meadow: Farmers and Land in Colonial Concord* (New Haven: Yale University Press, 2004) as "a story of sustainable human-environmental interaction and adaptation that has important prescriptive implications." (106.)

312   Sutter, 110.

313   *Breathing Space: How Allergies Shape Our Lives and Landscapes* (New Haven: Yale University Press, 2007).

expansion of cities and agricultural production into new regions, allergies appeared and yielded "a growing tribe of hay-fever sufferers who
perceived themselves to be distinctly sensitive to the world around them
and who, using their bodies as barometers, searched for environments in
which their symptoms subsided." Health resorts and conservation movements responded to such concerns, and the idea took root that moving to
a "healthy environment" was the solution. In urban areas, the correlation
of allergies and asthma with air pollution and poor living conditions presented a target for environmental activists. Today chemical sensitivity to
human products within indoor environments (e.g. the "sick-building syndrome") provides a new focus for inquiry and action.[314]

So at least in studies of disease and health, historians do not seem
reluctant to make evaluative judgments. However, there are instances where making them is problematical. Sutter comments at length on
Nancy Langston's work on links between chemical exposure and genetic expression.[315] Beginning in the 1940s, diethylstilbestrol (DES) was first
prescribed for women as a treatment for menopause and then as a way to
reduce miscarriages and premature births. Eventually its use extended to
cattle and chickens to increase milk and meat production. The cumulative
but delayed effects of exposure to small doses meant that the effects on
human health were not immediately recognized. When those effects were
detected, some evaluative judgments were noncontroversial, i.e., obvious
harms were "increasing cancer rates, growing incidences of reproductive
tract abnormalities, sterility, and impotence." However, what are environmental historians to say about "growing rates of intersex conditions
among amphibians, fishes, and humans"? Are these changes harms? Some
worry that "essentialist notions of normative sexuality [are] dangerously
driving the discourse on harm, while some in the intersex community
worry that these epidemiological connections risk branding their bodies
as mutant products of polluted environments."[316]

Such worries complicate the making of evaluative judgments. What
standards are environmental historians to rely on in assessing such changes? What is "biologically normal" when talking about sexual development? When environments and bodies interact in ways altering the range
of actual genetic expression, can we any longer assume the latter follows a
pre-ordained or "normal" path? Must talk of natural or genetic determin-

---

314   Sutter, 111.
315   *Toxic Bodies: Endocrine Disruptors and the Legacy of DES* (New Haven: Yale University
Press, 2010).
316   Sutter, 112.

ism give way to talk of a range of conditionalities?[317] Without formulating the questions in these terms, Sutter does conclude that Langston's study makes a very powerful case for the hybrid view of environments and culture.

> The issue is not merely that humans have become saturated with artificial toxicity and thus have polluted the natural state of their bodies and environments; it is that, in the process of trying to master nature, they have contributed to the biological transformation of bodies and ecological systems in ways that cannot be described as either natural or artificial/cultural.[318]

Before concluding his survey, Sutter takes up a problem inherited by the second generation of environmental historians. What he terms the "built-environment problem" arose from an early separation of nature from supposedly distinct urban environments. While the latter clearly affected the former, some historians thought a "built environment" should be left to "urban, architectural, technological, social, and cultural historians."[319] At work was the old distinction between nature and culture. Cities represent human mastery over nature. Even their parks are part of a designed environment, one that preserves a semblance of nature in the midst of more obvious signs of human construction.

Sutter cites William Cronon's work as an early challenge to this pre-hybrid notion of a "wild" nature and a tamed urban landscape.[320] The author detailed the dependency of Chicago on natural resources, financial assets and flows of goods and services; he then proclaimed the result a "second nature." In doing so, Sutter believes, Cronon anticipated the notion of hybridity; however, his category, second nature, remained largely undifferentiated. Still, the basic insight of mutual dependency was

---

317 Relevant to answering these questions is Chapter Three's discussion of the abstractness and conditionality of classical laws and the need for statistical frequencies in accounting (1) for the flexibility of schemes of recurrence and (2) for what appears to be "natural" or "normal." Within an explanatory context these two terms refer to an understanding of statistical ranges outside of which random deviations occur.

318 Sutter, 113. While some issues may resist facile evaluative judgments, Sutter is not hesitant to endorse Langston's prescriptive view that "precaution" is the appropriate stance to take regarding new environmental policies. In the absence of knowledge of causal links between new policies and harms, we should be cautious. Why? Given limited knowledge of environments and their complex interacting variables, and given our tendency to operate with hidden cultural biases and our past mistakes, we should err on the side of caution. Presumably the norm here is, "First, do no harm."

319 Ibid.

320 *Nature's Metropolis: Chicago and the Great West* (New York: W.W. Norton, 1992).

present. Cities distanced themselves from nature only by relying on the materials it supplied, e.g. lumber, water, soil and animals. The flows of production and consumption in an urban economy may be a second nature, but they are made possible and sustained by the first.[321]

Again, recent practitioners have generally accepted the hybrid thesis. However, Sutter raises a series of questions that may imply problems for the thesis. If it is far too simplistic to think of the persons inhabiting a metropolitan area as all thinking alike about "nature" and their relations to their environs, how are environmental historians to track this diversity of views? Hybridity is useful in avoiding the nature versus culture divide, but is it less useful in revealing much about diverse cultural views and practices?[322] Sutter cites Matthew Klingle's study of Seattle as an investigation of such hidden complexities.[323] Targeting Seattle's "public image as a city in harmony with its natural setting," Klingle recounts how politically contested plans went forward, landscapes were manipulated to the benefit of some while maintaining environmental inequalities for others, and hidden or largely ignored were the social disharmonies left in place. To refer back to the remarks above on moral judgments, Klingle proposes a new "ethic of place" or "civic environmentalism" that more explicitly recognizes and responds to real disparities in environmental conditions within urban populations.[324]

Sutter closes his review of the recent literature by an extended discussion of what he considered "a model for other environmental historians to follow."[325] Thomas G. Andrew's *Killing for Coal: America's Deadliest Labor War* studies how mining altered the history of labor and of the American West.[326] In doing so he "convincingly integrates environmental with other causal forces." For example, the transition from dependence on organic sources of energy to dependence on fossil fuels transformed Colorado from a frontier state into a prosperous "urban-industrial region,"

---

321 Nash seconds this view. "Built environments are surely products of social relations, but those social relationships are mediated and ultimately reinforced or undermined through existing material environments and nonhuman species: rivers, tidelands, coal seams, seismic faults, and rats, to name only a few." Linda Nash, "Furthering the Environmental Turn" in *Journal of American History*, (June 2013), 133.

322 These questions about diversity are implicit in Sutter's remarks about a "third crucial insight of recent metropolitan history." (114) They also bring to mind the earlier reservations about the adequacy of "energy" as a category for explaining the diversity of variables in an ecosystem.

323 *Emerald City: An Environmental History of Seattle* (New Haven: 2007).

324 Cited in Sutter, 115. This "ethic of place" may remind readers of the economic fantasy of the preceding chapter and its expectation that local, economically literate populations might learn to adapt their activities to the rhythms of an economy.

325 Ibid. 118.

326 Cambridge: Harvard University Press, 2008.

spurred a migration of labor forces and eventually provided an impetus to "labor solidarity." Andrews gives the last consequence special attention. He writes of coal mines as "workscapes" in which miners interacted with diverse environmental variables, e.g. animal labor (primarily that of mules), unstable rock formations, fluctuating air quality, varying groundwater levels and ever present gases and fire dangers. To stay alive in such a "'close, complex, and sometimes fatal relationship with a capricious environment,'" miners had to depend on one another and animals to be alert to changing conditions. Such dependency under harsh conditions promoted the emergence of labor solidarity and even "'workscape militancy.'"[327]

Sutter praises *Killing for Coal* as "the book that has come closest to my inchoate vision for a critical rethinking of nature and agency in environmental history." His reasons summarize the developments he has detected in recent decades.

> Andrew's story is not one in which an abstract and singular nature has agency, but one in which "mules and molten steel, arid climates and Irish potato plots, explosive gases and, most of all, a humble rock that burns all have roles to play" – roles that are inseparable from human labor and power. More than that, it is not just environmental history but also encompasses deep history, energy history, animal studies, sensory history, envirotech, environmental justice, and other facets of the fruitfully fragmenting field.[328]

The next section will arrange these perceived signs of development in a more structured way. For now some general comments will suffice. First, the shift from talk of nature as a single, undifferentiated "agency" to talk of diverse sources of dependency, e.g. animals, labor conditions, climates, minerals, agricultural practices, is evidence of an increasingly more comprehensive and detailed understanding of historical patterns of relations among persons, institutions, organisms and ecosystems. The price of such refinements in understanding is fragmentation of a field into an increasing number of specialties. But what is purchased is a "moving viewpoint" that leaves behind previous generalizations and category sets that inadequately framed inquiries. No longer is nature always the victim and humankind the despoiler. No longer is it assumed that inquirers

---

327   Andrews quoted in Sutter, 117.
328   Sutter, 117-118.

are making unbroken progress toward enlightenment about "the natural world, how it works, and what is required to protect it." Humans "have sometimes overestimated their capacity for environmental mastery [and environments have sometimes proven] resilient in the face of [human] transformative powers. As a result, the stories environmental historians tell are more complex, contingent, and counterintuitive."[329] Second, as Sutter observes, these developments make for complex and messy narrations. However, "they offer truer and more satisfying renditions of the human-environmental past."[330]

Sutter's article was part of a roundtable discussion with other environmental historians. In replying to their comments on his paper, he composed a brief set of reflections.[331] His primary aim was to reply to the charge by two participants that he wanted to return to the pre-hybrid division of nature and culture and the facile moralizing it encouraged.[332] While denying that was the case, he did worry that "environmental historians have not done a great job of reengaging metanarratives of environmental decline after the hybrid turn." For him the turn was an advance since it had immensely enriched historians' understanding of causal dependencies among so many variables. However, he saw their task as twofold: understanding the past and using the resulting insights to guide action in the present. The latter goal requires a more complex ethics of environmental action than in the past, and his concern was that hybridity fell short of supplying one.[333]

Bron Taylor, an environmental ethicist participating in the roundtable exchanges, shared the same concern.[334] More so than Sutter, he was suspicious of critics of preservationist movements who alleged they masked efforts to "secure privileged access to and use of the earth's lands and waters [and were] indifferent to the plights of marginalized peoples who struggle for access to basic environmental goods."[335] In short, critics charged the affluent cared about trees and wildlife but ignored how preservation efforts have harmed indigenous populations.

329   Ibid. 118.
330   Ibid. This conclusion reflects implicit stances on questions about RKO and will be key to comparing different claims about what has been going forward in environmental history.
331   "Nature Is History" in *Journal of American History*, Vol.100, 1(June 2013), 145-148.
332   Gregg Mitman, "Living in a Material World" in *Journal of American History*, 128-130. Linda Nash, "Furthering the Environmental Turn," in *Journal of American History*, 131-135.
333   Sutter, "Nature Is History," 147.
334   "'It's Not All about Us': Reflections on the State of American Environmental History" in *Journal of American History*, 140-144.
335   Ibid. 141. Taylor is criticizing the generalization that a "biocentric ethics [masks] privilege, self-interest and even misanthropy."

Taylor challenges this new version of victims and victimizers. On the one hand, he wonders "why scholars who are alert to and even outraged by human on human imperialism are so often indifferent to the ecocidal domination of humankind over the rest of the living world." But when some scholars do "apply an anti-imperial logic to their own species," the result is often a dismal record of habitat destruction and nonhuman extinctions followed by claims to the moral rightness of preservationist efforts.[336] Might the issues and motivations of preservationists be more complex than simply caring for nonhuman species and being indifferent to their own kind? Some preservationists desire to protect environments for aesthetic and spiritual reasons. Thoreau easily comes to mind. Others more commonly cite pragmatic reasons. Biodiversity is worth protecting because of "ecological interdependence." Oxygen-consuming humans depend on rain forests wherein yet-to-be-discovered flora and fauna may contribute to medical breakthroughs. In addition, natural settings provide opportunities for recreation and restorative psychological experiences. Psychological and ecological "health" can be synergistic.[337] So Taylor "complicates" the question of environmental protection. To frame the issue in terms of nature and its despoilers was an oversimplification in the first generation, and Taylor thinks it no more useful today in doing environmental history. Still, a strong theoretical rationale for environmental advocacy may be difficult to formulate and justify.

Taylor dismisses a type of moral relativism as a way of dodging this difficulty.[338] Instead, he endorses the search for what Donald Worster in the 1970s called an "ecological ethic of interdependence." The latter thought developing one might require a "quasi-religious conversion."[339] In mentioning this possible prerequisite, Taylor may have been trying to

---

336   Ibid. 142.
337   Ibid.
338   Taylor worries that, "if either cynicism or indifference is the outcome of our scholarship – then environmental historians will be complicit in the erosion of biological and cultural diversity. Given what I see in the academy today, I do not think this is an idle fear." (Ibid. 143.) Nash perhaps provides some evidence for this fear when she writes: "there is little payoff in returning to moralizing narratives of environmental decline. Such narratives risk reproducing the very nature-culture division that environmental historians thought they were overcoming. Moreover, from a purely strategic perspective, narratives of decline and environmental prescription are as likely to produce apathy and resistance as they are to motivate change. For every narrative of decline there is one of material progress that can be mustered, and now that scholars have historicized both nature and science they cannot easily invoke those ideas to authorize some stories over others." Nash, 135.
339   Worster is quoted in ibid. 144. For many persons talk of a "quasi-religious conversion" may seem out of place; yet, this book series has repeatedly stressed how types of "displacements" are central to moving beyond initial viewpoints and toward more developed ones.

avoid the naturalistic fallacy, but a type of conversion or displacement is arguably a precondition to a more comprehensive understanding of how entangled human living is with natural processes. As a precedent for this claim, consider how Chapter Three exposed the fiction of the discrete individual existing independently of institutions. The thesis there was that as organisms are to ecosystems so individuals are to institutions. The correlates in either relation are not explainable apart from one another. To arrive at this conclusion does require some displacement from a world of imaginable organisms and persons. If one understands ecological and institutional patterns of relations in some detail and if misanthropy is absent, then developing a theoretical ethic of environmental protection will be more likely.[340]

III. What Has Been Going forward in Environmental History?

Mitman identifies two fundamental questions that can serve as reference points for tracking differences in how the cited authors have assessed recent changes in their specialty.

> Where does the explanatory weight of environmental
> history reside: in biology, in culture, or in an adamant
> rejection of what Donna Haraway refers to as the "Great
> Divide"? As a field deeply committed to relationality,
> environmental history is also a field deeply resistant to
> embracing a relational ontology in which things exist
> not in themselves, or in Haraway's words, "partners do
> not precede their relating."[341]

The first question is, how much "weight" do the natural sciences and their explanatory correlates have in the specialty, especially since historical narration is the usual mode of presentation? In terms familiar to readers of this book series, the question might be: Is the first horizon more

340 Developing such a theory and applying it to policy debates are two distinct tasks. For example, Taylor acknowledges that ethical generalities about respecting other species and preserving biodiversity fall short of supplying insights into specific cases and into what courses of action are realistic options. As he says, "the move from general principles to concrete judgments is usually fraught." Ibid.
341 Mitman, 129. He is quoting from Donna J. Haraway, *When Species Meet* (Minneapolis: University of Minnesota Press, 2008), 10 and 17.

important than the second horizon for doing environmental history or is it a false dichotomy to think the two are not complementary? Regarding things and persons, the second question is whether environmental historians should embrace a relational ontology, whatever that might be.[342]

Before turning to the first question, we can revisit the sequences of views of environments and ecosystems in Chapter Two and relate them to the views identified in this chapter. In the earlier chapter one question was whether there were any signs of development in the ways ecologists (and artists) understood their objects of inquiry. Nisbet described four "clusters" of views.

1. A first understanding of environment (associated with environmental art) was of an encompassing or bounded space within which objects appeared.

2. A second understanding (associated with land art) moved beyond fixed boundaries (e.g. galleries) to placing artworks in situ thereby making the material conditions of an environment part of the work.[343] Images of the earth from space suggested that all objects and their sites belonged to a unified living whole, a single ecology in which all parts were interconnected.

3. A third view (associated with ecological art) shifted from a focus on singular works and their locales to thinking of patterns of relations among conditioned objects that existed in and through interdependent and mutable ecosystems that were dynamic because of instances of random variation.

4. A fourth understanding (associated with process art) emphasized what all systems had in common, namely,

342   Mitman clearly favors a relational ontology of some sort. See his brief contrast of two different histories of the spread of yellow fever and malaria. His concluding remark about these studies is revealing: "we exist only as a result of symbiotic relationships, with each other, and with other living and non-living things on this earth." (Ibid. 130.) Readers of the preceding chapters can surmise these writers' general answer to the second question. How one answers it will have implications for subsequent evaluations of differences in views of agency, environment, mutual conditioning between cultural and natural processes and environmental ethics.
343   In effect, and in anticipation of critiques of the nature versus culture dichotomy, environments and artworks were mutable and interdependent.

energy exchanges. The generalized understanding of environments, whether cultural exchanges of information or biological exchanges of nutrients, was of systems dependent on variable conditions, changes in which required adaptations.

Chapter Two was in part an exercise in FS3 and so presented a series of different views of ecosystems and environments that could later be studied for signs of development. To identify differences in views, that chapter surveyed Golley's reading of the history of ecology and identified his three "periods" and their views of ecosystems.

1. A very minimal meaning of ecosystem noted the embedding and dependency of organisms on environments. Added to it was the notion that organisms and their habitats formed hierarchies of systems with less complex systems supporting more complex ones.

2. A second view of ecosystems was that they were self-regulating systems that responded to disturbances and returned to equilibrium or steady states (though catastrophic breakdowns were always possible).

3. A third understanding reflected a rejection of the deterministic machine (read "computer") model of the second view. Instead, it emphasized random variations and development within ecosystems, with equilibrium being relatively short lived. In brief, ecosystems were dynamic and conditioned "wholes" with emergent properties.

In applying FS3 to Nisbet's four views, the authors placed them in a sequence moving from the less developed to the more developed, with the criterion being greater comprehensiveness. The minimal view operated within the first horizon of imaginable objects and settings. The second marked an advance because it conceived of intelligible relations among artists, artworks, materials, art history and mutable settings, e.g. seasonal changes. The third cluster represented a breakthrough to thinking about art and environments in terms of constitutive relations among physical properties, biochemical processes, political systems and technologies. In doing so, it clearly moved beyond what was imaginable. With its talk of energy flows, the fourth view manifested an even greater distance from both the first realism and a naïve model of knowing. To focus on energy exchanges is to assume that phenomenal organisms and artworks exist in and through what eludes sensory detection.

There were criticisms of this fourth and most general view of environments. Energy as a category is too undifferentiated and so loses touch with the "unruly complexity" of so many diverse classes of organisms and processes. Furthermore, it does no work in explaining how ecosystems develop, and, as a fundamental category in an explanatory framework, it may mark a retreat to the Pre-Socratic search for the "common matter" allegedly making all things what they are. Still, the push for more comprehensive understanding was at work during the 60s and into the 70s, making the third and fourth views more developed positions.

What signs of development appear in Golley's account of views of ecosystems up to the 90s? The earliest view mixed both imaginable organisms embedded in picturable settings and hierarchical systems with more complex systems dependent on less complex ones. Talk of hierarchies presupposed a limited departure from the first horizon. The departure was still incomplete in the second view with its machine analogy of self-regulating systems adapting to disturbances and tending toward routine functioning. The third view of ecosystems was more clearly representative of thinking within the second horizon. Talk of ecosystems as developing through random variations and having emergent properties reflected a more developed understanding of relations among classes of variables, relations that were both systematic and nonsystematic, deterministic and probabilistic. Despite criticisms of Golley's comments on the "concept" of ecosystem as but one "device" for imposing order on the flux of experience, the authors concluded that the third view he identified was more comprehensive than its predecessors.

Presumably further developments in understanding environments and ecosystems have occurred since the 1990s. We return then to the two surveys of environmental history. The leading question again is: What difference, if any, did operating in the second horizon have on understanding how humankind was related to environments?

McNeill's survey in 2003 identified a variety of negative and positive changes over the thirty-year history of the field. Left behind were early generalizations about the origins of environmental degradation.[344] McNeill rejected the "Hegelian" view of some of his colleagues because

---

344   Targets for blame were Judeo-Christian culture, capitalism, colonialism and patriarchy.

it privileged ideas and culture in the shaping of human behavior. He also dismissed the exaggerated emphasis in the 90s on the social construction of reality. More positively, he endorsed the acceptance of multiple types of "agents" in understanding environmental change, e.g. population numbers, animals, climates, ideas and technologies. He also tracked the waxing and waning of environmental activism and defended its revival in an increasingly complicated field.

What specific changes did McNeill see as signs of development? He listed several. The multiplying ties of environmental history to other specialties (e.g. climatology, genetics, archaeology and disease history) "fragmented" the field but aided in its maturation and relevance to the broader discipline of history. The gradual deepening of insights into how peoples and their environments were entangled prompted his call for internationalizing inquiries beyond political borders. When he wrote in 2003, he was able to cite a few regional studies that reflected such a broadening of perspective. Studies of this kind led to complaints that human actors were vanishing from the expanded narratives, but McNeill thought this was inevitable given the "scale" of such histories.[345] These authors suggested that, as environmental studies increasingly reflected operations in the horizon of theory, one should expect a decreasing emphasis on particular actors and events. However, McNeill noted that historians tended to be "thin on theory." While he meant they avoided constructing their own theories, opting in some cases to borrow theories from other fields, he did not mean they avoided the effects of science on environments, e.g. agrarian revolutions and industrialization. In addition, the focus in Nisbet's fourth cluster on energy exchanges McNeill finds replicated in several European environmental histories.[346]

So what, if any, difference did the horizon of theory make in the period of environmental history that McNeill surveyed? Apparently the effects were indirect. That is, as environmental historians drew upon findings from various scientific fields, they were gradually recognizing the range of diverse conditions that sustained and, in some cases, degraded environments. One result was to make the overgeneralizations of the first generation more obsolete and even embarrassing. Another result was to fragment the specialty into various subspecialties. The very complexity of

---

345   Recall how some commentators diagnosed the lessening of "moral engagement" among environmental historians as due to increasing "scientific sophistication." While it is likely they may have been measuring scholarly progress in terms of the fact-value distinction, might they have overlooked the demand of theoretical explanations for "abstracting" from particular cases and focusing on patterns of relations among kinds of objects and events?

346   McNeill, 19-20.

the conditions they were investigating and the troubling questions about the terms appropriate for talking about those conditions (e.g. agency, nature and environment) put pressure on the next generation to examine the categories they used. That focus on language became much more apparent for practitioners in the first decade of the new century, a period included in Sutter's article in 2013.

What changes did Sutter see as signs of development in environmental history? The first significant advance he detected was the replacement of old dichotomies, e.g. nature versus culture, by the notion of hybridity. The new view implied both that natural environments already bear a human imprint and that societies are rarely, if ever, explainable apart from their natural environments. Historical interactions change both terms in this correlation. But then human actions are but one class of variables in the dynamic relations among so many diverse kinds of mutually conditioning variables.

All the same, Sutter thought hybridity a "transitional" view. It did represent an advance over earlier views that separated natural and social environments—the first found, the other made or built. However, it was too undifferentiated a notion. Still, recognizing this deficit contributed to another advance; namely, historians began to question the basic categories in use in their specialty. Was it at all clear what "nature," "environment" and "agency" meant? To pay attention to such fundamental issues and to differentiate classes of variables previously left aggregated were both signs of a maturing field of inquiry.

An enduring challenge for environmental historians has been justifying normative judgments about human acts and policies affecting environments. Sutter and Taylor believed an environmental ethic was possible. Even in its absence, normative judgments may be inescapable in writing histories of health and disease. However, making such judgments is the easy part; actually constructing a theory justifying them proves far more difficult. Donald Worster's mention of a "quasi-religious conversion" as a prerequisite to such an ethic signaled one of the difficulties.[347] Earlier references to the naturalistic fallacy and to the fact-value distinction signaled others. At least some of the obstacles are explicit and do not foreclose in any obvious way the possibility of an environmental ethic.

---

347   In defending various types of displacements as preconditions to differentiations of consciousness, the authors of this book series have not found Worster's prerequisite an obstacle but a sign that the nineteenth-century positivistic ideal of science is dead. This does not preclude remnants of the ideal from lingering within common-sense views of objectivity and subjectivity.

IV. Doing FS4

The preceding section surveyed a number of authors to identify what they thought was going forward in ecological studies and in environmental history. Several lists of changes followed and reflected different assessments made at different times over the past forty years. Ideally the later assessments detected advances not yet available to earlier commentators. Still, there was no expectation that advances would occur on some linear time-line such that later views would necessarily be more developed than earlier ones. Just as changes in an ecosystem can harm previously thriving organisms dependent on it, so changes in how ecologists or historians understand their practices and objects of inquiry can fall back behind an earlier level of insight.[348]

In this book series one measure of development is the demand of further why-questions for more comprehensive understanding, a demand that, if it is to be met, requires entry into the horizon of theory. So the first leading question was what differences have a few steps into the horizon of theory made for the specialty of environmental history? Departing from views of nature either as a single, undifferentiated "agent" of change or as always a victim of human depredation and moving on to distinguish a wide range of classes of mutually dependent variables are evidence of a shift from pre-theoretical images of "pushing and pulling causes." While the proliferating types of variables have made the tasks of historians more complex, a more comprehensive "moving viewpoint" promises, in Sutter's words, to produce "truer and more satisfying renditions of the human-environmental past."[349]

Such prospects are warranted, these writers believe, because further why-questions demand ever more comprehensive accounts of what at first are descriptive views, and the advances noted so far have reflected such expansions in understanding.[350] Some developments have undoubtedly

---

348   McNeill claimed as much in preferring the practices of cultural-environmental historians of the 70s over the enthusiasm in the 90s for constructivist accounts of nature and society.

349   Sutter, 118.

350   To summarize the major expansions in understanding environments: development occurred (1) in moving from the ancient view that geography determined a population's character to the view of mutual dependency between a population and its environment; (2) in transcending the bifurcation of nature and culture by talk of hybridity; (3) in accepting that the human species is but one type of variable in complex patterns of relationships among many types of organic and nonorganic variables; (4) in understanding environments in terms of variable conditions such that random deviations among them lead to developments in and emergent properties of organisms and ecosystems.

been due to the increased exposure of environmental historians to the findings in fields such as genetics, biology, climatology and social theory. As a result, historians have accepted a wide range of classes of variables as relevant to understanding hybrid environments. Working out patterns of relations among such mutually conditioning classes of objects and processes requires a departure from the first horizon. Recognizing that ecosystems develop through random variations and have emergent properties erodes the plausibility of machine analogies and any exclusively deterministic viewpoint. But what new vocabulary is adequate for talking about all these new developments? Traditional dichotomies and categories have become targets of criticism, a sign that the descriptive terminology of the first horizon is inadequate for inquiries within the horizon of theory. As well, the ongoing debates over normative judgments in doing environmental history are phrased in ways too indebted to earlier views of science and objectivity. What new and more adequate vocabulary can help resolve this problem?

Both the debates about normative judgments within environmental history and any project trying to find a more adequate terminology for expressing recent developments in the field, e.g. moving beyond the categories of hybridity and human agency, belong to the "future-oriented" specialties within the eight functional specialties. Some clues, nevertheless, have appeared in this chapter's "backward looking" exercises in FS3 and FS4. For example, a first step in formulating a new vocabulary for talking about ethical judgments and objectivity might rely on an analogy between dependencies among intentional acts and an understanding of ecosystems as flexible ranges of schemes of recurrence dependent on only relatively stable conditions.

To highlight the similarities, normative judgments and decisions about environmental policies and actions are functionally dependent on prior intentional acts, e.g. raising and answering questions. New questions may effect random deviations from prior answers. Answers to new questions may undermine established schemes or habits in judging and deciding and begin to form new patterns that, in turn, future questions may eventually disrupt.[351] Put another way, instabilities among the conditions

---

351   A concrete example of questions disrupting settled views and schemes of recurrence (in this instance questions about schemes of constitutional order and military strategy) appears in Philip Bobbitt's work. "*The Shield of Achilles* presented the thesis that revolutions in military affairs induced transformations of the constitutional order and that transformations in the constitutional order bred revolutions in military affairs. For the historian, it is an arbitrary choice where one steps into this river of causal currents: the interaction between these two phenomena is mutually affecting such that nothing fundamental happens in the constitutional realm that does not have fundamental consequences in the strategic

supporting organisms and ecosystems have parallels in conditions in any field of inquiry. The capacity to raise new questions is a principle of indeterminacy and destabilization that, when exercised, can undermine established viewpoints in a field. For example, the nature versus culture dichotomy endured for centuries. The facile generalizations about capitalism and patriarchy as sources of environmental harm had a shorter life span. What destabilized those views? The first generation had not yet exploited the findings of multiple scientific fields that provided later environmental historians with a much broader range of questions about hybrid environments and types of causal dependencies. One result was to complicate their narratives because they brought more complex patterns of analysis to their work.

What new terminology might someday replace talk of "human agency"? Paralleling the complex perspective of environmental historians on "causal" dependencies among variables, the determinate conditions for human action are multiple, ranging from neurophysical and neurochemical processes within persons to their educational histories and social-political relations. Human living is so entangled with institutions that the range of determinate conditions for action includes political, technological and economic schemes of recurrence. And nothing yet has been said about human entanglement with impersonal environmental conditions. These multiple conditions interact and eventually shape the subsequent "contexts" persons bring to making judgments and decisions. Perhaps the general contribution of this chapter to future inquiries about human agency is the general insight that understanding a wide range of relations among types of variables is indispensable in explaining human actions and their antecedent conditions.[352]

The second leading question was whether environmental historians needed to operate with a "relational ontology." What might this mean? Haraway's quip that "partners do not precede their relating" seems to be no more than a linguistic form of dependency. The classic example of all bachelors being unmarried illustrates the limits of this appeal to language. What environmental historians face is the more difficult challenge of explaining how so many human and nonhuman variables can be mutually conditioning. One clue to meeting this challenge was the

arena, and vice versa." *Terror and Consent: The Wars for the Twenty-First Century* (New York: Random House, 2009), 168 (footnote).

352 *A Theory of Ordered Liberty* attempted to understand intentional operations, ranging from acts of paying attention to acts of decision-making, in ways consistent with this general insight. The book attempted to meet the need for a new vocabulary, one evading the traditional terms still common in debates about free will and determinism.

earlier analogy of proportion: as organisms are to ecosystems so individuals are to institutions. The basis for this analogy is the insight that one cannot adequately understand either organisms or individuals apart from their relations to other organisms and individuals. But are those relations part of the being of particular entities? Answering this question requires several distinctions that already appeared in Chapter Three. First, to understand the being of something is to answer distinct types of questions. What-questions anticipate discovering what makes something what it is while is-questions anticipate determining if answers to such what-questions are correct or if what is correctly understood actually exists.[353] In asking these distinct types of questions, we presuppose a distinction in being, i.e. what the medievals debated as the difference between *essentia* and *esse* and what some contemporary philosophers debate as the difference between concepts or "constructs" and either one's relation to something real.

Second, as Chapter Three suggested, a distinction between natural being (*esse naturale*) and intentional being (*esse intentionale*) is crucial to affirming the reality of institutions. The latter are patterns of relations constituted by acts of meaning and sustained by the same. Without such continuing constitutive acts institutions cease to exist. Does this understanding of institutions provide clues for understanding how a "relational ontology" might apply to ecosystems? Again, an earlier distinction proves helpful.

While not constituted (in the *ordo essendi*) by intentional acts, ecosystems as understood patterns of relations among organisms and multiple types of inorganic conditions presuppose the inventive or constructive operations of inquirers in the *ordo cognoscendi*. In other words, inquirers proceed from puzzling data through questioning to preliminary syntheses or answers. Is-questions about such answers anticipate distinguishing between correct and incorrect answers both about what something is and about whether it exists. In some cases what has been invented or constructed by intentional operations turns out to be some limited knowledge of what in fact is real.

More widespread familiarity with the third horizon, especially with the functionally related operations in coming to know, may one day reduce resistance to thinking of things as unities that exist in and through intelligible patterns of relations, some of which are internal and many of which are external to those things. For example, the chemical processes

---

353   To exemplify these two different ends of is-questions, we can ask: (1) Is this an accurate account of what Homer meant by Cyclops? (2) Did a Cyclops ever exist?

of its digestive system condition the mobility of an animal, and climatic regularities condition the availability of food toward which it can move. Let either type of condition be unfulfilled, and the animal may perish.[354] Insight into this sort of dependency may persuade some to take a relational ontology seriously.

To exploit another insight from the third horizon, since inquiries produce syntheses or constructs, it makes a difference who is doing the constructing and then the judging. More developed or less developed inquirers are the "contexts" for specific intentional operations. Thus, for example, to know something of the history of environmental studies is to be better prepared to avoid categories, generalizations and procedures that predecessors tried and found wanting. This simple observation implies that knowing the history of one's field, its advances and missteps, can be a precondition to making more competent judgments.[355]

As already claimed, more competent work in environmental history occurred as inquirers began to move into the second horizon. These advances in understanding the objects of their inquiries presupposed developments, even displacements, in the inquirers. The earliest views of organisms and environments belonged to a common-sense horizon of imaginable objects and events. The language in use was largely that of the same horizon. Both were signs the earliest generation of environmental historians was at home primarily in the first horizon. Only gradually did an understanding of organisms, their conditionalities and development through random variations replace the earlier pictures. Perhaps without noticing their shift from picture thinking to thinking in terms of invisible, conditioned relations among classes of variables, environmental historians were actually departing from the first horizon. They were becoming more adequate "contexts" for operating in an increasingly more complex field. Development of inquirers permits development of the field they study and vice versa.

---

354   These simple examples of different internal and external conditionalities are evidence for (1) the claim that talk of "energy exchanges" is too general to capture the diversity of relations occurring in ecosystems and (2) the charge that the category energy does no work in explaining how ecosystems develop. They also reinforce the critique of talking about "nature" as some single agent.
355   This observation may also bring to mind the claim in the two previous books that a certain type of developing subject was the "remote criterion" for reliable judgments and knowing. As well, basing new judgments on an acquired understanding of the history of some debated issue, "its advances and missteps," anticipates the future practice of GS across the functional specialties.

A slow and incomplete shift between the two horizons is detectable in McNeill's complaint against social constructivist views during the 90s. To repeat his words:

> I think the cultural construction of nature just isn't all that important compared to what has happened and is happening to real nature, and how nature has affected and still affects us (there is some reality out there independent of our perception!).[356]

He seems to assume that "cultural construction" and "real nature" are antithetical. The former is perhaps a world of ideas while the latter is something real "out there" and not just ideas. This antithesis may presuppose the first type of realism and reflect an oversight of the distinction between acts of understanding and acts of judging. All the same, McNeill's performance (1) in criticizing facile generalizations about the "causes" of environmental degradation and (2) in affirming relations of mutual dependency as true of humankind and environments alike is compatible with the position that reasonable judgment is the criterion of what is true and what gives meaning to the term "real." Contradictions between authors' performance and their explicit comments on its results are not uncommon and usually reflect their unfamiliarity with the third horizon, i.e. with their own performance in first constructing and then judging meanings.

Since this chapter has been concerned with what has developed in the field and not with what has become obsolete, we can end in the way previous chapters have concluded, i.e. by asking what the new comparative interpretation can contribute to a developing field of inquiry, in this case, environmental history.

Previous chapters employed FS3 to identify different sequences of views ranging from the less developed to the more developed and then applied FS4 to trace some of those differences back to implicit and more basic stances on the meanings of reality, knowing and objectivity. This chapter has compiled different views appearing at different times over a forty-year period and then assessed their degree of development primarily in terms of how comprehensive they were. While a few explicit criticisms based on UV appeared, e.g. remarks about McNeill's attack on constructivism and questions about the focus in the 90s on energy exchanges, the direct references to UV were minimal. Implicit uses of the

---

356   "Observations on the Nature and Culture of Environmental History," 17.

basic positions on reality, knowing and objectivity occurred in various criticisms of some of the views surveyed. Those criticisms focused, for example, on the indebtedness of early views of environments to the first horizon and its picture thinking, on simplistic views of causation and agency, on talk of energy exchanges as inadequate for understanding the diverse variables within ecosystems, on ways of talking about normative judgments that remained tied to nineteenth-century views of science and objectivity.

The major positive applications of UV appeared (1) in identifying more developed positions as those reflective of the second horizon, (2) in suggesting some changes in how we think and talk about normative judgments and human agency, and (3) in commenting on and defending a relational ontology.

Both positive and negative applications of UV to the various views of environments and environmental history allow us to identify these major developments, as well as some unfinished work, in the field.

> 1. Environmental historians have gradually shifted away from the first horizon by applying the findings of different scientific fields to their own works.

> 2. They have made advances by leaving behind deterministic models of ecological processes and by accepting the instability of environments and their inhabitants because of their dependence on complex patterns of relations among multiple types of variables.

> 3. In making such advances they have begun to question the adequacy of some of the basic categories in use in the profession.

> 4. An earlier resistance within the profession to some sort of relational ontology may be weakening.

While McNeill and Sutter identified other developments in the field and cited specific works as evidence, the preceding list reflects judgments based on UV.

V. In Retrospect

What has this chapter contributed to the pursuit of the elusive meaning of environment? Sutter announced the chase was on by noting his discipline's use of "the encompassing and surprisingly undertheorized term 'environment.'" As commonly used the term has no more precision than most of ordinary language. However, to "theorize" it is either to replace it with a neologism or to stipulate a technical meaning for the common term. The first option is not promising since multiple disciplines employ the term and neologisms are unlikely to transfer successfully across those conventional boundaries. The second option presents its own problems. To stipulate technical meanings for commonly used words is not to ensure that future usage (even by the same author) will not slip back into ordinary usage. Perhaps subscripts to the term might track variations in the term's meaning. For example, $environment_1$ could refer to some variable common-sense meaning of the term while $environment_2$ could alert readers to its technically defined meaning. A bit cumbersome?

Then there is a more basic problem. Whatever theoretical meaning the term environment acquires, different readers will bring different degrees of development to the reading of it. If the technical meaning is to be more than a series of words anyone with a decent memory can repeat, the readers will have had to accumulate the insights that led up to its formulation. Again, formulae and "concepts" can be passed around without the users having an adequate understanding of what they mean.

So what effective response can we offer to this problem of an "undertheorized" category? While Chapter Seven offers our detailed response, this chapter and those that preceded it have taken some preliminary steps. For example, exposure to the findings of different scientific fields prompted environmental historians to recognize that some of their basic categories were surprisingly vague and in need of scrutiny. This is a step toward what commonly occurs in the second horizon, namely, control over meaning. Next, a later generation of historians shifted to an understanding of ecosystems as "open" (or non-deterministic) because they understood that complex patterns of relations among multiple classes of variables were mutually conditioning and subject to random variations. To accept this much about the objects of their inquiries is a step toward accepting a relational ontology. To these writers such steps contribute to a more controlled use of basic categories and signal a more comprehensive understanding of the objects of their inquiries.

Still, these steps are preliminary, and the destination lies ahead. The next chapter shifts focus in perhaps a surprising way. What can the neurosciences have to contribute to puzzling out the meaning of environment? Asking how neurons discovered or even invented themselves hardly seems relevant to the primary question of this book. These authors think otherwise and trust readers who have come this far will continue the slow pursuit of the elusive meaning of environment.

CHAPTER SIX:
HOW NEURONS DISCOVERED THEMSELVES

Might the meaning of environment depend on neurons? The strangeness of this question is matched by the title of this chapter and by the claim that any sensitively integrated environment is part of someone's central nervous system. Question, title and claim will all play roles in applying FS4 to two impasses in contemporary fields of neuroscience. First, reductive analyses that assume psychological states and intentional acts are wholly explainable in terms of neural activities come into conflict with "folk psychology," i.e. common-sense views of human control over mental acts. Second, the terminologies in use by reductionists and by their critics have deficiencies. Often there is a mingling of ordinary language (e.g. voluntary motions and free will), eighteenth-century mechanistic metaphors (e.g. "mechanisms in the brain") and metaphors borrowed from information theory. The linguistic challenge is to be able to talk about relations among psychological variables and neural variables without denying both the real distinctions and the mutually conditioning relations among them. Meeting this challenge will help provide more detailed answers to two questions pervading these chapters: Is an environment reducible to its components? What language is appropriate for talking about relations among organisms, ecosystems and the environment?

I. Background to the Two Impasses

The previous chapters have laid the groundwork for providing critical assessments of, if not solutions to, debates about reductive analyses and the linguistic difficulties facing neuroscientists and some of their critics. Chapters Two and Five on natural environments and Chapters Three and Four on social environments responded to impasses in various fields, and those responses have implications for this chapter's puzzles. Those chapters advanced two general theses: (1) we cannot adequately understand biological organisms apart from their relations to ecosystems; and (2) we cannot adequately understand persons apart from their relations to institutions. An analogy of proportion followed: organisms are to ecosystems as persons are to institutions.[357] The fifth chapter exploited this analogy in shifting from talk of "hybrid environments" to talk of mutually conditioning variables forming flexible ranges of schemes of recurrence among organisms. A question for this chapter is whether this way of speaking of organisms and ecosystems can assist in evading the two impasses of reductive analysis and linguistic deficiencies.

This new way of talking is an alternative to thinking of economies or natural environments either as mechanistic processes or as energy or information exchange systems. First, why object to the mechanistic metaphor? In regard to economic institutions, one complaint is that the analogy ignores how intentional acts constitute and sustain businesses as ongoing enterprises. The occurrence of those acts is not always systematic. Employees fail to show up, consumer tastes change and competitors use innovations to seize more market share. Fortunes are made as often as they are lost. Human plasticity and defensive schemes of recurrence provide some flexibility in responding to economic threats. The machine metaphor misses all this. In its place the language of schemes of recurrence is a way of capturing both the systematic and the non-systematic patterns of relations comprising institutions.

Second, why object to talking of ecosystems as energy exchange systems or of cultures and neural networks as information exchange systems? As argued in Chapter Two, "energy" is too undifferentiated a category and does no work in explaining how systems develop.[358] It is an oversized umbrella blocking so much rain that it becomes unwieldy to carry, so that its success is its failure. Also, in arguing for the status of institutions as intentional realities, Chapter Three posited intentional acts as the basis for their emergence, survival and adaptation, but it went on to distinguish between agreed-upon roles and the persons temporarily filling them. The intelligible patterns of relations among roles or functions are conditioned by the intentional acts of particular persons but are not reducible to those acts. The analogy used to make this point was the relation of insights to images. The former are dependent on the latter but

---

357   Even though the biological category has been applied metaphorically to social set-ups such as economies, our analogy is not that institutions are like ecosystems.

358   There was also the suspicion that those employing the category may have been asking the Pre-Socratic question about what ultimately made all things what they were.

are not themselves just more images. Similarly, a good of order depends on persons deciding to fill their institutional roles but is not just an aggregation of imaginable individuals exchanging information.

To discard stubborn mechanistic metaphors and the language of energy and information exchanges is not to provide positive solutions to the two puzzles about reductive analysis and linguistic deficits. The next section will survey previous chapters in this book and findings from even earlier works to assemble more positive solutions. Before proceeding to that survey, we can summarize basic questions and answers appearing in earlier works. Recalling some of those provisional answers is a step toward answering new questions about neurons and the language appropriate for talking about their relations to intentional acts.

Are ecosystems and institutions real? Organisms and individuals are presumably observable entities, but the patterns of relations among them are not; so might the former be said to be real but not the latter? Yet can any of the former be adequately understood apart from such patterns of relations? As an added problem, over time ecosystems and institutions appear to be quite mutable, but science requires stability in the objects of its inquiries or at least regular patterns of development in those objects. If there is so much chaos in matters ecological and economic, might a science of either be impossible?

Some distinctions can refine these basic questions. To begin with the question of whether patterns of relations are real, suppose it is more accurate to say (1) that organisms and persons exist in and through ecosystems and institutions and (2) that the latter do not exist in and of themselves as distinct things. The use of "thing" here presupposes Lonergan's distinction between body and thing.[359] The term "body" belongs to the first type of knowing, i.e. what is understood in relation to observers, what an object, for example, looks like to them. In contrast, the term "thing" can be reserved for use in pursuing the second type of knowing.[360]

What of the question about the stability of the objects of scientific inquiry? Again, the distinction between two types of knowing can prove helpful. We can ask further questions about whatever bodies we observe and describe. Specifically, we can wonder what makes objects

---

359   *Insight*, 270-279.
360   Just as ecosystems and institutions are not visible, so things, as distinct from describable bodies, are not imaginable. But what is a thing? The question of thing or "substance" has an ancient and contentious history. Most of the controversies have reflected both a failure to distinguish the two types of knowing and an implicit debt to the first type of realism, i.e. the view that a thing must be an imaginable something. For several chapters in this book, the less complex question is whether patterns of relations among things are real.

what they are in relation to one another. For example, we begin with descriptions of organisms but can move on to inquiries in biochemistry, genetics and evolutionary history. The complex systems that make up the functioning organism have internal conditions (e.g. chemical exchanges in digestive tracts) and external conditions (e.g. the operations of the hydrological cycle in varying locales, oxygen releases from plant life and even planetary cycles making life on earth possible). Disrupt conditions too radically and the organisms dependent on them may go extinct. So the stability of things and their ecosystems is never assured; it is a matter of probability.[361] But contemporary sciences are at home in talking about non-systematic relations and statistical probabilities. Graphing pressure readings and assembling actuarial tables are routine ways of finding hidden order amid apparent chaos.

These are at least some of the broad questions and provisional answers relevant to understanding ecosystems and institutions. The following section will more directly reveal their relevance to understanding relations among neural events and psychological acts.

II. The Two Impasses and FS3

A. An Emergentist View

Currently most inquiries in the neurosciences focus on the antecedent and more basic conditions that support both localized brain functions and basic intentional acts. Study of the dependency of intentional acts on organic functions and of the latter on chemical transmitters and genetic substrates is an attempt to understand the more complex in terms of the simpler. However, might these relations of dependency also go in the other direction? For example, might acts of understanding and deciding exercise "executive control"[362] over simpler conditions?

---

361   For example, deforestation in Brazil impacts different species in different ways. Though both species are faced with habitat loss, birds are able to fly away, but sloths have no option but to hold on tight. The probability of survival varies for each species.
362   Various definitions of "executive control" are offered in the literature. For example, Gruber and Goschke propose "a neurocognitive model of executive control according to which the human ability to flexibly adapt to changing behavioral requirements, i.e. executive control, depends on dynamic and context-sensitive interactions between... brain systems." Oliver Gruber and Thomas Goschke, "Executive Control Emerging from Dynamic Interactions between Brain Systems Mediating Language, Working Memory and Attentional Process" in *Acta Psychologica* Vol. 115 (2004), 105. Regardless of the definition,

The literature on such "top-down" ordering is sparse. Posner and Synder detected the problem in 1975. Forty years ago they speculated about the future of attention studies and foresaw a "kind of research schizophrenia" with one focus being on "mechanisms that subserve" neural processing and conscious attention and the other focus being on conscious strategies that "modify and build upon 'automatic processes.'"[363] Most of the literature over the past forty years reflects an opting for the first focus and does not answer their original question:

> To what extent are our conscious intentions and strategies in control of the way information is processed in our minds? This seems to be a question of importance to us both as psychologists and as human beings. Yet... most theorists in psychology have avoided consideration of the relationship between conscious and unconscious mental events.[364]

However, twenty years earlier at least one author wrote of mutual dependencies between intentional acts and some of their antecedent and more basic conditions.

> Human intelligence and reasonableness function as the higher integration of the sensitive flow of percepts and images, emotions and feelings, attitudes and sentiments, words and deeds. It follows that as the cognitional and volitional appropriations of truth are solidary with each other so also they condition and are conditioned by adaptations of human sensibility.[365]

---

most subsequent research into executive functioning focuses on brain locales and neural activities. "The involvement of the prefrontal cortex in the ability to engage executive control constitutes one of the fundamental results of cognitive neuroscience. Current research focuses on the respective roles of frontal lobe structures such as anterior cingulate cortex (ACC), dorso-lateral prefrontal cortex (DLPFC), or orbito-frontal cortex (OFC) in this general process of control." Lionel Naccache et al. "Effortless Control: Executive Attention and Conscious Feeling of Mental Effort are Dissociable" in *Neuropsycholgia*, Vol. 43, No. 9 (2005), 1318.

363 "Attention and Cognitive Control" (1975), reprinted in *Cognitive Psychology: Key Readings*, A. Balota and Elizabeth J. Marsh (eds.) (New York: Psychology Press, 2004), 221-222.

364 Ibid. 205. Implicit here is a rudimentary critique of reductive analyses. One way of expressing it is to ask how deliberate mental acts might exercise some "control" over or integrate lower-level conditions.

365 *Insight*, 585.

First, what does it mean to say, "Human intelligence and reason-ableness" integrate the lower-order "sensitive flow of percepts and imag-es, emotions and feelings, attitudes and sentiments, words and deeds"? Presumably persons are "integrating" when they understand sights and sounds and when they recognize their moods and then support or resist them. But conscious ordering is only half the story. The integrating op-erations are themselves "conditioned by adaptations of human sensibili-ty." Negatively, for example, a student's illness interferes with taking an exam; foul moods disrupt a writing schedule; anger undercuts a resolve to mend a relationship. Positively, "adaptations of sensibility" promote more complex operations. For example, a love of dance helps the aspiring ballerina practice despite pain. The cultivated and discriminating eye of the painter sees variations in color and texture where the untrained eye sees none. The compassion of a skilled nurse allows patients to reveal fears they hide from family members lest they add to the latter's worries.

So how are sensibility and intelligence mutually conditioning? From a "top-down" perspective, actual developments in understand-ing through professional training can alter sensitivity and alertness to the contents of sensibility. For example, engineers and physicians were less frequently fooled than other test subjects in Kolers' famous experi-ments in apparent motion.[366] They witnessed the same scenes but made more careful inferences about what they were seeing. Similarly, trained therapists detect deceit in clients far more reliably than nonprofessionals talking with the same persons. Training in forensic science prepares in-vestigators to be more alert for relevant clues. On the other hand, from a "bottom-up" perspective, we suppose that persons develop in under-standing and improve deliberate acting by raising and answering ques-tions prompted by sensitive presentations and imaginative representa-tions. The bottom-up argument is cogent: we would have nothing to question without the lower-order contents of human sensibility, and, without questioning, intellectual and practical development would not occur. So training or intelligent operations presuppose data as the "material" for their own occurrence.

Do the preceding claims about sensibility and intelligence make the case for a mutual conditioning of intentional acts and biological and neurochemical events?[367] At most they provide a model of how such

366   See the review of Kolers' experiments in apparent motion in Nelson Goodman, *Ways of Worldmaking* (Indianapolis: Hackett, 1978), 71-89. The reference to the populations less frequently deceived occurs on page 92.

367   As an example of mutual conditioning, Chapter Two cited "process art" as recognizing that achieving the intention of the artist depended upon materials used, variable conditions at a

acts are conditioned by and, in turn, integrate some more basic materials, e.g. sensations and images. But what does this model suggest about nonconscious processes in the brain? When researchers are studying antecedent neurochemical conditions for intentional acts, they are studying conditions that make their own performance possible. That is, they are studying the unconscious conditions for their own conscious operations in doing research. As Posner and Synder hoped forty years ago, might neuroscientists and their fields benefit from shifting the focus of their inquiry to their own performance? What are the conditions for such performance? In exploring those conditions, are the researchers "ordering" those very conditions in themselves? A simple example may help. Suppose the phone rings while you are counseling a troubled client and you choose to ignore it and to continue the conversation. Your deliberate attending to the client and not to the phone affects neural events, suppressing some and allowing others to occur. In the "competition" among stimuli for attention, the "winner" owes its victory to what some authors called a "higher level template."[368] Yet how is any such victory possible?

Deliberate interventions in brain disorders through pharmacological means are evidence that intentional acts can alter neurobiological conditions. Experiments in bio-feedback produce evidence of test subjects deliberately altering patterns among neural activities. There are similar results associated with meditation techniques and hypnotism.[369] Further examples are plentiful. We have all experienced sustained attention, i.e. "the volitional maintenance of the current focus of attention. This may mean awaiting the change from red to green in traffic stoplights..." or simply waiting for water to boil.[370] But what does "volitional" control of conscious acts of attention mean? How can intentional acts effect nonconscious changes in brain activities? Descriptively we can all recount how, at some time or other, we deliberately shifted our attention away from disturbing sights or distracted ourselves from painful memories by staying busy. We were trying to control our emotional responses by controlling our attention.[371] In doing so, did our intentional acts have reper-

specific site, available technologies, sources of financing and the history of art.

368   Cohen et al. "A System-Level Perspective in Attention and Cognitive Control" in *Cognitive Neuroscience of Attention.*" Michael I. Posner (ed.) (New York: Guilford Press, 2004), 76.

369   "A number of human practices, including ingestion of drugs, meditation, and hypnotism, are known to alter attention." Michael I. Posner, "Progress in Attention Research" in ibid. 7.

370   Melinda Beane and Richard Marrocco, "Holinergic and Noradrenergic Inputs to the Posterior Parietal Cortex Modulate the Components of Exogenous Attention" in ibid. 318.

371   Such deliberate acts to "control" attention are evidence that attention is not monolithic but occurs in gradations. Damasio provides support for talking about various levels or gradations of attention by citing cases of epileptic automatisms. During seizures patients are awake but exhibit only a low-level attention to the activities they carry out. After the seizure

cussions on what neurobiological events were or were not occurring?[372]

If such examples are so commonplace, why is there any controversy about reductionist views? The fact is such views do appear in the
literature. For example:

> Given that a true understanding of the nature of cogni-
> tive function can only be derived from an understand-
> ing of its underlying mechanisms, an overarching theme
> of our research program has been to focus on the pro-
> cesses of attention in infancy....[373]

To interpret these remarks descriptively, the author envisions a one-
way street leading to an understanding of intentional acts.[374] But why
should "true understanding" only be possible through reducing cognitive functions to "underlying mechanisms"?[375] If one assumes that any
explanation must be reductive, this view of scientific understanding follows. However, the puzzles are if and how a complete explanation might
include evidence of cognitive functions altering their underlying conditions. Presumably a "true understanding" of the "nature" of something
will leave out nothing relevant, i.e., it will account for all the known
variables. References to the "nature" of something are initially anticipations of some unknown "x" much like that found in algebraic equa-
tions. To solve for it is to proceed from the known variables to unknown
variables and then on to an understanding of how relations among all of

---

they have no recollection of their actions during it. *The Feeling of What Happens* (New York:
Harcourt, Brace and Company, 1999), 96-99.

372   Cf. Seth D. Pollack and Stephanie Tolley-Schell, "Attention, Emotion, and the
Development of Psychopathology" in *Cognitive Neuroscience of Attention*, 359.

373   John Colombo, "Visual Attention in Infancy" in ibid. 329. What does "mechanism"
mean here? Is it a descriptive category hiding the absence of explanatory understanding?
Furthermore, will understanding attention in infancy supply reliable data for understanding
attention in trained diagnosticians? Of course, the basic question is what does "true
understanding" mean to this writer or to any reader?

374   While the preceding citation is evidence of a reductionist stance not uncommon in
contemporary sciences, an intermediate stance between it and other positions may be the
following: "'...no attempt is made to discard the notion that attentional selection is controlled
by an intelligent agent, but a serious attempt is made to relieve the burden on the agent by
placing a powerful mechanism at its disposal.'" C. Bundsen, "A Theory of Visual Attention"
in *Psychological Review*, Vol. 97 (1990), 523. Quoted in Gordon D. Logan, "Attention,
Automaticity, and Executive Control" in *Experimental Cognitive Psychology and Its Applications*.
Alice F. Healy (ed.) (Washington, D.C.: American Psychological Association, 2005). Does this
talk of "mechanisms" reveal a tendency to dodge the complexity of what "intelligent agent"
might mean?

375   The same assumption appears in metaphysics when many insist that "substance" must
mean something out there, just beneath the surface of a thing, somehow making it what it is as
a unity.

them reveal a correct solution. But are intentional acts of questioning, imagining, surmising, deliberating and deciding relevant variables in a more complete explanation of what neuroscientists investigate? They are if neurochemical events are ever dependent for their occurrence on such intentional acts.

How are we to understand mutual dependencies between bio-chemical conditions and intentional acts? Much of the literature in neuroscience reflects an interest in model building. References to an "interactive model, which assumes that pattern recognition is not simply controlled by the stimulus but is aided by pre-existing memory representations" is one way of portraying both bottom-up and top-down processes in acts of attention. How and why the interaction occurs is the neglected puzzle. Still, some features of the puzzle are well documented.

Feed-forward processes include genetic, neurochemical and organic processes in the brain that make possible intentional acts. The routine occurrence of the latter makes possible inquiries (e.g. the intelligent operations of neuroscientists) that seek to trace intentional acts back to biological, chemical and physical roots. The aim of the inquiries has been to move from descriptive studies of individual specimens (e.g. the test subjects of PET and fMRI) and static accounts of brain locales to explanations of the dynamic processes investigators assume are occurring. The other side of the puzzle is less frequently visited.

As already noted, folk psychology is not short of examples of top-down control. But research provides its own examples. Experimental programs in treating dyslexic students by means of computer instruction have demonstrated how such instructional techniques can modify brain functions and improve reading skills. This much suggests that feedback processes from intentional acts can modify underlying organic and biochemical conditions. Yet how are conditioned acts able to act back on their conditions? Posner provides a helpful clue in remarking: "...attention is the emergent property of the cognitive system that allows it to successfully process some sources of information to the exclusion of others, in the service of achieving some goals to the exclusion of others."[376] What might "emergent property" mean here?

The literature on emergence has been expanding in recent decades. In abbreviated form, the diverse views on emergence have been struggling to integrate two distinct types of processes. First, there are regularly occurring and continuous processes, e.g. the cycle of seasons and planetary motions. Second, there are processes that admit of irregularities

---

376 *Cognitive Neuroscience of Attention*, 71.

and discontinuities, e.g. weather patterns and survival rates of species. Integrating both types of processes requires an understanding of how systematic and non-systematic processes are related. So neuroscientists study how various neurochemical events routinely generate localized brain activities associated with facial or spatial recognition. As a result, we get systematic correlations among chemical, organic and conscious events. However, clinical psychology cites its individual cases of departures from the "norm" (e.g. Cotard's syndrome) and so presents the systematic view with irregularities. Subsequent research discovers both the ideal frequencies according to which correlations are expected to show up and the rates of departure from them in large populations.

What has this to do with "emergence"? One linkage between the two types of processes and emergence occurs in thinking about the evolutionary development of species. Initially genetic and chemical conditions are open to an indefinite number of organic possibilities, i.e. any number of biological integrations could emerge from different possible combinations of those prior conditions. But in any range of possible integrations, some will be more probable than others because of existing resources or schemes of recurrence in actual environments, and so some organic combinations, given enough time and enough numbers, will actually emerge. To emerge is one thing, to survive is another. In a given environment an emergent organism will interact with routinely available resources (those forming the initial conditions or schemes of recurrence for its appearance) and with novel conditions occurring after its emergence. Survival then becomes a question of whether the systematic operations of the organism and the systematic relations among it and its initial conditions are sufficiently flexible to adjust to non-systematic variations occurring in schemes of recurrence within and outside of the organism. So we find a range of animals flourishing in a given environment only to diminish in number and variety when physical and chemical resources change or when a new predator appears. Some animal types will exhibit greater flexibility in their "routines" and so adapt to changed conditions, i.e. to non-systematic variations.

How can we comprehend together both systematic processes and the flexible responses of organisms to non-systematic variations? The notion of schemes of recurrence that already appeared in earlier chapters provides some help.[377] First, organisms interact routinely with available resources to meet their demands for nutrition, procreation and survival.

---

377   As in those previous discussions, these authors' comments on conditioned series of schemes of recurrence are indebted to Longeran, *Insight*, 140-148.

Thus, the systematic processes of nitrogen and seasonal cycles supply general conditions for an herbivore's cycles of foraging, mating and hibernation. Departures from regularly occurring conditions tend to disrupt cycles, so the schemes of recurrence through which a species exists need to be a flexible range of possibilities if a species is to survive.

To the notion of flexible ranges of schemes of recurrence (incorporating both routine cycles and adjustments to variations in initial conditions), we need to add an account of how more complex schemes emerge from simpler ones. Some of the literature in cognitive psychology simply assumes this routinely happens. Thus, we find references to "volitional control" over acts of attention. Such comments assume: (1) in evolutionary history cognitive schemes have emerged from organic schemes; and (2) the former depend on but also can modify, to some degree, the latter. Now, in regard to both assumptions, scientific inquiries are in their infancy, i.e. explanatory accounts remain remote possibilities. The barely recognized question is how development from one ordered series of schemes to a new series, not reducible to the former, can occur. For instance, cognitive operations form their own flexible schemes in raising and answering questions of various types. But how do such routinely occurring intentional schemes emerge from organic schemes and, through further development (e.g. through stages of infancy, adolescence and maturation), exercise increasing control over those organic schemes?[378]

These questions, anticipated by Posner and Synder in 1975, are worth formulating even if answers remain elusive. As anticipations of possible answers, the questions can serve a heuristic function. That is, without specifying answers, they direct inquiry along certain lines. For example, questions about systematic or ordered processes anticipate that any answers will (ideally) take the form of invariant correlations among classes of events. Questions about non-systematic processes anticipate answers in terms of probabilities or ideal frequencies in the relations among such classes of events. The heuristic notion of schemes of recurrence integrates both of the preceding types of processes. How do systems adjust to novel conditions? The question of emergence anticipates answers in terms of developmental stages, i.e. when new systematic processes emerge from prior ones. For example, how does embryonic development in humans occur and give way eventually to the stages studied by child psychologists and the less studied stages of adult self-control?

---

378   Examples of control range from suppressing yawns in public to deliberately enduring hunger during Ramadan.

How emergence and development occur in plants and animals continues to be the focus of intense inquiry. The same is not yet true in regard to cognitive schemes and their organic and neurochemical conditions. As previously noted, the focus has largely been on the underlying conditions for such cognitive schemes but not on the latter's emergence from and capacity to alter those antecedent conditions. From an evolutionary perspective, most will agree that radical alterations in initial conditions threaten existing organisms with extinction, but, to the degree that those organisms exist in and through flexible schemes, a range of alterations in underlying conditions may be not only survivable but a step toward novel developments. However, is there any explanation of how variations in initial conditions make possible the emergence of novel, intelligent things? How might this happen? An appeal to probability is common: what is possible, given enough time and enough numbers, becomes probable and, in the long run, becomes an almost guaranteed development. So in a very old universe, we should expect to find complex molecules, plant species, animal species, patterns of psychological development and structured intentional acts that deliberately modify their initial conditions.

Asserting the preceding is not the same as explaining how these processes of emergence and mutual conditioning occur. Why should explaining them be so remote from current inquiries? One author identifies the "foundational problem" behind this difficult challenge.

> On the one hand, there is the tendency to consider conscious activities as unconscious and to reduce them to lower-level conjugate forms; the other tendency is to consider conscious activities without any reference to the lower levels which set the conditions for the emergence and maintenance of these higher conscious schemes. Behind these two tendencies is the foundational problem of integrating the higher human sciences with the lower natural sciences.[379]

This "foundational problem" sets a cultural task far beyond the limits of a single chapter or even a single book. The task of integrating the

---

379   Joseph Flanagan. *Quest for Self-Knowledge* (Toronto: University of Toronto Press, 1997), 171.

intentional operations producing commonsensical, artistic, religious, scientific and scholarly meanings with the processes studied in neuroscience and biochemistry is a project spanning generations of researchers, a project more anticipated than actually underway. Still, what can be done now? What Part II offers is a sketch of different alternatives to a reductive viewpoint and then an ordering of them as an exercise in FS3. This section has outlined a first alternative relying on an inchoate theory of emergence. What follows next is a somewhat different stance taken by Daniel Dennett.

B. Dennett's View

One commentator on Dennett's work has identified his fundamental purpose:

> Dennett's project…is a highly original and ingenious
> attempt to show…how it can be the case both (1) that
> human beings are conscious, thinking, free, responsible
> agents, and (2) that human beings are purely natural
> products of evolution, composed of simple biochemical
> components, arranged in complex, self-maintaining
> configurations.[380]

At first his purpose of reconciling these two viewpoints seems impossible to achieve. Common-sense views of free agents as the "causes" of their deliberate actions run counter to conventional scientific accounts of how more basic neurochemical processes in the brain or nervous system cause human behavior.[381] But at least the puzzle is out in the open. For example, how can sounds emitted by human speakers and received by their audiences have both biochemical antecedents and be instrumental acts of meaning, i.e. words deliberately spoken and understood? The antecedents are non-conscious and intelligible processes, but the latter

---

380   Tadeusz Zawidzki. *Dennett* (Oxford: Oneworld Publications, 2007), 2. Dennett's attempt to unify these two perspectives on human operations and origins continues a theme in modern philosophy. Spinoza, Kant, Hegel and Schelling made earlier attempts.

381   Consider how remote the following view of thinking is from common sense. "When we are thinking, our 'orienting networks' develop such that new neural pathways are forming in our right parietal and frontal hemispheres; and, when we are actually attending to our intentional acts, various neurochemical events (e.g. dopamine releases) are occurring in our lateral prefrontal regions, the anterior cingulated cortex and basal ganglia. How strange is it to think about thinking in this way, but can we be serious about understanding inquiry if we neglect such strangeness?" *The New Comparative Interpretation: A Primer*, 45.

are intelligent acts communicating and interpreting meanings. The former are detectable as neural activities, but examining nervous systems does not detect intelligent acts of meaning.[382]

Historically a project of reconciliation has had competitors. Galileo's distinction between primary and secondary qualities was one way of handling the apparent opposition between conscious experiences of colors, images, variable sensations and the findings of the sciences of his day. Secondary qualities belong to a world of appearances while primary qualities "get at" the objective properties of real things. Cartesian dualism preserved the common-sense view of a mental world of intentional acts by strictly separating it from a world of measurable objects and events. Of course, another option, a reductive one, is to eliminate an "inner world" entirely by declaring that psychological states and intentional acts are epiphenomenal and will eventually be "explained away" by even more scientific inquiry.

Dennett's project makes use of Galileo's distinction and rejects Cartesian dualism, but he stops short of banishing common-sense talk of consciousness to a realm of illusion. How does he go about providing a new and reconciling viewpoint? He begins by endorsing a qualified form of reductive analysis.[383] In *Darwin's Dangerous Idea*, he distinguishes between two types of reductive analyses regarding conscious states and intentional acts. The good or acceptable type attempts to unite or to explain everything in "one big overarching theory." Consciousness, thus, must be linked with organic processes and neural mechanisms and not left as an isolated phenomenon inaccessible to science. The unacceptable or "greedy" type of reductive analysis asserts that higher-level sciences need to be explained using the categories of more basic sciences, e.g. physics.[384] Dennett's most developed position seems to be less an explanation of how more complex patterns of operations are dependent on less complex ones and more a statement of what any explanation must

---

382   Failures to communicate are evidence of the differences here. The meanings speakers intend to communicate may be quite different from what an audience interprets the sounds to mean. Different members of an audience may interpret the same emitted sounds quite differently, so what is one set of neural activities in the speaker can give rise to multiple, and even incompatible, meanings in an audience.

383   Dennett's explicit claims about reductionism have ranged from early denials that his work is reductionist to statements in later popular works that seem to be an affirmation of reductive analysis. Cf. Zawidzki (157) for the relevant loci.

384   *Darwin's Dangerous Idea* (New York: Simon and Schuster, 1995), 81-82. Dennett diagnoses the problem with "greedy" reductionism: "[I]n their zeal to explain too much too fast, scientists and philosophers often underestimate the complexities, trying to skip whole layers or levels of theory in their rush to fasten everything securely and neatly to the foundation. That is the sin of greedy reductionism...." (82)

avoid. It must not identify the more complex with the less complex and must not think that the latter wholly explain the former. In other words, conscious phenomena are dependent on neurobiological antecedents without being identical with them,[385] and understanding those antecedents will go only so far in explaining the more complex operations upon which they are dependent.

An analogy for understanding these relations of relative dependence and relative independence is found in biological evolution. Different species of plants and animals have biochemical preconditions that must be met if they are to survive; however, they are not identical with those preconditions. The photosynthesis occurring in a plant may be studied as a chemical process, but the plant as a living thing is not explained simply by reference to the chemicals it exploits in its development. Similarly herbivores remain dependent on the ingestion and chemical transformation of plants; yet they are not explained simply by reference to their plant diets and the chemical exchanges occurring in digestion. Furthermore, animal psychology (e.g. reflex responses of fight, flight and freeze) is dependent on the biological state of the specimen. Too little food or too many injuries and the animal is unable to escape the digestive tract of the predator. All the same, the alertness of the animal to danger, its "vigilance" network, is a rudimentary form of consciousness that is dependent on but relatively independent of fluctuations in an organism's health.[386]

Having such a vigilance network presumably favors survival, and a further advantage accrues to animals routinely alert and able to adapt to changes in their environments. The regularities that obtained in the past may vanish and new ones appear. Species that are alert and adaptive to the new conditions are ones able to respond not only with routine patterns of behavior but also with novel solutions. The qualitative "leap" here is that surviving specimens exhibit a flexibility in adjusting to new conditions, i.e. they can learn both to recognize changes and to find effective means for responding to them. Dennett writes of how this flexibility appeared in a very limited but still intelligent way in pre-human species:

> Consider what the behavior of our hypothetical primate
> ancestor looked like:...an animal capable of learning

---

385   Recall the difference above between emitting sound waves and making sense of them. Dennett generalizes about the difference: "...we have access – conscious access – to the results of mental processes, but not to the processes themselves." *Brainstorms* (Cambridge: MIT Press, 1978), 165.
386   Dennett. *Consciousness Explained* (Boston: Little, Brown and Co., 1991), 180.

new tricks, and almost continually vigilant and sensitive to novelty, but with a 'short attention span' and a tendency to have attention 'captured' by distracting environmental features.[387]

But "learning new tricks" means not having to wait upon shifts in rates of reproduction and genetic mutations for new ways of responding to the challenges an environment presents. Instead of taking generations to appear, novel adaptations can emerge within the life span of individual specimens. Two forms of natural selection, thus, are at work when animals achieve even a minimal consciousness that routinely allows them to monitor their environment and to learn new ways of interacting with it.

For humans there is a third medium of evolution. While socially acquired routines are found in other species, humans experience both mimicry and deliberately designed ways of efficiently transmitting cultural information across generations.[388] Educational institutions and popular media convey new and old tricks that individuals would never discover on their own. Innovations are thus preserved and added to at an accelerating rate, and so improvements in human capacities to anticipate and to plan further changes appear with greater frequency.[389]

Following Dawkins, Dennett calls the carriers of cultural innovations "memes." The play on words with "genes" is deliberate; as biological reproduction transmits the latter, so cultural practices transmit the former.[390] In both cases survival and reproduction are dependent on individual organisms surviving and replicating themselves. Of course, the modes of transmission are far more complex with memes since they can be communicated in ways that require no proximity in time or place between senders and recipients. Language plays the key role in sharing "at a distance" information about environmental challenges and effective responses. In addition, mutations in cultural ideas and practices can occur

---

387   Ibid. 189.
388   "Cultural evolution, and the transmission of its products, is the second new medium of evolution, and it depends on phenotypic plasticity in much the same way phenotypic plasticity depends on genetic variation. We human beings have used our plasticity not just to learn, but to learn how to learn better, and then we've learned better how to learn better how to learn better, and so forth. We have also learned how to make the fruits of this learning available to novices." Ibid. 193.
389   *Darwin's Dangerous Idea*, 381.
390   The etymology of "meme" may also recall the Greek *mimesis*. Culture supposedly reproduces itself through mimicry and mutation. However, we suspect that shifting from DNA to culture in discussing development can leave intact the assumption that both types of growth are explicable in terms of an underlying material manifold, to the exclusion of "top-down" integrations.

with greater frequency and spread quite rapidly because of language.

How do these three modes of evolution contribute to Dennett's understanding of the emergence of conscious acts and states? Since he is committed to a philosophical naturalism, any explanation of intelligence must cite non-intelligent antecedents as its origin. Theistic options and Cartesian dualism are not options for him. But how might intelligence emerge from something non-intelligent? A plausible response employs an analogy between heterarchies organizing the brain and evolutionary "leaps." Complex capacities may depend on the cooperation of multiple brain locales, their internal functions and lateral communications, all without any one of them being a "central switchboard." As long as each cooperating component does its work and passes along the result, the cumulative effect may be the emergence of a more complex order or system that is not identical to any single component.[391] Might a similar cumulative effect yield more complex orders of being?

No one doubts that conscious intentional systems have appeared relatively late in evolutionary history. This fact evokes questions that point ahead to challenging tasks: (1) to account for the emergence of intentional systems in evolutionary history and (2) to explain how psychological states and intentional acts are related to their biochemical antecedents. While Dennett offers some speculative comments about the evolution of consciousness and so contributes to the first task, his primary interest has been to reconcile competing accounts of conscious states, intentional acts and biochemical processes. In pursuit of that goal he talks (1) of complex physical systems, not all of which are of the same type, and (2) of three different "stances" one can adopt in explaining them.[392]

The first he calls the physical stance. Imagine watching someone pushing coins across a counter to a sales clerk. The observable objects in motion could be explained in terms of their physical properties and the relevant laws of physics governing their motions. But one could also go on understand the same scene in terms of what he calls the <u>design stance</u>. Then the observed objects are understood as part of a web of purposeful motions and of objects designed to achieve various purposes. For example, the counter is an artificial surface belonging to the furnishings used to run a business, and the coins are instruments facilitating

---

391 A common analogy here is the view of a market economy as an ongoing flow of goods and services which no one designs and over which no one has control. The analogy is subject to a standard objection cited by Dennett: "The whole is a very clever assemblage of coordinated *parts* that at its best acts with a unity not unlike the unity of a single person, but still, it has no soul of its own, even if some of its parts do." Ibid. 152. The next chapter will revisit and criticize the use of the part-whole metaphor in talking about environments.

392 Dennett introduces the three stances in *Brainstorms*, 3-5.

economic exchanges.

Dennett's third way of understanding physical systems is the intentional stance.[393] It differs from the design stance insofar as one approaches the system assuming that not only is it designed to achieve purposes, it will pursue them in the most rational way. "Rational" here seems to mean choosing efficient means to desired ends, i.e. Max Weber's "instrumental rationality." Once one assumes this about a system, one can predict its behavior in terms of what one knows about its purposes and the resources available for achieving them. Human beings and animals are appropriate candidates for this third stance. We observe cats hunting mice and shoppers hunting bargains and can attribute to them deliberate acts in pursuit of goals. The observed behaviors could be described from the physical stance or from the design stance, but the intentional stance does a better job in making sense of them. As in the example of pushing coins across a counter, the conventional gestures of customer and sales clerk make more sense if we attribute shared beliefs and intentional acts to both of them, e.g. they have desires and know what efficient steps they need to take to satisfy them.

Dennett's point appears to be that no one of these descriptions is a complete explanation of all the others. Rather, the three are potentially complementary and so reconcile both some of the terms of folk psychology and some of the demands for scientific accounts of human behavior.[394] Still, those doing research in the cognitive and neurosciences will need to discover the empirical details of how a complex physical system is best explained by shifting among all three stances. It is possible to begin by describing human behavior from the intentional stance and so attribute psychological categories to it. But then one could adopt the design stance and suggest how components of the system operated both separately to achieve micro-purposes and cooperatively to achieve a macro-purpose that was "rational" in the limited sense of practical intelligence. Finally, one could adopt the physical stance and describe each component as operating according to physical laws such that neural processes receive signals and send them on to other brain locales. While

---

393   "I wish to examine the concept of a system whose behavior can be – at least sometimes – explained and predicted by relying on ascriptions to the system of beliefs and desires (and hopes, fears, intentions, hunches...). I will call such systems intentional systems...." Ibid. 3.

394   One commentator endorses this reading of Dennett's methodology as beginning with cognitive psychology and moving "down" to physical processes. "First, we determine, from what Dennett calls the intentional stance, the intelligent competence that we want to explain. Then, we hypothesize more limited capacities that cooperate to approximate the competence we want to explain. Finally, we investigate how these more limited capacities might be physically implemented in biological brains." Zawidzki, 43.

such a view affirms cognitive psychology is not a field of illusions and so avoids a reductionist stance, it remains largely within the first horizon of description.[395]

Why conclude this? Talk of "stances" can easily give way to talk of "conceptual frameworks." Just as there is no single best description of an object under all circumstances so there is no privileged conceptual framework suitable for every line of inquiry. Stances, descriptions and conceptual frameworks vary with purpose. Thus, Dennett's alternative to the greedy type of reductive analysis is an acceptance of legitimate multiplicity in how one decides to think and to talk about objects of experience. But why is this multiplicity legitimate? What is the ontological status of any of these objects? What is it about any object that prevents it from being reducible to a single stance? These questions do not seem to receive more than matter-of-fact answers, i.e. we can make more sense of some objects of experience by employing more than a single stance.

C. Gazzaniga's View

What alternative to a reductive analysis does Michael Gazzaniga provide? Some clues are in his response to the question about the emergence of psychological acts and states from organic antecedents. He holds that the brain has a modular organization comprised of multiple subsystems that make conscious experience possible. That is, there is no central switchboard in charge of all the subsystems; instead, human "consciousness is distributed everywhere across the brain."[396] He favors talking of the brain as a "complex system...composed of many different systems that interact and produce emergent properties that are greater than the sum of their parts and cannot be reduced to the properties of the constituent parts."[397] An analogy he employs is of a traffic pattern composed of individual vehicles that, in turn, are composed of multiple parts interacting with one another, as well as with weather conditions, traffic laws, various drivers etc. The traffic pattern emerges from such interactions, but analyzing the properties of cars, drivers and weather conditions will not allow you to predict the particular traffic flow.

---

395   Lonergan concluded that reductionism was likely if one remained in that horizon and held to the first type of realism. Cf. *Insight*, 282-283.
396   Ibid. 64.
397   Ibid. 71. A similar argument appeared in regard to institutions or a "good of order" as more than an aggregate of parts.

Whatever the merits of the analogy, Gazzaniga endorses a view of consciousness and intentional acts as emergent from a large number of distinct systems. When persons are conscious of something it is because some of those systems have won the "competition" in pushing the results of their processing to the surface. What justifies talk of competition among systems? In writing of "local consciousness systems...enabling consciousness," Gazzaniga presumably is not committed to asserting that each system is conscious; rather, each is processing different "inputs" that may or may not contribute to what eventually enters a person's conscious operations. Only some sensory inputs "come to the surface," and it seems plausible to posit a selection process that might be described as a competition for attention. This descriptive language is not beyond criticism. However, he modifies his terminology when he discusses the question about the emergence of psychological states and intentional acts from neurobiological antecedents.

> Emergence is when micro-level complex systems that are
> far from equilibrium (thus allowing for the amplification
> of random events) self-organize (creative, self-generated,
> adaptability-seeking behavior) into new structures, with
> new properties that previously did not exist, to form a
> new level of organization on the macro level.[398]

He distinguishes two schools of thought about emergence. The "weak" viewpoint holds that, through their interactions, more basic systems give rise to new properties belonging to more complex systems that are reducible to, are explainable in terms of, the different components of those more elementary and antecedent systems. In other words, psychological states can be wholly explained in terms of antecedent neurobiological processes. In contrast, the "strong" viewpoint denies such reducibility and holds that the laws governing more basic processes do not explain the operations of more complex systems or allow predictions about what systems will emerge.[399] According to the strong view, psychological states

---

398   Ibid. 124. Gazzaniga cites R.W. Byrne and A. Whitten as sources of this view of emergence in their *Machiavellian Intelligence* (Oxford: Clarendon Press, 1988).
399   Gazzaniga adheres to the strong viewpoint, and one argument he cites in its defense draws upon the history of physics. "Although some neuroscientists think we may prove that specific neuronal firing patterns will produce specific thoughts and that they are predetermined, none has a clue about what the deterministic rules would be for a nervous system in action. I think that we are facing the same conundrum that physicists dealt with when they assumed Newton's laws were universal. The laws are not universal to all levels of organization; it depends which level of organization you are describing, and new rules apply when higher levels emerge. Quantum mechanics are the rules for atoms, Newton's laws are

and intentional acts emerge from more elementary systems but are really distinct from those antecedents.

Still, to affirm emergence is not to explain more complex orders or to give a detailed account of their genesis. Perhaps the adjective "emergent" functions as a linguistic warning sign: "Don't expect the prior laws and explanations to work here." Going beyond this negative conclusion about emergence, Gazzaniga offers a positive insight borrowed from Robert Laughlin: "'What we are seeing is a transformation of worldview in which the objective of understanding nature by breaking it down into ever smaller parts is supplanted by the objective of understanding how nature organizes itself.'"[400] A shift occurs, then, in how one searches for answers. Instead of focusing on the elementary building blocks of complex phenomena, the new inquiry is into how, from the "far from equilibrium" or disorganized conditions occurring in simpler organizations, more complex organizations can arise.[401] For example, a new line of inquiry might investigate how thinking that is dependent on patterns among neuronal firings manifests a new type of organization, one exploiting those firings without standing in any one-to-one correspondence with them.[402]

Gazzaniga affirms Laughlin's shift in focus and notes the pressing need for a new language to describe interactions between physical and mental systems. In the last sentence of his Gifford Lectures from 2009, he remarks: "Understanding how to develop a vocabulary for those layered interactions, for me, constitutes the scientific problem of this century."[403] But we do not have that new language, and in its stead, the "terms of art" continue to be a loose mix of categories including eighteenth-century

the rules for objects, and one couldn't completely predict the other." *Who's in Charge?* 130.

400   Robert Laughlin. *A Different Universe: Reinventing Physics from the Bottom Down* (New York: Basic Books, 2006), quoted in ibid. 135. This shifting of inquiry from a "building block" or "ingredients" focus to one of emergence may escape the misstep of searching, with the Pre-Socratics, for the basic elements of all realities. These authors believe this to be a key breakthrough in neuroscience.

401   A promising analogy here is to think of how questions lead to further intentional operations that synthesize "disorganized" materials into more complex unities ranging from descriptive generalizations to theories of chemistry, biology, psychology and history.

402   Gazzaniga cites two cases of how one outcome may be reachable in an indefinite number of ways (i.e. "multiple realizability"). The hypothesis is that a more elementary system sets a range of possible combinations that may occur as a more complex system; however, which ones actually occur is not predictable from the laws applicable to the first system. He cites in support the work of Eve Marder on the nervous system of the spiny lobster and John Doyle's example of how, from nine letters in English, 362,880 sequences of just those nine letters are possible. Which of those many possibilities become actual words in the language cannot be predicted by simply knowing all those possible combinations. Ibid. 130-132.

403   Ibid. 220.

mechanistic analogies, sports metaphors about competition and attributions of psychological acts to nonconscious processes.[404] So we need a new and more complex language flexible enough to track the interdependent relations between conscious and unconscious variables.

D. The Question of Language

How is anyone to meet the challenge Gazzaniga identifies? The mixing of categories from psychology, biology and physics presents one obstacle. The historical fragmenting of fields of inquiry into subspecialties continues to generate such mixing of terminologies.[405] Dennett's recognition of multiple legitimate stances in talking about the same series of events is one way of responding to this mix of discourses. Complex realities are approachable from more than one line of inquiry, and a range of disciplines may contribute partial insights into those realities. However, while this approach evades "greedy" reductionism, it does not explain how neurochemical variables and psychological states and events are interdependent, nor does it supply a vocabulary for expressing those relations of mutual dependency.

Does the language of schemes of recurrence offer a way forward? Any proof of its worth will lie in the future, assuming those doing neuroscience attempt its use. Why should anyone make the attempt? Lonergan's distinction between bodies and things offers one benefit in thinking of variables as unities explainable only in terms of relations. Left behind are imaginable bodies "out there" and problems of accounting for invisible relations among them.[406] The hard questions about types of relations become muddled when inquirers employ the distinction between inter-

---

404   An example of the last linguistic deficit occurs in Gazzaniga's Gifford Lectures, an admittedly non-technical presentation in front of a diverse audience. "This is something that neuroscientists don't tend to think about much, but the brain is a decision-making device. It gathers information from all sorts of sources to make decisions from moment to moment. Information is gathered, computed, a decision is made, and then you get the sensation of conscious experience." Ibid. 127.

405   This mixing of terms includes those belonging to ordinary language. While neuroscientists legitimately employ such terms after assigning them technical meanings, two problems usually follow. First, the stipulated meanings may not be observed even by the same author. Second, when those technically defined terms are repeated in reports of scientific research in the popular media, audiences will "hear" their non-technical meanings. Ambiguity seems inescapable unless new terms are invented, but this tactic generates its own set of problems.

406   The shift to the second horizon is not easily made here. Consider how easy it is to continue talking about organs "in" bodies, organisms "in" ecosystems and objects "in" their environments.

nal relations (i.e. those imagined as "within" the thing) and external relations (i.e. those obtaining among distinct things). The language of schemes of recurrence is a way past this misleading distinction. Some schemes belong to an organism (e.g. the digestive system of an herbivore), but their functioning depends on other schemes, e.g. the physiological processes enabling the herbivore to move, the nitrogen cycle supporting plant growth that provides nutrients to the animal's digestive system that returns nutrients to the soil sustaining future plant growth and so on. This way of talking appears to respect the mutual conditioning and distinctions among types of variables.

What is promising about such talk when it comes to neural impulses and psychological states and intentional acts? For decades technologies have allowed the detection of how psychological states (e.g. fear and anger) and intentional acts (e.g. paying attention and deciding) are associated with neural activities occurring "at" certain brain locales. They have, thus, identified distinct types of variables as possible terms in correlations. If strict reductionism is an obsolete issue, the pressing question is how to understand the relations among these correlates. Talk of flexible ranges of schemes of recurrence is compatible with an understanding of such variables as mutually conditioning.

Descriptive examples offer a starting point without doing the hard work of explaining mutual conditioning. For example, environmental sciences have produced studies of how systemic exposure of urban populations to toxins have affected brain development and subsequent educational performance in children. Recurrence schemes in learning depend obviously on brain development, but schemes in a hybrid environment may impair the latter because of past intentional schemes (e.g. policy decisions) to locate industries in certain locales, thereby increasing the exposure of young brains to avoidable risks. However, not all those exposed suffer the same ill effects. Differences in how persons respond to exposure offer evidence of the flexibility of the schemes occurring in brain development. Policy initiatives to reduce exposure (e.g. to lead in paint and in fuels) offer evidence of flexibility in intentional schemes. Recent cases of post-trauma brains shifting functions to undamaged locales and permitting "lost" capacities to re-emerge offer evidence of organic flexibility and neural plasticity.

In short, all three terms in the general correlation of intentional, neural and organic variables manifest flexibility in responding to threats. Still, shifting such descriptive materials into the second horizon is a task foreseen but not yet accomplished. Carrying it out is not among the functions of comparative interpretation. What FS4 tries to achieve is to evade obsolete impasses and to bring forward what seems most promising from what has already been accomplished. Doing so is primarily achieved today by comparing different stances to UV. Without repeating these authors' commitments to positions on the meanings of reality, knowing and objectivity, this chapter can move toward some assessments of the three alternatives to strict reductionism.

E. Two Sequences

Before moving on to Part III, we need to offer two sequential orderings of the earlier alternatives to a reductionist view. Such sequences are what practitioners of FS3 pass on to those doing FS4. The following orderings rank alternatives to what Dennett called "greedy" reductionism and what Gazzaniga labeled the "weak" form of reductionism. Both authors repudiated the stance that more complex systems were reducible to or explainable in terms of the components of antecedent and less complex systems. To add to their judgments, might this type of reductionism represent an obsolete view? Why entertain this possibility of moving beyond the terms of an old debate?

The practice of FS4 will eventually lead to the formation of an acquis, a series of settled questions, regarding previously disputed matters. Just as views of alchemists and astrologers no longer are subjects of debate among scientists, so the practice of FS4 will someday dismiss as outdated views that scholars have long disputed in their different fields. As a small beginning, uses of comparative interpretation in previous books in this series have assembled reasons for relegating a strict reductionist view to the status of an obsolete issue. The basic reason, drawn from GEM, has appeared several times: insights depend upon but are not identical with or reducible to images. More detailed reasons also appeared. For example, the earlier analysis of the problem of induction concluded that any intellectual apprehension of what made a thing what it is did not require a thorough enumerating of instances, i.e. the empirical surveys and sensitive apprehensions identified with a "swan psychology" of human knowing. Explanatory accounts of types of things are not achieved by such surveys of particular instances. Insisting, along with Hume, that all empirical generalizations be reducible to and justified by an adequate number of observed particulars reflects an oversight of the type of insight found in the second type of knowing.[407]

407   Further contributions in these texts to an emerging acquis have included a denial of the primacy of argumentation and conceptual analysis in philosophy, a rejection of a strictly social

In addition, a strict type of reductionism reflects a deterministic view that ignores non-systematic relations and random deviations from established patterns. The basic oversight of such a view is the conditionality of classical laws. While the functioning of organisms and their ecosystems may be relatively stable and operate according to classical laws, they do so only because initial conditions remain stable. Changes in those conditions can threaten extinction but can also allow for the emergence of more complex forms of both. Either outcome is a matter of probability.[408]

A further reason for abandoning debates about strict reductionism is to notice how inquiries in the second horizon generate a type of knowing that, while dependent on initial descriptive materials, exceeds and is not reducible to that starting point.[409] Such, at least, seems to follow from taking a position on the two kinds of knowing and the two kinds of realism. Of course, UV is not universally acknowledged, and the displacements it requires do not occur of necessity. In their absence outmoded debates may continue and their participants may think they are addressing serious issues. However, the claims of the new comparative interpretation are blunt: (1) the remote criterion is a certain type of developing subject; (2) in the absence of needed displacements, subjects can be operating hundreds of years out of date and needlessly sustaining debates that should have ended long ago.

So, if defenses of a strict form of reductionism do not merit attention, what are alternatives to it and how might practitioners of FS3 order them in developmental sequences? First, this section identified three alternatives: an emergentist view (associated with the work of Lonergan and his language of schemes of recurrence), Dennett's strategy of employing multiple stances, and Gazzaniga's endorsement of a shift in questioning from asking what are the basic building blocks of nature to asking how nature organizes itself.

Suppose a first sequence privileges Dennett's philosophical naturalism as well as his qualified or "good" form of reductionism. If the issue is explaining how psychological states and intentional acts are related to biochemical antecedents, the philosophical naturalist will hold that any

---

genealogy of the principle of double effect and two critiques of relying on what-questions to work out the meanings of consciousness and being.

408   Examples are not in short supply in human living and its deliberate manipulation of organisms and ecosystems. Fertilizers modify agricultural output and aquatic ecosystems, breeding modifies dog species, chemical additives in food modify, for good and ill, human health.

409   The counter-argument sometimes appears in the form of a claim that anything the contemporary physicist understands should be translatable into the language of common sense.

explanation of the former must trace them back to the latter. However, the restricted version of reductive analysis (1) does not identify the former and the latter and (2) does not assert that the latter will wholly explain the former. What is potentially attractive about both restrictions?

Dennett's ambitions are to avoid both Cartesian dualism (generally put, the mind-body problem) and any theistic grounding of the special status of human intelligence (e.g. defending human capacities to know things-in-themselves in terms of Christian Platonism). At the same time, Dennett's concern is to avoid the metaphysical quagmire of debates about knowledge of things themselves. Recall how he pursued these ambitions and addressed this concern. First, he acknowledged competing ways of talking about psychological states and intentional acts. To grant legitimacy to these diverse views and to avoid eliminating all but one, he advanced his three different stances toward different types of physical systems. In insisting that all were ways of talking about physical systems, he was fulfilling both ambitions, i.e. there was no need to posit separate spiritual substances (whether human or divine) apart from physical systems. Furthermore, to affirm the legitimacy of these three ways of talking is to skirt the metaphysical quagmire. Precedents for this maneuver include talk of language games and conceptual frameworks.

A practitioner of FS3, who shares these ambitions and this concern (and many contemporary philosophers do), may find Dennett's view the most developed of the three alternatives. Since the emergentist view associated with Lonergan's work is more explicit than Gazzaniga's view about the ontological status of things known *priora quoad se*, this same practitioner might keep the former at arms length and prefer the latter for second place in the first ordering.

Suppose a second historian affirms that operations in the second horizon sometimes yield a limited knowledge of what makes things what they are. To this historian Dennett's concern to avoid metaphysical debates will seem less pressing. Similarly, minimal insight into the two types of knowing and the two types of realism will reduce interest in debates about language games and conceptual frameworks since they usually limit themselves to descriptive understanding and its variable formulations. How might the second specialist handle Dennett's ambitions to avoid Cartesian dualism and theistic assumptions?

In regard to the first ambition, the historian could use a notion of emergent probability to account for the appearance of complex organizations in evolutionary history. Plant sensitivity seems a rudimentary form of the alert systems of animals, and the latter seem simpler forms of human capacities to fantasize, anticipate and plan. There is no need to posit a radical discontinuity among these functions. In keeping with Dennett's "acceptable" type of reductionism, the functions are not identical, and the more complex are not reducible to the less complex. Still, the second historian may notice that Dennett does not suggest how the former functions emerge from the latter, but this hypothetical specialist may find a plausible answer in talk of movement from empirical possibility to probability and on to actuality. In other words, given enough time and large enough numbers, even the remotely probable occurrence becomes actual. Thus, in a very old and very large universe, it is not strange that intelligent beings should appear. This "natural" explanation does not make an explicit appeal to a theistic grounding of any type of beings. It does not require a special creation of "spiritual substances;" indeed, it need not speak of any origin of the universe. The latter may be without a beginning, and the former may be emergent properties of such an enduring universe.[410]

With Dennett's concern deflated and his two ambitions achievable by a notion of emergent probability, the second specialist may reverse the first historian's ordering of the three alternatives. Instead of Dennett's view being the most developed of the three, the emergentist view indebted to the work of Lonergan may occupy that rank while Gazzaniga's less specific view of emergence may come next in the ordering with Dennett's representing the least developed stance.

III. Doing FS4

The title of this chapter will have seemed strange. Ordinarily we read that scientists discovered neurons and not that neurons somehow discovered themselves. So why this unusual wording? Comparative interpretation includes GEM as one of its elements, and readers of this

---

410   Some readers may recall Aquinas' stance. While Aristotle could hold that the universe was without a beginning, Christian revelation included a creation narrative, and so Aquinas affirmed such a beginning. When one shifts from the first horizon to the second, talk of creation *ex nihilo* can dispense with analogies to human making and a descriptive understanding of efficient causality. Leibniz' question can play a role in the shift: Why is there something and not nothing? The demand for a sufficient reason for the existence of anything is not a demand for something imaginable or for anything analogous to human making. Section three of Chapter Four in *Cracking the Case* presented some insights from Classical Greek Philosophy relevant to this issue.

book series may suspect that element has something to do with the choice of title. For the moment let's imagine the standard textbook account of how neuroscientists came to talk about neurons.[411] Centuries of formal research on animal and human brains began with the ancients and their interest in anatomy. Speculation on the organ, its components and functions antedated the technologies and sciences required to detect chemical, electrical and neural activities. Researchers gradually invented complex diagrams and novel vocabularies to stabilize what they were beginning to discover about brains. Eventually textbooks summarize all these discoveries for new generations, and, after giving some pioneering figures credit, they describe the neural activities occurring at different brain locales. Specialized journals announce more recent discoveries and occasionally predict what new technologies and expanded research projects hope to discover. Talk of neurons discovering themselves would indeed seem a strange intrusion into such narratives. Even stranger would be talk of neurons inventing themselves.

All the same, parts of this book will have prepared readers for such strange intrusions. First there is the primary question: What is an environment? Chapters Two and Five surveyed responses over several decades and pointed out signs of developments in understanding environments, organisms and ecosystems. What was left implicit up to now in this book (but was explicit in the *Primer*) was a specialized meaning of environment appropriate to the study of perception. There a sensitively integrated environment, i.e. the recognized panorama of familiar objects and events, is said to be part of the central nervous system.[412] For someone at home in only the first realism, this will seem strange enough. However, to say that what is apparently outside is actually inside is a shorthand version of a puzzle first-year graduate students encounter in their studies of psychology of perception. In the previous books some of the examples from clinical psychology implied this puzzle, and an exercise employing the first three stages of Hegel's dialectic of consciousness implied the same while challenging readers to break the dominance of the first type of realism over their thinking.

Without repeating those clinical cases and that exercise, we can justifiably claim that recognized objects and their "encompassing" environments are integrations of minds.[413] At a basic level of intentional

---

411 A parallel would be textbook accounts of how Newton discovered the law of gravity.

412 The implications of this claim are the focus of the fifth chapter of McShane's *Wealth of Self and Wealth of Nations*.

413 Here we are using "environment" as it occurs in ordinary language and so reflective of the first horizon.

operating (what Aquinas called sensitive apprehension and what Hegel called perception), environments and their objects are first made, constructed, invented or whatever synonym one prefers for what results from a synthesizing act of understanding. To alleviate worries of idealism, one might recall from one's own performance as an inquirer the distinctions between acts of understanding and acts of judging and between the proper objects of each type of act. One could also appeal to the medieval distinction between the *ordo cognoscendi* and the *ordo essendi*. What is first understood is not necessarily what is the case. It is not unusual to ask whether one's surmises, bright ideas or whatever meanings one makes of things are correct. Newton raised and answered questions in working out his laws of motion, and among his types of questions was the is-question or question for judging. This is the kind of question that sometimes ends with a claim that what began as a bright idea or construct has turned out to be a discovery of what is the case.[414]

What has this digression to do with explaining how neurons discovered themselves? Recall that GEM has two foci: one attentively circles around both intentional operations and their intended objects. Doing so is not yet common practice. Nevertheless, it is not outlandish to claim that those investigating brain functions are using their own brains; thus, they are specimens of what they are studying. While legitimate worries abound about relying on personal experiences as the touchstone for empirical claims, GEM is productive of results that others can test against their own empirical performance.[415] For example, claims about question types and their proper objects are traceable to common experiences in inquiry. Positing developmental patterns among intentional acts and parallel patterns among intended objects is similarly grounded. More specifically, attending to both operations and to the objects operated on can reveal both conditions of dependency (e.g. insights require images) and emergent integrations (e.g. insights are more than the images first attended to and puzzled over, and objects as explained are more complex integrations of what was earlier sensed and described). Furthermore, insights occur not of necessity but as conditioned events occurring as matters of

---

414 Despite its potentially misleading spatial metaphors, the movement between the two orders and between the question types can be suggested by the formula: "the outside is first inside but sometimes the inside is outside." The formula will make more sense when one is thinking of examples of explanatory knowledge as well as adopting Aristotle's view that knowledge is by way of identity. Then there is no expectation that the problem of knowledge requires getting "outside" one's mind to inspect what is really "out there."

415 This position presupposes that, besides the data of sense, there are data of consciousness that permit others to check anyone's claims about intentional acts and their proper objects. Were there no such data, inviting readers to re-enact Hegel's dialectic of consciousness would be an exercise in futility.

probability.[416] Since new insights are first possibilities, given enough time and enough inquirers, they will emerge to develop or to correct prior integrations. A common enough insight in learning is that, to increase the frequency with which insights occur, one should change prior conditions. Thus, students change their study habits, scientists refine their procedures, educators experiment with computer-based learning and classroom instructors constantly search for examples effective with new generations of students.

Such deliberate changes are dependent on prior conditions, but they achieve a relative independence from them. Thus, new inquiries can develop or correct the previous integrations (e.g. the answers with which they began) and, in turn, can give rise to further questions leading to newer syntheses. In short, thinking occurs as a flexible pattern of dynamic relations among variables. Among these variables are neurons, or better, neural impulses. They are some of the prior conditions for psychological states and intentional acts. Simply put, it takes neurons to know neurons. Neural activities are necessary though not sufficient conditions for knowing anything at all. In this sense neurons did play a role in their own discovery.

Is this conclusion at all significant? Does it amount to more than saying brains are prerequisites to understanding brains? Perhaps it has some worth in strengthening the case for Gazzaniga's "strong" type of reductionism and in remedying some of the language deficits he detected in his field.

First, to acknowledge that multiple interacting variables condition our thinking as well as its intended objects, e.g. organisms and ecosystems, is to affirm relations of dependency or mutual conditioning among types of intentional acts and intended objects. Second, to grant those mutually conditioning acts and objects only a relative stability is to anticipate that intelligible syntheses and explanatorily understood systems, whether social or natural, are incomplete and open to change. Third, the conditionality of such syntheses and systems permits the successive emergence of modified insights, things and processes as a matter of probability.[417]

---

416   The conditionality of insights and of classical laws was the basis for understanding how organisms and their ecosystems were stable only relative to initial conditions.

417   This third claim assumes conditionality both in thinking and in intelligible objects and processes. A critic might object that the emergence of new insights is not grounds for expecting the emergence of new forms of intended objects and processes. After all, just because an inquirer learns more about the latter does not entail they must change or become more complex. A response to this common-sense objection draws upon insights from the second and third horizons: (1) thinking is one of many types of processes due to interacting variables; (2) insights, organisms and ecosystems are explainable only in terms of patterns of

These three statements are compatible with Gazzaniga's "strong" type of reductionism.[418] For instance, neural impulses and the patterning (integration) of them by experiences are processes upon which new intentional acts and their intended objects depend, but any laws governing those processes will not explain or allow for predictions about what specific objects are noticed and investigated, what insights are reached and what meanings are made.[419] It is one thing to treat neural patterns, acts of thinking and intended objects as correlates; it is another to conclude any term in the correlation completely explains the others. To do so would be to ascribe stable one-to-one correspondences seemingly at odds with both the instability of meanings (e.g. the ease with which false memories are created by embittered individuals) and the instability of ecological relations among organisms. Still, brain trauma and diseases can erase capacities to think, so there is no denying a dependency of those capacities on neural processes. Similarly, both intentional acts and brains are dependent on variable ecological conditions, e.g. whether or not chemical toxins enter ecosystems and food chains. To reverse the relations of dependency, new intentional acts and insights can develop or correct prior meanings and practices and so presumably alter both established neural patterns and environmental policies. If those new acts and insights are to occur, however, we must assume that "free" neural impulses, i.e. ones not already monopolized by existing patterns, are available for new forms of integration.[420] Further, inquiry into incompletely understood objects

relations among variables; (3) developments in insights, organisms and ecosystems occur not of necessity; (4) their conditionality entails the possibility of new developments in accord with probabilities. Thus, changes in understanding entail that intended objects have changed in the *ordo cognoscendi* but not necessarily in the *ordo essendi*; however, the possibility of both types of changes has the same source, namely, the conditionality of all world processes.

418   Again, the strong version affirms the dependency of more complex processes on less complex ones but denies that the laws governing the latter explain the former or allow predictions about what new objects or processes may emerge.

419   Lonergan noted a relative independence from prior conditions as understanding developed. "The higher system of the organism or of the psyche develops in an underlying material manifold of physical, chemical, cytological events that are subject to their own proper laws. The higher system of intelligence develops not in a material manifold but in the psychic representation of material manifolds. Hence the higher system of intellectual development is primarily the higher integration, not of the man in whom the development occurs, but of the universe that he inspects." *Insight*, 494.

420   "The average human brain consists of about 100 billion neurons (or nerve cells). However, it is more concrete to think of the brain not as an assembly of bodies - nerve cells - but rather as a collection of events – nerve impulses. Nerve impulses are essentially waves of electromagnetic potentials that vary in complicated ways and surge along the pathways of our nerve cells. Most nerve cells are capable of 1000 electrical impulses per second. Not every nerve cell fires this frequently, and estimates of how often they do fire on average vary widely. Still, an average of about 100 impulses per cell per second is frequently used in the literature. This would mean that there are something like 10 trillion nerve impulses per second in the active adult brain." Patrick Byrne, "Neuroscience, Consciousness, Freedom and Lonergan,"

and processes can produce surprises undermining established habits of thought (i.e. "paradigms" or publicly adopted "memes") thereby leading to new insights and neural integrations. Tracking these complex relations among variables demands a new vocabulary free of images of linear causality and simple categories.

The linguistic challenge here is to give the distinct classes of variables and relations their due.[421] To attribute psychological acts (e.g. communicating meanings, remembering them and deciding among options) to neural processes is at best to speak analogously, but it may also signal that language deficits persist. What the preceding review of alternatives to strict reductionism has offered are a few guidelines for evaluating new vocabularies. Foremost is the need to retain the complex, non-linear relations among variables and to respect the distinctions among different classes of related acts and objects. Finding appropriate terms will not be easy. For example, talk of top-down and bottom-up relations suffers from ties to descriptive terms belonging to the first horizon. Talk of "levels" of conditions, with some being higher-order operations or processes and others lower-order ones, has the same limitation. Talk of dialectical or reciprocal relations is perhaps an improvement since it reflects an understanding of mutual conditioning and does not have an apparent debt to picture-thinking.[422] Talk of interactive systems perhaps falls short of what environmental historians recognized and began talking of as hybrid environments. Still, even the latter, more inclusive language offers little help in preserving distinctions among classes of variables. As subsection D of Part II affirmed, the language of flexible schemes of recurrence seems a plausible alternative in talking about organic and intentional types of variables.

It has the added merit of being compatible with UV. But Dennett's "acceptable" type of reductive analysis and Gazzaniga's "strong" type are also compatible with UV. All the same, neither author explores how relations of mutual dependency might be explained. In Dennett's case the source of his omission is perhaps his desire to avoid entanglement in

---

unpublished paper given at the Lonergan Philosophical Society session at the American Catholic Philosophical Association (November 2007), 9.

421   "Weak" reductionism evades this challenge and its linguistic difficulties by eliminating whole classes of variables. This chapter and earlier ones cited an analogous problem. To talk of ecosystems as "energy exchange systems" eliminates too much of the diversity observed in ecosystems that different disciplines explore. The category also fails to do much work in explaining how organisms and their ecosystems develop and generate more complex forms.

422   The medieval language of *et motus et movens* already reflected an understanding of mutual conditioning. The eye as an organ is stimulated (is moved) by visible objects, but selective attention focuses on only some part of the field of possible objects of attention, i.e. it moves some features or objects and not others into focus.

metaphysical debates. Gazzaniga goes further in favoring a shift from asking what are the basic building blocks of nature to asking how nature organizes itself. The language of emergence is of some help in answering the latter question, but Gazzaniga recognizes how much work remains in both understanding and talking about emergence. The alternative associated with the work of Lonergan, who first formulated UV, is obviously compatible with all three basic positions. Readers of the preceding pages on schemes of recurrence and linguistic deficits will not be surprised to find these writers endorsing this alternative as the most developed and linguistically promising of the three.

IV. In Retrospect

This chapter has added to the multiple uses of "environment." By its claim that a sensitively integrated environment is part of the central nervous system, it has taken a strange turn in our pursuit of the meaning of environment. Clearly a further reversal of the first realism is in the offing; yet resistance will be quick to appear. Who can doubt that, whatever they are, ecosystems and environments are "out there"? But this and previous books in this series have already replied to this objection from the first horizon.

While we leave it to the last chapter to sort out the multiple meanings of environment, it may help to alert readers to a way they might track and classify usages of the term occurring in these chapters. The three horizons of common sense, theory and interiority are distinct from and irreducible to one another both in the questions persons find significant and in the types of responses they anticipate finding. The same term may take on different meanings depending on which horizon a person operates within. Tracking the differences and controlling how one uses the term varies with degrees of familiarity with those horizons. This, at least, is one benefit of GEM. It may be obvious, but this new use of "environment" reflects an understanding of how whatever we claim to know begins when we integrate, unify, "digest" and order the fragments of experience.

CHAPTER SEVEN: WHAT IS AN ENVIRONMENT?

Previous chapters have been asking, at least indirectly, the lead question of this book and of this final chapter. Various answers have already appeared. Part II surveys these answers and summarizes the developmental orderings of them that these chapters identified as a result of doing FS3 and FS4. Part III widens the scope of the question about environment by relating it to the conditionality of all objects and processes, whether cultural or natural. Part IV works out some of the implications of understanding the environment in terms of the conditionality of world processes.

I. The Basic Puzzle

One of the most important features of human life is the central role meaning plays in its constitution. Human life takes place against more than a cold background of severed, isolated facts. Cases in this and the previous volumes show how our lives do not move and grow and develop with the lockstep fixity, the self-assured direction, of a high-speed train. For all its obviousness, it remains an easy point to miss: our lives are more flexible, more open-ended and more unpredictable, partly because the universe within which they occur is likewise. As an empirical method set within such a meaningful context, comparative interpretation shows how different persons identify and pursue different answers. Person w thinks x because of y, all in contrast to another investigator, sure that x and y are in fact unrelated, that w is mistaken, and that another z is really a much better explanation of the entire issue. Thus, in part, a methodical form of comparative interpretation works to track the different answers persons deem worth pursuing and the routes their questions take along their way to those answers.

In distinguishing successes and failures, methods serve normative functions. They help us to get where we are going yet also encourage us to keep on track as we progress. In this way, comparative interpretation also evaluates the differences that it identifies or, more ideally, that other functional specialists hand over to it for evaluation. One key source of differences among persons and their questions is the horizon in which inquirers operate.[423] Any plausible answers to some question will reflect the horizons of the inquirers. More importantly, because the horizons in which persons operate are subject to change, comparative interpretation is not content to cite instances of diversity. It does not collect disagreements like others collect butterflies or antique cars. Multiplicity is not its final word. If it were, comparative interpretation could only add to the din, the babble of voices, it means to sort out. Though human life does not as a matter of fact simply or statically advance, though age and wisdom are not automatically in direct proportion to one another, comparative interpretation, by relying on H2, GEM and UV, may contribute order where there were previously many backtracks, detours and not a few wrong turns.

Have there been wrong turns in thinking about environments? Chapter Two reviewed Nisbet's account of how artists through the late 1960s pursued the making of environments. Eventually their goal to create a "total environment" (*Gesamtkunstwerk*) proved elusive; however, their attempts helped break down the dichotomies of nature and society, of pristine wilderness and human artifice. What environmental historians were discovering about the hybridity of environments artists also were uncovering through their failed experiments. Was there a wrong turn in thinking that an environment was a hybrid? Perhaps it was an incomplete turn.

To say that an environment is hybrid is not the same as to say it is imperceptible or to say that it is not an object. Nisbet cites Marshall McLuhan as asserting these further conclusions.[424] The latter's distinction between environment and anti-environment is perhaps less vague if one thinks of how possible objects (both artworks and organisms) appear, are empirically detectable, over against fields that do not appear as objects of perception in the same way. The former belong to foregrounds while the latter are concealed as backgrounds. Nisbet formulates an important implication: "an Environment is not an independent entity. It is not a thing that can be substituted in one place for another, erased,

---

423   Horizon is the *tertium quid* of interrogation. It unifies the asker with the asked. Because they take place within one and the same horizon, one's questions can be one's own. One's horizon conditions what will count as an answer by organizing answers into a field of possibilities.
424   Ibid. 63-64.

overwritten."[425] Thus, while the manipulation of objects is within the capacity of artists, their backgrounds elude direct control. Hence, the ambition to create a total environment was futile.

But here we may have strayed into a conundrum. Environmental history emerged as a specialty and quickly gained attention because of growing concern about environmental degradation. The moral aims of the first generation of environmental historians extended to understanding and preventing such harm. However, if the environment eludes direct control, were the ambitions of environmental historians also futile? Is the environment something that eludes human mastery, either to degrade or to rescue it?

This seems to be another intellectual impasse, but comparative interpretation may offer a way forward. Methods are sometimes antidotes to unproductive inquiries. Comparative interpretation introduces some methodical control where previously there has been little. But methods emerge and survive because we assume the world is meaningful and so worth exploring and understanding. Because human living occurs primarily within social worlds overwhelmingly constituted by acts of meaning and by durable relationships with others, it follows that a collaborative method can be part of an intelligent and "intelligible solution to living in a given environment." So how might comparative interpretation respond to the puzzle about the environment eluding human control either for harm or rescue?

One response might recommend talking of different kinds of environments, some of which may resist human manipulation.[426] The previous chapters have done so. Alternatively, it once was common to speak of economies as ecosystems, and perhaps that analogous usage can be adapted to speaking of ecosystems of diverse sorts. In this alternative, one might distinguish between environment and ecosystems with the latter being objects of concern to environmentalists. Still, this alternative only defers the problem. The question will recur: If ecosystems are of many kinds, what yet is the environment? A series of questions will likely follow. Is the environment a whole composed of subsystems, e.g. ecosystems or institutions, with those parts being further divisible into organ-

---

425   Nisbet, 63. Another implication deserves emphasis. An environment is not an entity or a thing. This will be an explicit topic in Part II. As a preliminary statement of the puzzle implied by saying an environment is not a thing, we can cite Nisbet's paraphrase of Niklas Luhmann's stance: "An environment is that which exceeds the system. It is the remainder. A system can draw upon its environment, but cannot grasp it in its entirety." (Ibid.) What does it mean to say an environment exceeds any system? Part III will provide an answer in terms of the indefinite range of conditions possibly affecting any system.
426   Sutter, 164.

isms and persons? To answer affirmatively is to think of the environment as a totality of related parts. Mereology would then have the final word in ontology. This way of thinking was popular once space images of the earth became available. A new perspective on the blue marble of our planet supposedly let us see the whole visible environment; "the earth is almost all that matters," writes one author.[427] This dependence of thinking on an image of the "whole earth" proved unsatisfactory for explaining what the environment was. Why this was so, what new possibilities are more promising and how we are to resolve the conundrum about human control are questions that will occupy the rest of this chapter. First, we will review earlier accounts of environments and what previous chapters detected as patterns of development in those views.

II. Different Views of Environments

We begin with Nisbet's history of how artists during two decades of the twentieth century conceived of environments. In his first cluster, environmental art, the understanding of environment is that of encompassing or bounded space within which objects appear. Environment in this sense is a setting or background, e.g. the wide-angle landscape, in which objects are situated and events occur. Visual experience tends to provide the dominant metaphors for presenting examples of such settings and their "contents." Talk of a panorama containing diverse objects and events relies on this initial understanding of environment as boundary.

The second cluster, land art, was indebted to the writings of Rachel Carson and the newly available photos of the earth taken from outer space. The latter provided an image of the earth that many read as depicting a single sphere, a material unity encompassing many diverse objects and processes. As diverse as the parts might be, beehives as well as megacities, they still belong to a unified, living whole. This perspective lent itself to talk of the environment as a single living ecology wherein all parts were connected.

In the third cluster, ecological art, the understanding of environment departed from talk of an imagined unity and, instead, favored talk of interactions among diverse systems. Physical, chemical, biological, technological and industrial systems formed a series of interdepen-

---

427   John Sallis, *Topographies* (Bloomington: Indiana University Press, 2006), 77.

dent and mutable ecosystems that were far from being a single unity. The emphasis within ecological art on mutability and incompleteness acknowledges randomness as a genuine feature of interactions among systems. But an environment itself is not a system or some fixed unity of systems. What then is it?[428]

Process art operated with the most generalized and hence abstract understanding of environment. The focus was on what was common to all ecological systems, namely, energy exchanges. Ecology becomes the study of how diverse systems distribute energy. The constitutive element of every ecological process is energy. Here the explanatory category marks a break with imaginable events in picturable settings, and the symbolisms of physics and biochemistry become more appropriate ways of conveying an understanding of what makes an environment what it is.

In brief, the meaning of environment changed from bounded space to self-enclosed whole and then to ecological systems as open and interrelated and finally to ecologies of energy exchanges.

What developmental sequences of these four views of environments appeared in Chapter Two and why? The first cluster of environmental art represents pre-ecological thinking inasmuch as it presupposes the first type of realism. That is, both the artwork as a discrete object and the environment as an imagined setting for the former seem to belong to a world of immediacy. Artworks with their surroundings or boundaries presumably comprise a field of objects "out there" to be sensed.[429] Since vision is but one mode of experience, the ideal of the total artwork, one providing a more complete sensory experience of the object and its settings, proceeds from the same realism. Sound and light shows follow in efforts to reach this ideal of immersion in some sensory experience of art.

The second cluster, land art, implicitly acknowledges that artworks have meaning only because of mediating acts of sensing and understanding. This generality supports talk of a web of intelligible dependencies, of conditionality, entangling and sustaining works, artists, material conditions, art history and future developments. Any extensive range of linked variables eludes sensible presentation; one has never literally seen a relation or pattern of relationships. Insofar as the conditionality of works includes such variables, it makes good sense to deny that those works are ever fixed or final. Practitioners of land art explored such dependencies and explicitly denied the notion of the self-enclosed artwork. Still, they continued to be tied to what Nisbet calls the "imaginary" of earth as a

---

428   "It is the remainder" according to Luhmann. But what does that mean?
429   But what is the "field" or environment of all these objects? Does it elude detection because it refuses presentation?

solid sphere, a <u>unified</u> whole containing singular objects. Despite their tie to the imaginable, they were slowly pushing beyond sensory experiences and environments as containers toward an understanding of dynamic relations among variables.

The third cluster, with its incomplete and mutable series of interdependent ecological systems, represents a breakthrough to thinking about art and environment in terms of constitutive relationships. For example, answers to the question about what makes an artwork what it is now focus on ecological relations among significant variables. In an advance over the imaginary of the previous cluster, new inquiries concentrate on the environmental conditions that constitute, sustain and modify artists, works and their settings. Talk of physical, chemical, biological, political and technological ecosystems, despite its metaphorical diction, is a more comprehensive way of accounting for things and the network of conditions in relation to which they emerge and pass away. Their conditionality comes more into focus as complex patterns of relations extending beyond the range of what is imaginable; the real artwork is more than whatever is given in sensing and imagining.

The fourth cluster, with its talk of energy flows, understands biological organisms as emerging and subsisting through such flows without themselves being the self-generating sources of such flows. Here we detect an increasing distance from the first realism of picture thinking. Talk of energy flows assumes that phenomenal organisms and artworks exist in and through what eludes sensory detection. The talk changes because the horizon expands to include more of what a less developed perspective neglects.

These authors concluded that, for Nisbet, process art and its understanding of environment seemed to represent the most advanced view of art and ecology during the two decades under study. We agreed with his sequence for all but the last view. Our shared judgments on the first three views were as follows.

First, land art moved beyond environmental art's static conception of environment as encompassing or bounded space. It understood the environment as diverse, interconnected systems forming an imagined totality. Still, while the second cluster represents environments as more dynamic settings for objects, its holistic view is still indebted to an imagined unity or totality of objects and events. The ecological view of the third cluster also conceived of the environment as a series of diverse, interdependent systems but understood the latter to be flexible in their interactions and open to novel changes. It was more reflective of the "unruly complexity" of biochemical mutations, global extinctions and artistic experiments departing from prior conventions. However, talk of ecological systems ranging from biological cycles to cultural institutions rests upon analogical thinking. It connects so many dots on the basis of their likeness, but, since the criterion of likeness is borrowed from the world of immediacy, the resulting order is confined there too. We imagine someone pointing and saying, "This is like this, which is like this, which is like this," and the pattern repeats as far as the imagination manages to rove. The further question is what intelligible similarity allows for such analogical comparisons? To this question the fourth cluster provided an answer in terms of the lowest common denominator of biochemical and cultural systems, namely, the absorption and distribution of energy. A beehive and a megacity have at least calories in common.

What goes forward in these varying estimates of environment is an expanding, increasingly more comprehensive series of viewpoints. Features of environments are present in later, more developed viewpoints that are missing from earlier, less developed ones. In its generalization about a common ground for all environmental processes, the fourth viewpoint seems the most comprehensive one in the series. Still, Nisbet and these authors voiced some reservations about it. For example, talk of energy flows among systems omits too many specific differences among types of systems and things. Furthermore, the single category of "energy" is inadequate by itself to resolve the puzzle about open and closed (i.e. deterministic) systems. In addition to these shared criticisms, these authors faulted some practitioners of the fourth cluster for discounting the limited legitimacy of common-sense knowing by promoting talk of energy flows as the right way of understanding artworks and their environments.[430] Among the relevant conditions for making sense of artworks are the describable materials available to audiences. This on its own is not a mistake. Without access to those materials audiences will have nothing to puzzle over, nothing to make sense of, but also nothing against which to check any guesses they may make.

Why should this be the case? One answer draws from the theory of intentionality familiar to readers of this series of case studies. If thinking requires images, carefully designed images may help to promote certain insights. Works of art, exactly because of their respective media, whether canvas or earth, are subject to interpretation. Artworks are to interpretation as images are to thinking. If answers and, by extension, concepts

---

430   Included in this criticism was the suspicion that an exclusive focus on energy exchanges might derive from the Pre-Socratic assumption that any real object was reducible to its material elements.

reflect prior questions, and prior questions reflect the desire to know, artworks reflect spontaneous demands for sensitive presentations and meaningful expression, and meeting those demands prompts questions of meaning and efforts to find interpretive answers. Norman Mailer was on to something when he wrote, "Art obviously depends on incomplete communication. A work which is altogether explicit is not art[;] the audience cannot respond with their own creative act of the imagination, that small leap of the faculties which leaves one an increment more exceptional than when one began."[431] Even when we leave behind the faculty psychology Mailer invokes, an artwork does seem to be the kind of object that gets us to pay attention to communication by frustrating the apparent seamlessness of the world and our relation to it. All facts are mediated; all art requires an interpretive leap. Since thinking can grasp the form in the image, artists show what their audiences are left to interpret. They leave behind carefully designed images for others to wonder about. In the existential project of our lives, art reminds us that we cannot rely on pre-drawn routes like a train does its tracks merely to arrive at the future. Art reminds us that meaning must be made, just as the future must be created rather than inherited.

Though access to describable materials mediated by sensory experiences is a prerequisite to interpretation, it is also insufficient. Such data are as important as they are incomplete. However, if art is an energy flow, then, first, it is altogether unavailable to sensing and to imagining, and, second, it is difficult or impossible to distinguish it from those other objects that also derive from energy flows, namely anything at all. On extrapolation this cluster ends in a closed, everything-is-everything-else thesis that undermines its own starting point. Think of Hegel's famous quip about the night in which all cows are black, an influential historical point about the fourth cluster's relevant shortcoming. Given these criticisms, we concluded that ecological art, the third cluster, offered answers to the question of conditionality superior to those of process art. Thus, we modified Nisbet's sequence and demoted the fourth cluster from its status as more developed than the third.

Chapter Two went on to summarize Golley's reading of the history of ecological thought and his ranking of views on ecosystems. He sketched three stages in the development of the concept of ecosystem: a formative period, an initial growth stage and a time of rapid growth.[432]

---

431   In fact, an artwork, as well as a work of any other type that is *altogether* explicit, is impossible; for they can serve only as images to provoke questions for intelligence and reflection. "Mailer on 'The Blacks.'" *The Village Voice.* VI, no. 30 (May 18, 1961), 14-15.
432   Golley, 185.

The formative period preceded the Second World War. The assembling of studies and their results for later organization under the heading of ecological studies was going forward, but the discipline, its objectives, terminology and methods were in formation and not yet a distinct field of inquiry. The minimal meaning of ecosystem was an understanding of how organisms were embedded in and dependent on environments.[433]

The initial growth stage was marked by efforts to integrate various forms of inquiry and their objects, and the term "ecosystem" lent itself to this unifying function. In particular, it was broad enough to include findings from physics, chemistry and physiology. But this generality came at a price. Golley notes the frequent use of loose analogies (e.g. the world as a heat engine) while advocates claimed the new discipline was relevant to more problems than it could solve.[434]

The understanding of ecosystem common in the second period, the initial growth stage, reflected two perspectives on ecological research. Theoretical developments allowed for sustained inquiries into (1) how ecosystems functioned, (2) what disturbances occurred in them and (3) what responses the latter provoked, responses usually effecting a return to a relative equilibrium. Ecosystems, thus, were dynamic patterns of relations among organisms and environments, flexible enough to survive most disturbances but occasionally succumbing to catastrophic breakdowns due to natural or human interventions. The second perspective reflected practical ambitions to do more than learn how ecosystems functioned; its further purpose was to learn how to preserve and exploit them for human benefit. The machine analogy in talk of self-regulating systems lent itself to both perspectives since breakdowns were outcomes to be avoided while understanding regular functioning could lead to greater productivity.[435]

---

433 Golley points out the absence of a common terminology for talking about the larger context within which an ecosystem functions. "Biosphere" and "landscape" were but two of the terms in use in the time frame he surveys. Ibid. 199. Presumably, "environment" usually meant no more than what contained ecosystems and their components.

434 Golley writes: "The condition of ecosystem studies at this time might be characterized by Claude Lévi-Strauss's term *bricolage*, which refers to the construction of an object or a theory from a variety of unrelated, found materials. The *bricoleur* arranges these and creates something new and unexpected from the disparate materials. Ecosystem theory was constructed from thermodynamics, from physical equilibrium theory, from information theory, from evolutionary history, from field natural history, and so on. In 1965 it did not yet form a coherent, organized body of knowledge." Ibid. 109.

435 The same analogy likely dictated the meaning of "environment." As a machine is the sum of its moving parts so an environment is an aggregation or totality of its energy-exchanging ecosystems and organisms.

Difficulties arose for both approaches to ecological studies. Golley notes two of them: (1) the abstractness or simplicity of the models ecologists employed for understanding ecosystems and (2) the reliance of many of them on a deterministic understanding of the relations among environmental and organic variables.

> The complex systems, sometimes consisting of thousands of species, were simplified by the theoreticians to sometimes as few as three or four components. The myriad environmental interactions between ecosystem components were reduced to a few flows of energy. The dynamic response of natural systems was made deterministic, being consistent with physical theory. The ecosystem was conceived as a machine, represented as a computer model.[436]

Besides this simplification, early environmentalism substituted one form of determinism with another. Dissatisfaction with both limitations inaugurated Golley's third period, a time of rapid growth, in modern ecological studies and with it a changed view of ecosystems. The introduction of evolutionary thought into mainstream ecology reflected a recognition both that simplified models missed too many of the real variables interacting in nature and that reliance on deterministic models from physics missed the temporal features of ecosystems, their evolutionary history and their potentialities for development, in other words, both their past and their future.

The understanding of ecosystem during the initial growth stage, approximately 1950-1965, had focused on how organisms and environmental conditions exchanged energy much like the moving parts of a machine. As well, that view had emphasized departures from and returns to equilibrium. In contrast, the view of ecosystems in the third period focused on variations and developments within ecosystems, with equilibrium or steady states often being comparatively short-lived and rare phenomena. Physical, genetic, chemical, biological, atmospheric and human variables were all relevant conditions for understanding how an ecosystem functioned and underwent changes. Analogies were still in use but under more control, and the understanding of ecosystems as "flows of energy and cycles of materials in well-defined systems" was,

---

436   Ibid. 4.

with some dissenting voices, widely shared.[437]

To shift from inquiry into ecosystems into the reach for a developmentally ordered way of talking about them, Golley's sequence identifies three ways of understanding ecosystems. The view he associates with the formative period was the simplest of the three. The term "ecosystem" referred to an understanding of (1) how organisms were dependent on biotic and abiotic components of their environments and (2) how there were hierarchies of systems within an ecosystem with less complex ones supporting more complex ones.

The view Golley detects in the initial growth stage reflected a cross-disciplinary object of inquiry. Multiple specialists were needed to investigate the relations among the interacting variables of complex systems. Their inquiries were guided by machine analogies derived from physics and information theory and by the assumption that systems were closed (i.e. deterministic) and tended toward equilibrium.

The period of rapid growth operated with a fairly uniform view of ecosystems as energy flows and the cycling of energy within and among systems. As well, though there were dissenting voices, most ecologists came to accept: (1) a holistic versus a reductionist viewpoint, (2) an understanding of systems as open versus closed and (3) multiple types of ecologies, including evolutionary or developmental ecology. These differences Golley loosely labels as "relativity." As noted in Chapter Two, one of his uses of the term may be synonymous with probabilistic patterns of relations among the components of an ecosystem. In any case, he seemed to endorse this third view as the most comprehensive of the three he identified. It evades the deterministic commitments of the machine analogy found in the second use of the term and, instead, incorporates historical variations and developments when trying to understand the relations between biological and non-biological components of an ecosystem.

We noted some problematic comments by Golley that revealed implicit stances at odds with UV. However, we concluded that these deficiencies did not undermine his claim that the third view of ecosystems was more developed than its two predecessors. At least it was arguably superior to the alternatives known at the time he ended his survey. But further developments in the understanding of ecosystems have occurred since the early 1990s. Some of these appeared in Chapter Five and its review of changes in how environmental historians have conceived of

---

437   Ibid. 204. The implicit meaning of "environment" remained that of a totality of such systems, and, given their complexity, multiple disciplines could contribute complementary accounts of how to understand them.

environments and ecosystems up to the present decade.

McNeill's survey in 2003 identified a variety of negative and positive changes over the thirty-year history of the field. Left behind were early generalizations about the origins of environmental degradation.[438] McNeill rejected the "Hegelian" view of some of his colleagues because it privileged ideas and culture in the shaping of human behavior. He also dismissed the exaggerated emphasis in the 90s on the social construction of reality. More positively, he endorsed the acceptance of multiple types of "agents" in understanding environmental change, e.g. population numbers, animals, climates, ideas and technologies. He also tracked the waxing and waning of environmental activism and defended its revival in an increasingly complicated field.

What specific changes did McNeill see as signs of development? He listed several. The multiplying ties of environmental history to other specialties, e.g. climatology, genetics, archaeology and disease history, "fragmented" the field but aided in its maturation and relevance to the broader discipline of history. The gradual deepening of insights into how peoples and their environments are entangled prompted his call for internationalizing inquiries beyond political borders. When he wrote in 2003, he was able to cite only a few regional studies that reflected such a broadening of perspective. Even so, studies of this kind led to complaints that human actors were vanishing from the expanded narratives, but McNeill thought this was inevitable given the "scale" of such histories. These authors suggested that, as environmental studies increasingly reflected operations in the horizon of theory, one should expect a decreasing emphasis on particular actors and events. However, McNeill noted that historians tended to be "thin on theory." While he meant they avoided constructing their own theories, opting in some cases to borrow theories from other fields, he did not mean they avoided the effects of science on environments, e.g. agrarian revolutions and industrialization. For example, the focus in Nisbet's fourth cluster on energy exchanges McNeill finds replicated in several European environmental histories.[439]

So what, if any, difference did the horizon of theory make in the period of environmental history that McNeill surveyed? Apparently the effects were indirect. That is, as environmental historians drew upon findings from various scientific fields, they were gradually recognizing the range of diverse conditions that sustained and, in some cases, degraded

---

438   Targets for blame included Judeo-Christian culture, capitalism, colonialism and patriarchy.
439   McNeill, 19-20.

environments. They started to realize just how large their puzzle was. One result was to make the overgeneralizations of the first generation more obsolete and even embarrassing. Another result was to fragment the specialty into various subspecialties. The very complexity of the diverse conditions they were investigating and the troubling questions about the terms appropriate for talking about those conditions (e.g. agency, nature and environment) put pressure on the next generation to examine the categories they used. Previous formulations were no longer appropriate to present circumstances. After all, if the words we use derive from the questions we raise and if technical vocabularies are meant to be consistent among uses, then the widespread detection of prior shortcomings helps to set the conditions for future innovations. Thus, the focus on language became much more apparent for practitioners in the first decade of the new century, a period included in Sutter's article in 2013.

What changes did Sutter see as signs of development in environmental history? The first significant advance he detected was the replacement of the old dichotomy of nature versus culture by the notion of hybridity. The new view implied both that natural environments already bear a human imprint and that societies are rarely, if ever, explainable apart from their natural environments. Historical interactions change both terms in this correlation. But then human actions are but one type of variable in the dynamic relations among so many diverse kinds of mutually conditioning variables.

All the same, Sutter thought hybridity a "transitional" view. It did represent an advance over earlier views that separated natural and social environments, the first found, the other made or "built." However, it was too undifferentiated a notion. Still, recognizing this deficit contributed to another advance; namely, historians began to question the basic categories in use in their specialty. Was it at all clear what "nature," "environment" and "agency" meant? To pay attention to such fundamental issues and to differentiate classes of variables previously left aggregated were both signs of a maturing field of inquiry.

During the decades studied by McNeill and Sutter, were there any signs of development in the meaning of environment? In this book series one measure of development is the demand of further why-questions for more comprehensive understanding, a demand that requires entry into the horizon of theory. So the first question is what differences have a few steps into the horizon of theory made for the specialty of environmental history? First, leaving behind views of nature or environment either as a single, undifferentiated "agent" of change or as always a victim of human depredation and, instead, distinguishing a wide range of classes of mutually dependent variables are evidence of a shift from pre-theoretical images of "pushing and pulling" causes. Second, while the proliferating types of variables made the tasks of historians more complex, a more comprehensive "moving viewpoint" promises, in Sutter's words, to produce "truer and more satisfying renditions of the human-environmental past."[440]

Such prospects are warranted, these writers believe, because further why-questions demand ever more comprehensive accounts of what at first are descriptive views, and the advances noted so far have reflected such expansions in understanding. To summarize the major expansions in the meaning of environment: development occurred (1) in moving from the ancient and one-sided view that geography determined a population's character to the view of mutual dependency between a population and its environment, thereby beginning to abandon the bifurcation of nature and culture; (2) in slowly escaping the ordinary usage of environment as that which surrounds or contains objects and processes; (3) in accepting that human agency is but one type of variable in complex patterns of relationships among many types of organic and nonorganic variables; (4) in understanding local environments as dependent on variable conditions such that random deviations among them can lead to developments and emergent properties; (5) in raising the suspicion that use of a part-whole metaphor might be inadequate in talking about environments;[441] and (6) in recognizing that terms such as environment and nature are "undertheorized" categories, commonly used but still problematical.[442]

What further developments might be next? Some possibilities about unfinished work turned up in Chapter Five and its review of recent advances in the practices of environmental historians.

1. Environmental historians have gradually shifted away from the first horizon by applying the findings of different scientific fields to their own works.

2. They have made advances by leaving behind deterministic models of ecological processes and by accepting

---

440   Sutter, 118.
441   Signs of this suspicion appeared in Nisbet's references to the works of Luhmann and McLuhan. Sutter's search for a new vocabulary that would "disaggregate the grand category of nature," and, we would add, the category of environment, is further evidence of problems with understanding an environment as a totality of objects. Sutter, 98.
442   Ibid. 107.

the instability of environments and their inhabitants because of their dependence on, conditioning by, complex
patterns of relations among multiple types of variables.

3. In making such advances they have begun to question the adequacy of some of the basic categories in use
in the profession.

4. An earlier resistance within the profession to some
sort of relational ontology may be weakening.

The last two possibilities are topics for Part III. First, we will summarize
earlier comment about a relational ontology.

A question in Chapter Five was whether environmental historians
needed to operate with such a relational ontology. Why might this be
the case? Environmental historians face the difficult challenge of explaining how so many human and nonhuman variables can be mutually
conditioning.[443] One clue to meeting this challenge was the analogy of
proportion cited earlier: organisms are to ecosystems as individuals are
to institutions. The basis for this analogy is the insight that one cannot adequately understand either organisms or individuals apart from
relations they have to other organisms and individuals. But are those
relations part of the being of particular entities? A preliminary answer to
this question required several distinctions.

First, to understand the being of something is to answer distinct
types of questions. What-questions anticipate discovering what makes
something what it is while is-questions anticipate settling both whether
answers to such what-questions are correct and whether what is correctly
understood actually exists. In asking these types of questions, we presuppose a distinction in being, i.e. what the medievals debated as the
difference between *essentia* and *esse* and what some contemporary philosophers debate as the difference between concepts or "constructs" and
either one's relation to something real.

Second, as Chapter Three suggested, a distinction between natural
being (*esse naturale*) and intentional being (*esse intentionale*) is crucial to
affirming the reality of institutions. The latter are patterns of relations
constituted by acts of meaning and sustained by the same. Without such

---

443   Sutter's admiration for Andrews' *Killing for Coal* is founded on his masterful handling
of so many different types of variables, e.g. labor forces, animals, rock formations, air quality,
groundwater levels, gases and fire dangers.

continuing constitutive acts institutions cease to exist. Does this understanding of institutions provide clues for understanding how a "relational ontology" might apply to ecosystems? Again, an earlier distinction proves helpful.

While not constituted (in the *ordo essendi*) by intentional acts, ecosystems as <u>understood</u> patterns of relations among organisms and multiple types of inorganic conditions presuppose the inventive or constructive operations of inquirers in the *ordo cognoscendi*. In other words, inquirers proceed from puzzling data through what-questions to preliminary syntheses or answers. Is-questions about such answers anticipate distinguishing between correct and incorrect answers about what something is and about whether it exists.[444] In some cases what has been invented or constructed by intentional operations turns out to be limited knowledge of what in fact is real. More simply put, hypotheses sometimes prove to be true.

As inquirers become familiar with these relevant distinctions between and among their questions, the scandal of affirming substantial unities or things together with their changing contexts may diminish. However, in the absence of these distinctions, we seem forced to choose between things and relations, between texts and interpretations, between persons and institutions, ascribing reality to one correlate and denying it to the other. In relying on GEM and UV, comparative interpretation evades such a forced choice.

More widespread familiarity with the third horizon, especially with the functionally related operations in coming to know, may one day reduce resistance to thinking of things as unities that exist in and through intelligible patterns of relations, some of which are internal and many of which are external to those things. For example, the chemical processes of its digestive system condition the mobility of an animal, and climatic regularities condition the availability of food toward which it can move. Let either type of condition remain unfulfilled, and the animal will perish. The animal and the wider context to which it belongs must both be real for it to emerge, change and pass away. Insight into this sort of mutual conditioning may persuade some to take a relational ontology seriously. As we will argue below, absent an understanding of the

---

444   This distinction between what-questions and is-questions can raise a further issue, i.e. the question of whether something is a thing, a substantial unity in older terms. Aristotle's reply, *what-it-is*, is less a tautology and more a stand-in for what has yet to be discovered. This text has not offered a detailed study of what a thing is or how it can be known. At best, the authors have contrasted bodies and things, reductionist views and emergentist views, as a way of indicating our implicit positions. The question, What is a thing? deserves its own book, and this is not it.

conditionality of objects and events, an adequate theoretical meaning of environment will remain elusive.

III. The Language and Ontology of Environments

The preceding parts of this chapter have reviewed how various authors have struggled with the meaning of "environment." Ecologists and environmental historians have been using the word without a consistent meaning. So the previous two parts contribute to our lead question by making these different meanings explicit. Inconsistent usages are compared not so much to one another but in relation to UV. This form of comparative interpretation allows us to rank different usages by assessing them according to their different and incompatible assumptions about reality, knowing and objectivity.

Regarding the term environment, Part I cited authors who distinguish between environments and ecosystems, the latter of which are parts that may be further divisible into organisms. To think of an environment as a totality of related parts and then to imagine that these parts can be further divided is to make the organism the basic unit, the "hero," of the story of nature. Much as a hero has a stage setting for the drama's rising and falling action, space images of the earth suggest how ecosystems perform together on the blue marble, the global stage for the widest environmental drama. Organisms on our spaceship called earth live within ecosystems, and ecosystems exist within the environment.

The part-whole relation that guides this way of thinking and speaking is at odds with UV. First, real things are not the same as imaginable bodies. If neither the ocean nor a whale is metaphysically primary, the issue will be further muddled when the latter is imagined swimming in the former. Second, there are no things within things. Common sense anticipates that beneath the surface or skin of something are its ingredients. The final chapter of *Cracking the Case* saw Graham Priest call these key ingredients, or hypokeimena, "gluons." In contrast, Heidegger defended the irreducibility of whole to part when he wrote, "Wholeness means that the organism is not an aggregate, composed of elements or parts, but that the growth and the construction of the organism is governed by this wholeness in each and every stage."[445] A better microscope will not

445 *The Fundamental Concepts of Metaphysics: World, Finitude, Solitude.* William McNeil and Nicholas

visually reveal the substratum that makes something what it is; still less will a more thorough inventory of ingredients, with or without one of Priest's gluons, explain what makes something what it is. The Pre-Socratic search for the basic unit of reality was a misstep then and now.

By the measure of the second horizon, there are no things inside other things because the appeal to imaginable ingredients will always be insufficient for explanation.[446] More complex integrations are always under-explained by their material manifolds. Why? A common-sense example may be that, contrary to advertisers' wishes, inside every adult is not an earlier child. Aristotle's type of explanation pushes past such misleading descriptions. When we raise scientific questions, we seek a demonstration's middle term to show the reason for a conclusion, a reason that would remain a mere fact without the middle term and the demonstration itself.[447] When we expect that some other thing is the explanation for something, a secret ingredient in the "sauce of nature," we beg the question and overlook the middle term. Contrary to common-sense expectations and speaking, there are no organs within persons, no cells within plants and animals because "within" designates a thing's spatial insides and not what makes it what it is.

The part-whole metaphor is also unsatisfactory because it makes what Dennett calls the mistake of "greedy reductionism," i.e. it assumes a complex object or event can be wholly explained by simpler realities. An explanation of environmental art in terms of energy exchanges was a previous example of this reductionist stance. Moving from environment to ecosystem and from there to organisms (or from institutions to persons) is marred by the same deficiencies noted in the preceding chapter. Again, the main criticism was based on findings from the third horizon.

Walker (trans.) (Bloomington: Indiana University Press, 1995), 261.

446   "As has been seen, when there is no possibility of observation, there is no possibility of a verifiable image; for the imagined as imagined can be verified only when what is imagined also can be sensed. Accordingly, there are no verifiable images for subatomic elements. But if subatomic elements cannot be imagined, then atoms cannot be imagined, for one cannot imagine a whole as made up of non-imaginable parts. It follows that no thing itself, no thing as explained, can be imagined. If atoms cannot be imagined, then by parity of reasoning, molecules cannot be imagined. If molecules cannot be imagined, then neither can cells. If cells cannot be imagined, then neither can plants. Once one enters upon the way of explanation by relating things to one another, one has stepped out of the path that yields valid representative images. No doubt, I can imagine the plant as seen, as related to my senses, as described. But if I apply the full principle of equivalence and prescind from all observers, then I also prescind from all observables. As the electron, so also the tree, insofar as it is considered as a thing itself, stands within a pattern of intelligible relations and offers no foothold for imagination." *Insight*, 275.

447   According to Aristotle, scientific knowledge culminates in understanding why something is the case. What begins as a matter-of-fact, a described state-of-affairs, a further why-question begins to transform into a reasoned explanation. Moving backward and forward through a puzzle, Aristotle begins with the fact of a lunar eclipse and seeks the reason for its occurrence.

For example, the intelligible integration of puzzling data or "material manifolds" does not occur by adding more data. Instead, the type of insight that responds to a what-question amounts to a new ordering or integration that adds to the data what they are lacking, namely, intelligible unity. Still, insights are dependent on prior conditions, and not just puzzling images. There are also antecedent conditions belonging to schemes of recurrence ranging from neurochemical releases to social practices (e.g. educational training) and economic agreements that provide the lighting by which one reads and writes.

Note how these relations of dependency on prior conditions are never given in the first horizon as so many parts of an imaginable whole. An ecosystem, to put it plainly, refers to something invisible. You do not use your eyes exclusively to understand a relation, and so you do not use them exclusively to understand an ecosystem. If we should not talk about objects or events <u>inside</u> an ecosystem and hope to say anything non-metaphorical about any of them, we also should not talk about ecosystems <u>inside</u> an environment. Doing so would just recommit the same error at a higher level of generality. As the ocean does not make the rain any more than the rain makes the ocean, as in fact they are co-dependent, we should not assign metaphysical priority to either organism or its ecosystem, to either ecosystem or its environment.[448] Among the relations an ecosystem may condition are recurrence schemes belonging to another ecosystem, so that widespread forest fires increase runoff, stifle rivers, kill fish populations and make April showers into wishful thinking. Picture thinking, e.g. the contrast between the forest browned and dead from drought and the forest green and flourishing from a reliable rainy season, would stubbornly endure where Tansley and others worked to overcome it. The environment does not analytically resolve into ecosystems any more than ecosystems analytically resolve into organisms; nor, despite the high hopes of federalism, does America analytically resolve into states and states analytically into citizens.

If the part-whole relation is misleading in understanding environments and if reductionist views are deficient, what other approach may be more promising? So far we seem to have said only what an environment is not. For example, an ecosystem is related to an environment, but the latter is not itself an ecosystem or the totality of ecosystems. Might earlier comments about the conditionality of objects and events point in the direction of a more positive understanding? To look back to the

---

448   The same response was given to the puzzle about relations between individuals and institutions in Chapter Three.

preceding chapter, the emergence of neural impulses in evolutionary history was possible long before it actually occurred in animals. It may have happened sooner because the relevant chemical and physical regularities of delicately patterned electrical currents were not impossible before grasses gave way to more sophisticated plant life, to simple animals and to rational persons who are clumsy and careless enough to corrupt the ecosystems on which their crowning achievements depend. Regardless, the possible became probable and then actual only after a long series of conditions had been fulfilled.

Chapter Six, with its strange question about neurons discovering themselves, reached some conclusions about the conditionality of objects and events. To review three related conclusions about both thinking and its intended objects: first, there are relations of dependency or mutual conditioning among types of intentional acts and among types of intended objects.[449] Second, because of such conditioning, both acts and objects have only a relative stability; thus, any intellectual syntheses and explanatorily understood systems (whether natural or social) are incomplete and open to change.[450] Third, the conditionality of such syntheses and systems permits the successive emergence of new insights, more differentiated things and more complex processes as a matter of probability.

What is the significance of these claims for the question of environment? Recall the response to a critic who granted the conditionality of thinking and the probable emergence of new insights but who saw no reason for thinking such "internal" changes were grounds for expecting any developments in things or processes. That is, just because someone learns something new about objects does not entail real changes in any of those objects. The response to this common-sense objection was in four parts:

1.   Thinking is one of many types of processes dependent on interacting variables (from the physiological state to the educational background of an inquirer).

2.   Insights, institutions, organisms and ecosystems are explainable only in terms of patterns of relations among variables.

---

449   For example, reflex responses and prior training condition acts of attention; acts of questioning presuppose puzzling images; intelligible sights and sounds are prerequisites to actually understood objects and events.
450   For example, specialized training can improve attention to detail; asking further why-questions can leave behind descriptive integrations of puzzling images; new data, questions and insights may modify whatever meanings one makes initially.

3. Developments in all four are grounded in their conditionality and occur in accord with probability.

4. While developments in understanding entail changes in intended objects in the *ordo cognoscendi* but not necessarily in the *ordo essendi*, the possibility of either type of change has the same source, namely, the conditionality of all world processes.

How does talk of the conditionality of all world processes help us move forward with the question of environment? First, prior conditions ground possible developments in organisms and ecosystems as well as in individuals and institutions.[451] Next, in regard to raising and answering questions, developments in understanding can achieve a relative independence from some of their antecedent conditions. As noted before, Lonergan affirmed this relative independence from prior conditions as understanding develops.

> The higher system of the organism or of the psyche develops in an underlying material manifold of physical, chemical, cytological events that are subject to their own proper laws. The higher system of intelligence develops not in a material manifold but in the psychic representation of material manifolds. Hence the higher system of intellectual development is primarily the higher integration, not of the man in whom the development occurs, but of the universe that he inspects.[452]

Where is the relative independence here? Insights are dependent on sensitive presentations, imaginative representations and "material manifolds," but, instead of being further images or reducible to neural impulses, insights are integrations of what initially are "representations" open to a range of possible integrations or meanings. While persons having

---

451 For example, the insights of adults were realizable in their youth but not actually realized. It is highly improbable that at the age of ten most would understand what they later would understand at the age of 30 because learning occurs according to probabilities, and it advances as a succession of incomplete insights. The child could not realize what the adult realizes because conditions are met later that are not met earlier. The fulfillment of conditions not only takes time, it depends upon the coincidence of a divergent series of prior conditions occurring in accord with probability. How many different paths may lead one toward or away from becoming a concert pianist?

452 *Insight*, 494.

these insights are changed as a result, the primary development is in the universe as intended and understood. That is, previously undetected differentiations and relations among variables come to light. For example, mountain building, once thought to be the result of volcanic activity, became a more complex process with the advent of plate tectonics. Or think of how much stranger and more puzzling the universe seems to us today because of Hubble's images and the astrophysicists' surmises about dark energy and dark matter.

Evidence of new differentiations and relations appeared in previous chapters. Chapter Two reviewed how over two decades artists gradually developed an understanding of their works as conditioned by more than artistic intentions and whatever materials they used. The dependencies among artworks, sites, seasonal changes, variations in lighting, available technologies and finances came into focus and expanded an understanding of the intertwined variables making artworks what they were. Similarly, Chapter Five's survey of four decades of environmental history noted the shifts from early dichotomies of nature and society, of pristine wilderness and human artifice, and from simplifications about agency and environmental degradation to more complex views of how human actions and ecosystems were mutually dependent. The increased exposure of environmental historians to various sciences both differentiated the universe they were investigating (hence subspecialties emerged) and expanded the range of conditions they found relevant to understanding their objects of inquiry.[453] In short, both artists and historians were changing during these decades, but the primary development was in the "regions" they studied and found to be more complex and differentiated than they previously had thought.

Further evidence of a more differentiated universe appears in the proliferating uses of "environment" and the fields that employ the term. The usages are usually pre-theoretical, and, as Sutter noted, unsatisfactory. Evidence of a reach for a more systematic and comprehensive usage appeared in talk of "energy and information exchanges" as basic to every biological and cultural system. While we earlier criticized that way of talking, we do think it reflected a demand for a theoretical understanding that would integrate so much diversity.

How is that demand to be met? It will not be met by listing the usages of "environment" in ordinary language. In both the *Primer* and

---

453   Thomas G. Andrew's *Killing for Coal* provided examples of such further differentiations and integrations. Sutter praised it as a model for future environmental histories because of the range of interacting variables he considered and how well he integrated them in his account of mining in Colorado.

Cracking the Case, that approach did not get to the basic question about the alleged problem of induction.[454] It holds no better promise for understanding what we might mean by environment in a theoretical sense. All the same, we do begin with an "undertheorized" term; the challenge is to lift the question of its meaning into a theoretical context. How is this to be done? We need both data and organizing ideas, both possible clues and initial hypotheses. The first terms without the second lack significance; the second terms without the first lack reality.[455] The pairs of terms together allow for a theoretical account of an environment.

But what are the relevant <u>data</u> and what are to be the organizing <u>ideas</u> for understanding the environment? Ecologists speak of "natural environments" and so are mediating the data of their experience by whatever meaning they assign the phrase. Sociologists speak of "cultural environments" and so are talking about the data of social relations that are mediated and constituted by acts of meaning. The sociologists may think the basic cultural data are the meanings people create and externalize in their activities.[456] The ecologists may think a biological species is "an intelligible solution to a problem of living in a given environment."[457] One organizing idea, then, is to suppose both cultures and species are solutions to living in concrete situations that are the cumulative effect of past actions and events.[458] Another is to posit that those solutions are only relatively stable because the initial conditions they met in order to emerge are not fixed for all time. Thus, concrete situations in the present pose new problems for living. What are such situations but environments?

If explanatory understanding requires that answers to further why-questions take the form of correlations among variables, what do we mean when we say an environment or a "situation" is a correlate of any species or culture as an "intelligible solution" to living? As already concluded, an environment is not an object for sensation; it is not something perceptible; it is not adequately understood in terms of a part-whole relation, e.g. the natural environment is misconceived as a totality of ecosystems and organisms. What is the question, then, to which a positive meaning of "environment" is an answer? What puzzling data does the term help integrate? The clues from the preceding chapters suggest an

---

454 As readers may recall, the suspicion was that reliance on ordinary language analysis was a symptom of a reluctance to engage the question of knowing things themselves.
455 *Method in Theology*, 251. Or, to paraphrase Kant: experience without concepts is blind; concepts without experience are empty.
456 Peter L. Berger. *The Sacred Canopy* (Garden City: Anchor Books, 1969), 8.
457 *Insight*, 290.
458 *Method in Theology*, 358.

answer. Individuals and institutions, organisms and ecosystems emerge, survive, develop and decline as matters of probability, and one can ask why all these varied phenomena undergo such changes. The general answer is in terms of the relative stability both of the initial conditions favoring their emergence and of later conditions challenging their continuance. "Environment" can refer to this understanding of their universal dependency or conditionality. Worth noting is that this general meaning tolerates multiple, field-specific usages (e.g. references to artistic, familial, economic, political and ecological environments) because the objects and events of those differentiated "regions" are conditioned realities.[459] No need then to stop at ordinary language analysis to understand the meaning of environment. Instead, as a correlate it refers to a grasp of why institutions and ecosystems, individuals and organisms enjoy only a relative stability; namely, the conditions under which they first function and later continue to function are subject to change.

To summarize the major steps in reaching this technical meaning of environment:

1. There were negative insights: the environment is not perceptible; it is not a thing; it is not a totality or aggregation of ecosystems and organisms.

2. We asked what is the question to which a positive meaning of the environment is an answer? That question was why do diverse phenomena emerge, continue, decline and sometimes recover as a matter of probability?

3. The first part of the answer took note of the relative stability of the initial conditions under which phenomena emerge. The second part generalized that all phenomena remain dependent on subsequent conditions that also are only relatively stable.

---

459   As an easily accessible reference point, we can ask readers to relate this usage of environment to talk of a "home environment." The personal experiences of one's early years can provide fascinating materials for reflecting on the conditionality of one's own life. To do so would be a study of a "regional" environment with all its variable conditions upon which depend the emergence of the adult. A home environment is a subset of the universe, but both can be understood as ranges of conditions for the possibility and actual development of things and processes. A relational ontology need not ignore either local or universal contexts; it can investigate regional environments but also can explore more difficult questions about the most general environment, i.e. the universe.

4. The term "environment" can, thus, refer to an understanding of the indefinite range of conditions phenomena depend on for their emergence, continuance, decline and recovery. In short, it expresses an understanding of the conditionality of all objects and events, i.e. their dependence on an indefinite range of potentially interacting variables.

5. As a correlate, the general category "environment" provides an answer to why ecosystems and institutions, organisms and individuals are mutable.

This understanding of environment is consistent with our reading of Nisbet's third cluster, ecological art, as superior to process art because of the former's emphasis on the conditionality of artworks. It is consistent with the critique of the deterministic and simplified views of ecosystems Golley found in the intermediate period of ecological studies. It agrees with Golley's estimate of the superiority of the third period's view because of its attention to variations and developments within ecosystems and the relegation of equilibrium or steady states to comparatively short-lived or even rare phenomena. It is consistent with McNeill's expansion of the category of "agency" in accounting for ecological change to include population numbers, animals, climates, ideas and technologies. Finally, this meaning does not make use of the part-whole metaphor in talking about environments and instead relies upon an understanding of how intelligible relations among diverse organic and nonorganic variables, among persons and institutions, depend upon an indefinite number of conditions such that those relations and the variables functioning through them are only relatively stable.

IV. In Retrospect

Arriving at this understanding of environment has been a slow climb, and one may wonder how useful this technical meaning may be for disciplines currently employing the same term in many different ways. In biology this new meaning may prove attractive since its generality extends to both relatively stable patterns of organic functioning and to catastrophic changes in such patterns. Volcanic eruptions and climate changes can erase entire ecosystems and species. To the dismay of dinosaurs the motions of asteroids turned out to be among the relevant conditions for their continuance. Cases of extinctions predominate in geological time, but they stand out only because of long-term survivals of ecosystems and species. Explaining both extinction and endurance in terms of environmental conditions is not a novel idea, and so this understanding of environment need not be a radical departure from current usages in biology.

Environmental historians may resonate with this technical meaning of environment because of an old problem in the field of historiography. While biographies and studies of particular periods and regional cultures are standard projects, some historians have posed the question of general historical process: What is the subject of this process in which individuals as well as entire civilizations come into being and pass away? What is history the history of? McNeill hinted at a similar puzzle when he complained in 2003 about the paucity of environmental studies extending beyond political borders. Some environmental studies have been regional in scope and so perhaps analogous to the study of a culture. Still, the further question turns up: what is environmental history the history of? Regional ecosystems with all their interacting variables come into being and pass away at varying rates, but do we want to say the same of the environment? Might environment in its broadest usage (the conditionality of all world processes that grounds the possibility of developments or declines, solutions or maladaptations to living) be the general answer to why objects and patterns of relations among them change at all? Consider how this very general answer leaves plenty of work for specialists to do in understanding and differentiating the range of conditions that bring about actual changes. One specialty could begin with the feeding routines of herbivores; another could study the growth patterns of plants and the roles of the nitrogen and hydrological cycles in how those patterns varied under different conditions; yet another could take note of periods of decreasing sun spot activity and the subsequent climatic changes affecting all of the preceding variables.

The term "environment" in an explanatory context expresses an understanding of the indefinite range of conditions for the emergence, continuation, decline and recovery of any of its correlates. As McNeill noted, environmental historians have gradually discovered the relevance of multiple scientific fields for their expanding studies of the environment.[460] This has been a development in the universe they were intending and further differentiating. To expect that future environmental historians will continue to generate new subspecialties is to assume that the environment with its indefinite range of potentially interacting variables can support an indefinite number of further differentiations.

Whether this meaning of environment takes hold in any disciplines is up to practitioners in those fields. These authors think it marks an advance over the mixed usages currently employed. As already noted, it is consistent with what we have earlier identified as advances in art history, ecological studies and environmental history. Of course, the conditionality we have identified with the meaning of environment applies to cultural products, and so we expect further refinements in this understanding of environment.

Finally, how does this understanding of environment affect the earlier conundrum about persons being unable to exercise direct control over an environment and so perhaps being unable to degrade or to restore it? Chapter Five cited the work of Gregg Mitman on the history of allergies and asthma and his description of suffering populations in search of "healthy environments." We might say they were seeking conditions other than those of urban environments; yet this would be too simplistic. Many of the conditions that made their lives in cities possible would also have to obtain wherever they moved if they were to survive. Imagine, if you will, a lunar space colony and what technologically replicated conditions would make survival there possible. Mimicry of earth-bound conditions would be needed, from recycling water and oxygen to plant cultivation and assignment of institutional roles. Would this not be a "built" environment, one ostensibly subject to human control and so liable to damage from carelessness and to restoration by deliberate action? An affirmative response need not rely on hypothetical cases. Policies removing lead from gasoline and reducing emissions from coal-fired power plants have already shown it is possible to improve an environment.

However, such "regional" policies alter only some of the conditions sustaining or threatening ecosystems and institutions, organisms and individuals. What remain indeterminate are their long-term effects. Why is this so? The range of potentially interacting variables that constitute the environment is so vast that deliberately designed regional improvements may prove to be small variations or even counterproductive in

---

460   Among those fields were genetics, climatology, demographics, archaeology, animal husbandry, disease history and the history of technology.

the long run. This does not mean such policies are pointless or never to be pursued under conditions of uncertainty; rather, the cautionary note is that future consequences are foreseeable in only a very limited way. Readers may recall Chapter Five in *Cracking the Case*. The inquiry there into the Principle of Double Effect noted how both positive and negative results can follow from even very carefully made decisions. Moral responsibility for either benefits or harms is limited to what was actually foreseeable by those deciding. But public policies should be judged not by the intentions of their makers but by their consequences, and the conditions affecting actual outcomes are never fully known in advance. It is in this sense that the environment eludes human control. Judgments about what will probably improve local conditions can be correct and policy decisions based on them can be justifiable. What eludes us is knowledge of and mastery over the vast range of conditions potentially affecting, for good or ill, us, our institutions and the organisms and ecosystems with which we interact.

We end by returning to McNeill's worry that the environmental activism of the first generation of environmental historians had waned. He and Sutter offered several surmises as to why. To those we add our own. The conditions under which we live, move and have our being, i.e. our environment, are so complex, so subject to surprising variations, that we make decisions rarely able to anticipate their long-term consequences. History goes on largely "over our heads." We tend but small garden plots but think them far grander. Activists of the first generation may have been blind to much of this hidden complexity. New activists, attuned to a far more complex understanding of the environment, need not despair of exercising some limited control over regional environments. They will, however, be less likely to overestimate human capacity for environmental mastery.

EPILOGUE

I. Prospects

The three books in this series reflect the authors' dissatisfaction with current practices in many of the fields traditionally classified under the Humanities. For years we have observed the periodic appearance of new "bandwagons" attracting attention for awhile and then departing the scene only to be replaced by new viewpoints and their proponents. We suppose scholarly practices should not mimic those of the fashion industry yet wonder what endures from season to season. Clearly questioning endures, but what of answers? Are there any cumulative and progressive results from so many inquiries or is there only intellectual salivation and fickle tastes?[461]

Our suspicion is that without method scholarly inquiries are going nowhere.[462] The preceding experiments with the five elements of FS4 are responses to our sense of what has been lacking. Of course, some academics may not suspect anything is lacking; they may believe all is well in Academus' grove.[463] However, the practical-minded among them

---

461   This second possibility brings to mind Samuel Beckett's scathing response to critics of Joyce's *Work in Progress*. "Here is direct expression -- pages and pages of it. And if you don't understand it, Ladies and Gentlemen, it is because you are too decadent to receive it. You are not satisfied unless form is so strictly divorced from content that you can comprehend the one almost without bothering to read the other. This rapid skimming and absorption of the scant cream of sense is made possible by what I call a continuous process of copious intellectual salivation. The form that is an arbitrary and independent phenomenon can fulfill no higher function than that of a stimulus for the tertiary or quartery conditioned reflex of dribbling comprehension." *Our Exagmination Round His Factification For Incamination of Work in Progress* (New York: A New Direction Book, 1972), 13. Quoted in McShane, *The Allure of the Compelling Genius of History: Teaching Young Humans Humanity and Hope.* (Vancouver: Axial Publishing, 2015), Chapter Five.

462   Lonergan remarked on his early education in philosophy: "I felt that there was absolutely no method to the philosophy I had been taught; it wasn't going anywhere." *Caring about Meaning*, 10.

463   "What is lacking is the appropriate set of conceptual definitions and linguistic expressions in which the triply conscious subject could convey to himself and to others what it is to be a human knower and what such knowing implies in the known. What is lacking is the cultural

might heed the injunction, "Follow the money." Which schools at universities attract the most external funding for new facilities and which ones attract the least? No need to mention sports programs and the revenue flows they enjoy to recognize that non-academic audiences have low expectations of what the Humanities will produce.

Are those expectations simply ill-informed and philistine? In areas of philosophy, evidence of feckless practices is not in short supply. How many "tired old debates" go on interminably?[464] Are they in principle unresolvable because they involve the "big questions" that no one can adequately answer or are the sources of disagreement too often left implicit? Readers will know that these texts presupposed the latter. UV formulates a set of positions for identifying some of those sources and for evaluating differences among interpretations that originate in them. GS anticipates that any sequence of interpretations from such a comparative analysis will represent an incomplete understanding open to further development. However, some viewpoints will no longer merit attention except as historical footnotes about what has been left behind.

Our efforts to introduce comparative interpretation as a new methodical practice presuppose our own belief that improvements in scholarly practices are possible. Lonergan's invention of functional specialization is, we believe, a way forward for scholars in any number of fields. Our experiments with FS4 are attempts to provide examples of the usefulness of one part of this new practice. The first element of this practice (H2) is already common in the natural sciences, and achievements there should interest scholars in at least this feature of the new practice. Why should the imperative "Be comprehensive!" be limited to natural scientists? Raising this question is a way of exposing some of what is lacking in current interpretive works. How many of them operate "below" the horizons of theory and interiority? Does talk of the possibility of a science of interpretation even seem plausible? If a new generation of students remains unaware of such a possibility, have their teachers swindled them

milieu habituated to the use of abstract concepts and trained in the techniques that safeguard their employment. What is lacking is a critical awareness of the polymorphism of human consciousness, of the alternative formulations of discoveries as positions or as counterpositions, of the momentum of positions for development and of the goal of counterpositions in reversal. Most of all, what is lacking is knowledge of all that is lacking, and only gradually is that knowledge acquired." *Insight*, 559.

464   These texts have presented case studies identifying various intellectual impasses that these authors believe are avoidable. For example, is nothing ever to be settled about questions regarding induction, strict moral dilemmas, reductive analysis in the neurosciences, the limits of conceptual analysis, the different but complementary aims of the two types of knowing and the two types of realism?

into accepting a conventional education several centuries out of date?[465]

If these initial books try to "get the show on the road," what are the prospects that FS will ever become part of conventional scholarly practice? We have already cited a number of obstacles, including the absence of various types of displacements. What are the chances that many scholars will significantly alter their expectations of themselves, their inquiries and their disciplines? To improve these chances, advocates of FS will need to reach new generations of young scholars not yet wedded to current conventions and not yet on the treadmill of pre-tenure productivity. To cultivate those new audiences is one purpose of the diverse case studies disentangling intellectual knots in a variety of disciplines. Most readers will need some evidence that this new way of doing comparative work is worth trying. The hope is that in time our initial efforts will seem amateurish[466] in comparison to future, more substantial projects benefiting from teams of functional specialists committed to recycling their works and gradually demonstrating that cumulative and progress results are possible.[467]

We are not there yet; hence, we noted multiple times the role of fantasy in composing these books. FS and a science of interpretation are fantasies. Suppose they are unrealized possibilities of human inquiry in history, in time. What is human inquiry in time? Does not the "whatness" of anything include its potential for further development? Is final causality the relic of a superstitious past, as Spinoza and Voltaire contended, or a dynamic function of the universe as it develops and decays? To envision the possibility of further growth is to sometimes be appalled by current levels of achievement. Frustration with all that is lacking in current practices finds a positive outlet in imagining a better future and

---

465   Henry Adams' judgment on the education his Harvard students were receiving at the end of the nineteenth century may still be applicable today. "...It would bore you to extinction to follow me through my daily struggle to find out how boys who have no minds can be made to understand that they had better be contented without the education of a Newton, and how boys who have minds can be made to understand that all knowledge has not yet been exhausted by Newton and such. This effort to get rid of rubbish and to utilize good material is one of my labors. I am preaching a crusade against Culture with a big C. I hope to excite the hatred of my entire community, every soul of whom adores that big C. I mean to irritate everyone about me to frenzy by ridiculing all the idols of the University and declaring a university education to be a swindle." Letter to Charles Milnes Gaskell (October 4, 1875). *Letters of Henry Adams (1858-1891)*. Worthington Chauncey Ford (ed.) (New York: Houghton Mifflin, 1930), 271-272.

466   McShane anticipates that first efforts will usually be amateurish: "And I would emphasize that the transition period ahead demands, for most of us, a commitment to teach and point beyond our own present competence." *The Road to Religious Reality* (Vancouver: Axial Publishing, 2012), 47.

467   Such results would be the forming of an acquis, a commonly accepted view of what questions about some issue were still open and which had been settled. Included in it would be developmental sequencing of answers-to-date.

in working to achieve its implementation.

GEM includes insight into our acts of deliberation and capacity to fantasize about new options. The meaning of "ordered liberty," already cited from a previous book, expanded upon that insight. In a brilliant passage Lonergan links both this frustration and the freedom to explore new options:

> That exploration is extremely important in our age, when philosophers for at least two centuries, through doctrines on politics, economics, education, and through ever further doctrines, have been trying to remake man, and have done not a little to make human life unlivable. The great task that is demanded if we are to make it livable again is the re-creation of the liberty of the subject, the recognition of the freedom of consciousness.[468]

Fantasy, whether in the arts, politics, economics or education, has a legitimate role because questioning expresses a human capacity to develop or to correct prior integrations of meaning. All the same, radical shifts in viewpoints and practices are the occurrence of the improbable. Nonetheless, given enough time and large enough numbers, even the improbable may become actual. Thus, while our vision of developments and departures rests upon little evidence of prior success and while the evidence of inertia is all around and deeply entrenched, we yet have hope for this project.

II. A Question of History

In Chapter One, we cited a view of historical development: "The challenge of history is...progressively to restrict the realm of chance or fate or destiny and progressively to enlarge the realm of conscious grasp and deliberate choice."[469] We went on to describe how that challenge has arisen within the context of the two times of the human subject and the slow emergence of the third horizon of meaning. FS with its eight-fold subdivisions is part of that second time and a further specification of how

---

468   *Topics in Education, CW* 10 (Toronto: University of Toronto Press, 1993), 232.
469   *Insight*, 253.

to control meaning and the deliberate making of history. Does it promise a new methodological culture in the academy and so a better way of meeting the challenge of directing history?[470] Its widespread acceptance as a way forward will not occur in our lifetimes. Perhaps its emergence belongs among the processes Braudel assigned to writers of *histoire de la longue durée*. Less descriptively we might think of time or history as what "grounds the possibility of successive realizations in accord with probabilities."[471] But then why are we confident that the developments and departures that are antecedent conditions for acceptance of FS will ever be realized? We expect no continuous advances along a timeline; in intellectual history there have been too many instances of earlier insights lost and of breakthroughs reversed. Additionally, we acknowledge that each new generation seems to struggle afresh with the differences between the two types of knowing and the two types of realism and so tends to fall into the same old confused debates about the three basic questions. Why should we expect any change in this pattern?

McShane posed a question challenging readers to take a personal stand: "Do you view [yourself and] humanity as possibly maturing-in some serious way-or just messing along between good and evil, whatever you think they are?"[472] The framework of the two times of the human subject offers some evidence of uneven and precarious progress. The criterion of development is movement toward the third horizon in response to the demand for more comprehensive understanding. Critics, of course, will find fault with this intellectualist criterion. They may easily cite how applied sciences have produced massive increases in the efficiency of war machines. But that line of criticism ends only with an insight into the moral ambiguity of tools. A better line of criticism would focus on the old puzzle about persons knowing but not doing what is good. Knowing about intentional operations and their proper objects (GEM and UV) and even understanding the potential of FS to make scholarship more efficient are intellectual advances. What effect might they have on performance? The historical evidence for minor and major betrayals of best judgments about what can and should be done is abundant. Populations of the last century were better educated than any of their predecessors, and yet the slaughter of millions evoked Thomas Mann's description of

---

470   McShane's strong response to a negative answer was: "to refuse FS is to be refuse." *FuSe* 10, 22 (philipmcshane.ca). FS is part of a fantasy about universities becoming more collaborative enterprises, increasingly as differentiated and integrated as the universe that is the environment for all inquiries.
471   *Insight*, 195.
472   *The Everlasting Joy of Being Human*, 77. The addition in brackets comes from a version of the question in McShane's correspondence with one of the authors.

"civilizational reversal" and Hannah Arendt's controversial diagnosis of the "banality of evil." The current century seems to be repeating the same old patterns of disorder and violence. Regress is all too common; progress is all too rare.

Lonergan advised practitioners of FS4 to "lay their cards on the table."[473] While he meant being explicit about one's own views regarding UV, the same advice to engage in direct discourse applies to answering McShane's pointed question. It asks us either to confine or to enlarge our viewpoints on human potential. These authors affirm their belief in a "friendly universe"[474] and pursue more mature scholarly practices accordingly. Cultural decline and threats to whatever progress has been made are not in doubt. However, our own scholarly efforts presuppose an underlying trust in the intelligibility of such efforts and the realities yet to be understood.[475] Why else would anyone continue to ask questions trying to push beyond the answers already available? Why should anyone care about making meaning? But there is a further reason for our personal stand.

For most of recorded history, whatever social order a population enjoyed they sustained by preserving some consensus about what their lives in time meant, whose version of reality they respected, whose rules were to govern their lives together. Traditional institutions with moral and intellectual authority were the instruments charged with preserving these shared meanings and solving the "generational gap problem," i.e. inducting each new generation into the consensus of the group. Today, especially in the West, institutions such as families, schools, churches and governments are less effective in fulfilling this age-old function. Multiple claimants to moral and intellectual authority vie with one another for the loyalties of audiences, and, in the resulting babble of contentious voices, confused listeners wonder what to believe and do. One challenge of higher education is not just to expose a new generation to the ever expanding range of views but to offer some guidance in sorting out and judging diverse meanings. Educators can easily dodge this challenge by saying students deserve the freedom to think for themselves. What "freedom" means in this case falls far short of an explanatory and normative under-

---

473   *Method in Theology*, 193.

474   "Faith places human efforts in a friendly universe; it reveals an ultimate significance in human achievement; it strengthens new undertakings with confidence." Ibid. 117.

475   Rilke wrote of this trust: "Catch only what you've thrown yourself, all is / mere skill and little gain; / but when you're suddenly the catcher of a ball / thrown by an eternal partner / with accurate and measured swing / towards you, to your centre, in an arch / from the great bridgebuilding of God: / why catching then becomes a power- / not yours, a world's." From the frontispiece of Hans-Georg Gadamer, *Truth and Method* (New York: The Seabury Press, 1975).

standing of freedom and probably is no more than the old descriptive notion of non-interference. However, left to their own devices students will face the need to judge and to decide among the contending voices but will find themselves ill equipped to do so.[476]

At a minimum might educators teach new generations how anyone goes about making meaning? GEM could be part of that instruction. Might a few be led to re-enact the cultural journey from the first to the second time of the human subject and so to a differentiation of the two types of knowing and the two types of realism? Then at least the puzzles pointing toward UV might become a topic of conversation. As well, some of the confusion about making meaning and about the multiplicity of viewpoints might become less prevalent; it might even be easier to diagnose the origins of some differences.

Caring about making meaning and about making judgments is a beginning but no substitute for being careful in doing both. What the elements of FS4 offer is a contribution to control over doing both. We see our efforts, then, as participating in a long climb, with no ropes to prevent falls, but hopeful that later generations will reach higher than they otherwise might have. Again, without method they will be going nowhere. The bandwagons will continue to roll, but the display will entertain without adding much to comprehension.

---

476   "New books pour forth annually by the thousands; our libraries need ever more space. But the vast modern effort to understand meaning in all its manifestations has not been matched by a comparable effort in judging meaning. The effort to understand is the common task of unnumbered scientists and scholars. But judging and deciding are left to the individual, and he finds his plight desperate. There is far too much to be learnt before he could begin to judge. Yet judge he must and decide he must if he is to exist...." Lonergan. "Dimensions of Meaning," 266.

BIBLIOGRAPHY

BOOKS

Adams, Henry. *Letters of Henry Adams (1858-1891)*. Worthington Chauncey Ford (ed.) (New York: Houghton Mifflin, 1930).

Andrew, Thomas G. *Killing for Coal: America's Deadliest Labor War* (Cambridge: Harvard University Press, 2008).

Berger, Peter L. *The Sacred Canopy* (Garden City: Anchor Books, 1969).

Berger, Peter and Luckmann, Thomas. *The Social Construction of Reality* (Garden City, N.Y.: Doubleday, 1967).

Bobbitt, Philip. *Terror and Consent: The Wars for the Twenty-First Century* (New York: Random House, 2009).

Cronon, William. *Nature's Metropolis: Chicago and the Great West* (New York: W.W. Norton, 1992).

Damasio, Antonio R. *The Feeling of What Happens* (New York: Harcourt, Brace and Company, 1999).

Dennett, Daniel. *Darwin's Dangerous Idea* (New York: Simon and Schuster, 1995).

---------- *Brainstorms* (Cambridge: MIT Press, 1978).

---------- *Consciousness Explained* (Boston: Little, Brown and Co., 1991).

Flanagan, Joseph. *Quest for Self-Knowledge* (Toronto: University of Toronto Press, 1997).

Friedman, Milton. *Capitalism and Freedom* (Chicago: University of Chicago Press, 1962).

Gabriel, Markus. *Transcendental Ontology: Essays in German Idealism* (New York: Continuum International Publishing, 2011).

Gadamer, Hans-Georg. *Truth and Method* (New York: The Seabury Press, 1975).

Gazzaniga, Michael S. *Who's in Charge? Free Will and the Science of the Brain* (New York: HarperCollins, 2011).

Golley, Frank Benjamin. *A History of the Ecosystem Concept in Ecology* (New Haven: Yale University Press, 1993).

Goodman, Nelson. *Ways of Worldmaking* (Indianapolis: Hackett, 1978).

Haraway, Donna J. *When Species Meet* (Minneapolis: University of Minnesota Press, 2008).

Hegel, G.W.F. *Elements of the Philosophy of Right.* Allen W. Wood (ed.) H.B. Nisbet (trans.) (New York: Cambridge University Press, 1991).

Heidegger, Martin. *The Fundamental Concepts of Metaphysics: World, Finitude, Solitude.* William McNeil and Nicholas Walker (trans.) (Bloomington: Indiana University Press, 1995).

Huddleston, John. *Healing Ground: Walking the Farms of Vermont* (Chicago: Center for American Places, 2012).

Klingle, Matthew. *Emerald City: An Environmental History of Seattle* (New Haven: 2007).

Kubler, George. *The Shape of Time: Remarks on the History of Things* (New Haven: Yale University Press, 1962).

Lambert, Pierrot et al. *Caring about Meaning: Patterns in the Life of Bernard Lonergan* (Montreal: Thomas More Institute, 1982).

Langston, Nancy. *Toxic Bodies: Endocrine Disruptors and the Legacy of DES* (New Haven: Yale University Press, 2010).

Laughlin, Robert. *A Different Universe: Reinventing Physics from the Bottom Down* (New York: Basic Books, 2006).

Lonergan, Bernard. *Insight: A Study of Human Understanding. CW* 3 (Toronto: University of Toronto Press, 1992).

---------- *Phenomenology and Logic. CW* 18 (Toronto: University of Toronto Press, 2001).

---------- *Philosophical and Theological Papers: 1965-1980. CW* 17 (Toronto: University of Toronto Press, 2004).

---------- *The Triune God: Systematics. CW* 12 (Toronto: University of Toronto Press, 2007).

---------- *Method in Theology* (New York: Herder and Herder, 1972).

---------- *Verbum: Word and Idea in Aquinas. CW* 2 (Toronto: University of Toronto Press, 1997).

---------- *For a New Political Economy. CW* 21. Philip J. McShane (ed.) (Toronto: University of Toronto Press, 1998).

---------- *Macroeconomic Dynamics.* Frederick G. Lawrence et al. (eds.) *CW* 15 (Toronto: University of Toronto Press, 1999).

---------- *Topics in Education. CW* 10 (Toronto: University of Toronto Press, 1993).

MacIntyre, Alisdair. *After Virtue: A Study in Moral Virtue* (Notre Dame: University of Notre Dame Press, 1981).

McIntosh, Robert P. *The Background of Ecology: Concept and Theory* (Cambridge: Cambridge University Press, 1985).

McShane, Philip. *Futurology Express* (Vancouver: Axial Press, 2013).

---------- *Randomness, Statistics and Emergence* (Dublin: Gill and MacMillan, 1970).

---------- *The Everlasting Joy of Being Human* (Vancouver: Axial Publishing, 2013).

---------- *Wealth of Self and Wealth of Nations* (Hicksville, N.Y.: Exposition Press, 1975).

---------- *The Allure of the Compelling Genius of History: Teaching Young Humans Humanity and Hope.* (Vancouver: Axial Publishing, 2015).

---------- *The Road to Religious Reality* (Vancouver: Axial Publishing, 2012).

Mitman, Gregg. *Breathing Space: How Allergies Shape Our Lives and Landscapes* (New Haven: Yale University Press, 2007).

Muller, Jerry Z. *Adam Smith in His Time and Ours* (New York: The Free Press, 1996).

Nisbet, James. *Ecologies, Environments, and Energy Systems in Art of the 1960s and 1970s* (Cambridge: MIT Press, 2014).

Nozick, Robert. *Anarchy, State, and Utopia* (New York: Basic Books, 1974).

Ormerod, Paul. *The Death of Economics* (London: Faber and Faber, 1994).

Proust, Marcel. *Remembrance of Things Past.* Vol. 2 (New York: Random House, 1981).

Sallis, John. *Topographies* (Bloomington: Indiana University Press, 2006).

Schor, Juliet B. *Born to Buy: The Commercialized Child and the New Consumer Culture* (New York: Scribner, 2004).

Shoppa, Clayton and Zanardi, William. *Cracking the Case: Exercises in the New Comparative Interpretation* (Austin: Forty Acres Press, 2014).

Voegelin, Eric. *The Ecumenic Age* (Baton Rouge: Louisiana State University Press, 1980).

---------- *From Enlightenment to Revolution* (Durham: Duke University Press, 1975).

White, Hayden. *Metahistory: The Historical Imagination in Nineteenth-Century Europe* (Baltimore: The Johns Hopkins University Press, 1973).

Worster, Donald. *Nature's Economy: A History of Ecological Ideas*, second edition (Cambridge: Cambridge University Press, 1994).

Zanardi, William. *A Theory of Ordered Liberty*, second, revised edition (Austin: Forty Acres Press, 2011).

---------- *The New Comparative Interpretation: A Primer*, second, revised edition (Austin: The Forty Acres Press, 2014).

Zawidzki, Tadeusz. *Dennett* (Oxford: Oneworld Publications, 2007).

ARTICLES, PAPERS and POSTINGS

Beane, Melinda and Marrocco, Richard. "Holinergic and Noradrenergic Inputs to the Posterior Parietal Cortex Modulate the Components of Exogenous Attention" in *Cognitive Neuroscience of Attention*." Michael I. Posner (ed.) (New York: Guilford Press, 2004).

Bruner, Jerome. "Possible Castles" in *Actual Minds, Possible Worlds* (Cambridge: Harvard University Press, 1986).

Bundsen, C. "A Theory of Visual Attention," in *Psychological Review*, Vol. 97 (1990).

Byrne, Patrick. "Neuroscience, Consciousness, Freedom and Lonergan," unpublished paper given at the Lonergan Philosophical Society session at the American Catholic Philosophical Association (November 2007).

Cohen et al. "A System-Level Perspective in Attention and Cognitive Control" in *Cognitive Neuroscience of Attention*." Michael I. Posner (ed.) (New York: Guilford Press, 2004).

Colombo, John. "Visual Attention in Infancy" in *Cognitive Neuroscience of Attention*. Michael I. Posner (ed.) (New York: Guilford Press, 2004).

Friedman, Milton. *"Free to Choose: A Conversation with Milton Friedman"* in *Imprimis*, Vol.35, No.7 (Hillsdale, MI: July, 2006).

---------- "The Social Responsibility of Business Is to Increase Its Profits." *The New York Times Magazine* (September 13, 1970).

Gruber, Oliver and Thomas Goschke, "Executive Control Emerging from Dynamic Interactions between Brain Systems Mediating Language, Working Memory and Attentional Process" in *Acta Psychologica* Vol. 115 (2004).

Haacke, Hans. "Untitled Statement" in *Theories and Documents of Contemporary Art: A Sourcebook of Artists' Writings*. Kristine Stiles and Peter Howard Selz (eds.) (Berkeley: University of California Press, 1996).

Hariman, Robert. "Prudence in the Twenty-First Century," in *Prudence: Classical Virtue, Postmodern Practice*. Robert Hariman (ed.) (University Park: The Pennsylvania State University Press, 2003).

Lawrence, Frederick G. "Editors' Introduction" in Bernard Lonergan. *Macroeconomic Dynamics*, *CW* 15 (Toronto: University of Toronto Press, 1999).

Logan, Gordon D. "Attention, Automaticity, and Executive Control" in *Experimental Cognitive Psychology and Its Applications*. Alice F. Healy (ed.) (Washington, D.C.: American Psychological Association, 2005).

Lonergan, Bernard. "Second Lecture: Religious Knowledge" in *A Third Collection* (New York: Paulist Press, 1985).

---------- "Dimensions of Meaning" in *Collection* (New York: Herder and Herder, 1967).

---------- "Healing and Creating in History" in *A Third Collection* (New York: Paulist Press, 1985).

---------- "Savings Certificates and Catholic Action" in *Shorter Papers*. *CW* 20 (Toronto: University of Toronto Press, 2007).

Mailer, Norman. "Mailer on 'The Blacks.'" *The Village Voice*. VI. no.30 (May 18, 1961), 14-15.

McShane, Philip. "One Hundred and One Damnations," *FuSe* 14, 2 (philipmcshane.ca).

---------- *FuSe* 10, 22 (philipmcshane.ca).

McNeil, J.R. "Observations on the Nature and Culture of Environmental History" in *History and Theory*, "Theme Issue 42: Environment and History," 4 (2003) 5-43.

Mitman, Gregg. "Living in a Material World" in *Journal of American History*, (June 2013), 128-130.

Naccache, Lionel et al. "Effortless Control: Executive Attention and Conscious Feeling of Mental Effort are Dissociable" in *Neuropsycholgia*, Vol. 43, No. 9 (2005).

Nash, Linda. "Furthering the Environmental Turn" in *Journal of American History*, (June 2013), 131-135.

Pluta, Joseph E. "Kenneth Boulding's Skeleton of Science and Contemporary General Systems Theory" in Wilfred Dolfsma and Stefan Kesting (eds.) *Interdisciplinary Economics: Kenneth E. Boulding's Engagement in the Sciences* (London: Routledge, 2013).

Pollack, Seth D. and Tolley-Schell, Stephanie. "Attention, Emotion, and the Development of Psychopathology" in *Cognitive Neuroscience of Attention*. Michael I. Posner (ed.) (New York: Guilford Press, 2004).

Posner, Michael I. "Progress in Attention Research" in *Cognitive Neuroscience of Attention*." Michael I. Posner (ed.) (New York: Guilford Press, 2004).

Posner, Michael I and Synder. "Attention and Cognitive Control" (1975), reprinted in *Cognitive Psychology: Key Readings*, A. Balota and Elizabeth J. Marsh (eds.) (New York: Psychology Press, 2004).

Schumpeter, Joseph. "The Analysis of Economic Change" in *Essays of J. A. Schumpeter* (Port Washington, N.Y.: Kennikat Press, 1969).

Sen, Amartya. "Rational Fools: A Critique of the Behavioral Foundations of Economic Theory" in *Philosophy and Public Affairs*. 6(1977).

Sutter, Paul S. "The World with Us: The State of American Environmental History" in *Journal of American History*, Vol.100, 1(June 2013), 94-119.

---------- "Nature Is History" in *Journal of American History*, Vol.100, 1(June 2013), 145-148.

Taylor, Bron. "'It's Not All about Us': Reflections on the State of American Environmental History" in *Journal of American History*, (June 2013), 140-144.

Voegelin, Eric. "Eternal Being in Time," in *Anamnesis* (Columbia: University of Missouri Press, 1990).

Zanardi, William. "Obstacles to a Basic Expansion" in *The Lonergan Review*. Vol. II, no. 1 (Spring 2010).

www.ingramcontent.com/pod-product-compliance
Lightning Source LLC
Chambersburg PA
CBHW062209270326
41930CB00009B/1694